Professional InfoPath™ 2003

Professional InfoPath™ 2003

Ian Williams and Pierre Greborio

WILEY

Wiley Publishing, Inc.

Professional InfoPath™ 2003

About the Authors

Ian Williams

Ian Williams is an information designer specializing in XML technologies and a software technical writer. He worked in the UK publishing industry before getting involved in information technology at OWL International, developers of one of the first commercial hypertext products. Ian was a product manager there, and later a consultant working with large corporate customers.

Since 1998 Ian has worked independently on technical writing and information design projects for customers like Nokia and Reuters. He lives with his wife in London, England, from which they regularly escape to a house on a beach overlooking the English Channel.

Pierre Greborio

Pierre Greborio is chief software architect of PEWay, an Italian software company providing services and Internet technologies for financial companies.

Born in 1971 in Belgium, he graduated as a telecommunication engineer from the University of Pavia in Italy.

His activity is characterized by a strong passion for technology. He participated in several talks at developer conferences and university workshops and wrote several articles for developer magazines and user groups about Microsoft .NET technologies and Microsoft Office InfoPath 2003. In the beginning of 2003, Pierre was given the award of Microsoft Most Valuable Professional for .NET.

Credits

Vice President and Executive Group Publisher
Richard Swadley

Vice President and Executive Publisher
Robert Ipsen

Vice President and Publisher
Joseph B. Wikert

Executive Editorial Director
Mary Bednarek

Acquisitions Editor
Jim Minatel

Editorial Manager
Kathryn A. Malm

Senior Production Manager
Fred Bernardi

Development Editor
Sharon Nash

Production Editor
Angela Smith

Text Design & Composition
Wiley Composition Services

Contents

Contents

Contents

Contents

Contents

Contents

Contents

Introduction

Welcome to Microsoft InfoPath 2003, the newest component in the Microsoft Office 2003 suite of applications. It's always exciting to get your hands on a totally new product to see what it adds to your knowledge and technical skills, and you'll find that InfoPath will not disappoint.

InfoPath is in many ways fundamentally different from existing Office applications. Whereas Excel and Word were originally (and still are) end-user tools, with VBA functionality added later, InfoPath is a developer's tool. It addresses an area of business activity that has been neglected by software vendors until now: tackling the task of forms-based information gathering head on. InfoPath makes full use of a full range of XML technologies, unlike other Office tools that have been retrofitted with XML parts. The development environment comes with a rich range of options: a design mode interface, declarative XML programming, conventional script-based coding with JScript or VBScript languages—or a combination of all three approaches. And last but not least, the whole environment is wrapped in an excellent user interface, which is up to Microsoft's usual high standards, and that will please both you and your users.

What Does This Book Cover?

Like all other books in the Wrox Professional series of books, we've provided a thorough introduction to the important features of InfoPath, you'll need as a developer. Starting with a general introduction InfoPath and the development environment, the book goes on to discuss the architecture of the XML form templates. We then take you, in two detailed chapters, through the structure of what Microsoft calls the form definition file. Then you can read about external data sources and back-end services you can connect to, and how to work with them.

We've already mentioned the InfoPath development environment and the options it provides. A chapter on business logic introduces the layers of validation from XML Schema, through interface controls, to scripting code. You'll learn more about the variety of controls that are available and how to customize them.

To round off the first part of the book, we cover the issues of updating forms during the development cycle and as business requirements change. Then you'll learn about the InfoPath security model, how to implement and deploy trusted forms, and about the use of digital signature.

A very comprehensive six-chapter case study follows. The study follows the development of a news and features syndication design and its implementation using a variety of techniques. This application includes the processing of story meta data from contributors, through the news desk, and out to RSS news feeds. There is also a section on exporting XML data to Excel for analysis.

Who Is This Book For?

If you're a developer with a good knowledge of XML and its related technologies, and solid experience of Microsoft Office and related applications, you are in an ideal position to get started with InfoPath and therefore with this book. That's because, as you'll see, InfoPath makes extensive use of XML technology throughout.

Here are some of the specifications and techniques that will help you quickly appreciate how InfoPath works and get started on building powerful applications:

- ❑   XML
- ❑   XML Schema
- ❑   XSLT
- ❑   XPath

As usual, the more you know in this area, the faster you'll get up the learning curve. We've assumed that you are well along the curve already. However, if you aren't an XML expert, don't be discouraged from digging into what we think is one of Microsoft's most innovative developments in recent years. InfoPath includes a large number of out-of the box sample forms that you can modify and use in different contexts as a learning tool. You can also build forms just by using the built-in XML schema. We also hope that this book will give you a head start, with tips on how to get the most results for the least effort. For example, if you can work out how to use XPath in an InfoPath form, that's enough for a start. You don't need to imbibe the whole XPath recommendation from the W3C Web site!

Learning the basics of XML and its multiple related standards isn't difficult, just a little time-consuming. But we hope you'll forgive us for assuming that you have enough knowledge and experience for us to leave most explanations to other sources of information. As you read through the book, we'll point you at plenty of URLs that will assist you in broadening your knowledge if you need to.

What You Need to Use This Book

Here's the minimum that you'll need to make use of most of the book.

- ❑   InfoPath 2003 in either the standalone version or the version that is supplied as part of Microsoft Office 2003 Enterprise Edition
- ❑   Microsoft Internet Explorer 6, which is required to run the InfoPath on the desktop
- ❑   A text editor such as Notepad or the editor in Visual Studio, though specialized XML validating tools are preferable

    Additionally, we recommend the following if you want to follow all the examples and the entire case study:

- ❑   Microsoft Access or Microsoft SQL Server
- ❑   Microsoft Excel 2003
- ❑   The InfoPath 2003 Developer's SDK
- ❑   Code examples download from the Wrox Web site

How Is This Book Structured?

Following is an outline of the structure. Check the Table of Contents for more detail. There's no particular need to follow the early chapters in sequence. In particular, you might want to skim Chapters 3 and 4 and return to them as you get more familiar with InfoPath. However, we do recommend that you read the case study Chapters 11 to 17 in order.

1. **About InfoPath**

   Why does MS Office 2003 need yet another XML processor? The answer is forms, possibly the last arena in office systems that is pretty much untouched by XML technology. Here we look at similarities and differences between different form-processing approaches, review the InfoPath development options open to you, and take a look at the design user interface.

2. **Form Template Architecture**

   This chapter provides an overview of the architecture of an InfoPath form template and gives you an insight into the purpose of the various form files that may be combined in a template to meet business requirements. Templates can vary in complexity, depending on the requirement they are addressing, so you won't necessarily need to use all these file types in a given application.

3. **Key Form Elements**

   Using standard InfoPath features in design mode, you can build a form interface using menus or objects on the task pane. Here you'll dig into the details by looking at the key XML element groups that shape the InfoPath user interface and see how interface controls relate to sets of XML tags in the form definition schema.

4. **Meta Data Elements**

   This chapter develops your knowledge of the XSF structure in greater depth, by looking at a number of element sets that contain meta data, or information about the form as a whole.

5. **Integrating Secondary Data Sources**

   Data gathering is normally a task that requires productive interfaces, where users don't waste time. Experienced users may know product, category, and area codes. However, new employees and infrequent users need support. In this chapter you will see how to solve this kind of problem while maintaining a high level of flexibility and usability.

6. **Adding Business Logic**

   Any data form you have to fill out in a real-world application must follow some predefined rules. It doesn't make a difference if the form is on paper or electronic; it must be completed correctly. InfoPath provides a rich support for business logic definitions, making it an ideal application for creating complex forms for business use. This chapter examines the different means of validating forms and reporting errors.

7. **Back-End Services**

   XML is a lingua franca, which makes InfoPath interoperable with back-end processes and applications, such as databases, Web services, application services and so on. This chapter will provide you with a general overview of the back-end integration process, giving you an understanding of how to incorporate your forms in several business scenarios.

8. Component Types and Controls

Here you expand on your understanding of the different component types supported in the form definition editing elements. You'll look further into the way InfoPath handles the six editing component types: xField, xTextList, xCollection, xOptional, xReplace, and xImage You'll also examine the potential of some other interesting InfoPath form controls.

9. Upgrading Forms

In this chapter you'll consider the issues around upgrading your InfoPath application, including changes to the main schema and modifications to external data sources. The chapter also covers XSF upgrade parameters and form versioning information. Much of this section also applies to the development and testing cycle. Even if you have had plenty of experience in developing applications, you will find that InfoPath has some specific requirements.

10. Security

The InfoPath security model is based on the Internet Explorer model, which attempts to protect your computer from unsafe operations by using security zones and levels. In this chapter you'll explore the model in more detail and see how InfoPath also allows for other form security measures, including protecting form design, managing operations such as form merging and submission, and trusting installed forms. You'll also review the way digital signatures are implemented in InfoPath and take a brief tour of the features of XML Digital Signature.

11. Customizing Forms

In this chapter, as a preliminary to the case study, you'll review the different approaches you can take with interface customization in InfoPath forms. The goal is to help you give your users a better experience when they work with your form application. Partly it's a question of good design practice, but you'll also find that InfoPath has some useful features that you can exploit.

12. Introducing the Case Study

In this chapter you'll learn about the background to the case study that you'll work through in the remainder of the book. It details the business requirements of NewsLine, a news and features service, and provides information about workflows and data structures. You'll learn about the three interrelated standards specified in the requirements: Publishing Requirements for Industry Standard Metadata (PRISM), the Resource Definition Format (RDF), and RDF Site Summary (RSS). To round off this section, you'll also have a look at our first thoughts on a design solution

13. Input Data Structures

In this chapter you'll look at the XML schema for the meta data capture form. As you develop the form schema, you'll also need to consider the data output requirements in conjunction with meeting the PRISM and RSS standards. To help things along, we've created a form template showing one possible solution to the application problem. As we go along, we'll suggest alternative approaches that you might want to explore. Your overall task in schema design is to create a robust set of data structures for capturing and processing the meta data. This means developing schemas that express the data content at each processing stage and the constraints that will contribute to validating user input.

14. Implementing the Template

In this chapter you'll assemble your form components into three views, and you'll look at techniques for merging stories using an XML source file and adding a task pane to help your users.

We'll illustrate how our proposed user interface looks and how you might go about dealing with some specific design issues. Essentially, you'll step through the three views in sequence, looking at the more interesting points, dealing with some simple scripts and some XSLT as you go. Rounding things off, you'll examine ways to construct a basic help system, with functions to switch views from the task pane.

15. ADO Scripts for Rates

In this chapter, you look at how to calculate the payment for each contribution approved by an editor. The calculation is based on some form information and contract details from a local Access database. We also introduce the Access database structure, the XML source elements, and computation scripts needed to calculate the payments to contributors. You'll see also how to update and complete information on the contributor and the story.

16. ADO Scripts for Posting

When stories are approved for publication, NewsLine archives them to a server, where customers can query the meta data. In this chapter you'll see how story meta data is posted to the server using ADO from scripts in InfoPath. The database model shows how to balance the need for easy access with the minimum amount of code, by storing some meta data as a binary object and using just a few keys for queries.

17. Output Data Structures

In Chapter 13 you analyzed the input data structures for the NewsLine application. Now its time to look into the output data structures and transforms needed to push your InfoPath meta data to Excel and RSS news feeds, and to serve the NewsLine customer Web site. First we've included a brief digression into the new XML features in Excel 2003. If you are already completely familiar with XML lists, the mapping interface and procedures, and importing and exporting XML, you can skip this section. Then you'll look into the InfoPath-to-Excel export data schema and how to map the output on to a payment analysis spreadsheet. To wind up the case study, you'll consider a modular structure that will support both the RSS output for the news feed and the XML/RDF archived and delivered as HTML in the Web site interface.

At the back of the book we've included the following appendixes:

A. InfoPath XSF Schema

This is the XML schema for the InfoPath form definition file (XSF). The schema is reproduced from the Microsoft Office 2003 Reference Schemas with minor formatting changes.

B. InfoPath Form Definition Reference

This reference lists the types, groups, elements, and attributes in the form definition schema in separate alphabetical sequences.

C. InfoPath Object Model Reference

The InfoPath Object Model (OM) provides extensive facilities for programming using JScript or VBScript. This reference provides details of the interfaces for all the objects, collections, events, methods, and properties that you'll need to develop code.

D. References

In this section we have included references to the primary references to standards and specifications likely to be of interest to InfoPath developers Also included are relevant Microsoft Developer Center URLs and Web sites on meta data standards.

Conventions

To help you get the most from the text and keep track of what's happening, we've used a number of conventions throughout the book.

> **Boxes like this one hold important, not-to-be forgotten information that is directly relevant to the surrounding text.**

Tips, hints, tricks, and asides to the current discussion are offset and placed in italics like this.

As for styles in the text:

❑ We highlight important words when we introduce them

❑ We show keyboard strokes like this: Ctrl+A

❑ We show filenames, URLs, and code within the text like so: `persistence.properties`

❑ We present code in two different ways:

```
In code examples we highlight new and important code with a gray background.
```

```
The gray highlighting is not used for code that's less important in the present
context or has been shown before.
```

Source Code

As you work through the examples in this book, you may choose either to type in all the code manually or to use the source code files that accompany the book. All of the source code used in this book is available for download at `www.wrox.com`. Once at the site, simply locate the book's title (either by using the Search box or by using one of the title lists) and click the `Download Code` link on the book's detail page to obtain all the source code for the book.

Because many books have similar titles, you may find it easiest to search by ISBN; for this book the ISBN is 0-7645-5713-0.

Once you download the code, just decompress it with your favorite compression tool. Alternately, you can go to the main Wrox code download page at `www.wrox.com/dynamic/books/download.aspx` to see the code available for this book and all other Wrox books.

Errata

We make every effort to ensure that there are no errors in the text or in the code. However, no one is perfect, and mistakes do occur. If you find an error in one of our books, like a spelling mistake or faulty piece of code, we would be very grateful for your feedback. By sending in errata you may save another reader hours of frustration and at the same time you will be helping us provide even higher quality information.

To find the errata page for this book, go to www.wrox.com and locate the title using the Search box or one of the title lists. Then, on the book details page, click the Book Errata link. On this page you can view all errata that has been submitted for this book and posted by Wrox editors. A complete book list including links to each book's errata is also available at www.wrox.com/misc-pages/booklist.shtml.

If you don't spot "your" error on the Book Errata page, go to www.wrox.com/contact/techsupport.shtml and complete the form there to send us the error you have found. We'll check the information and, if appropriate, post a message to the book's errata page and fix the problem in subsequent editions of the book.

p2p.wrox.com

For author and peer discussion, join the P2P forums at p2p.wrox.com. The forums are a Web-based system for you to post messages relating to Wrox books and related technologies and interact with other readers and technology users. The forums offer a subscription feature to e-mail you topics of interest of your choosing when new posts are made to the forums. Wrox authors, editors, other industry experts, and your fellow readers are present on these forums.

At http://p2p.wrox.com you will find a number of different forums that will help you not only as you read this book but also as you develop your own applications. To join the forums, just follow these steps:

1. Go to p2p.wrox.com and click the **Register** link.
2. Read the terms of use and click Agree.
3. Complete the required information to join as well as any optional information you wish to provide, and click Submit.
4. You will receive an e-mail with information describing how to verify your account and complete the joining process.

    You can read messages in the forums without joining P2P, but in order to post your own messages, you must join.

Once you join, you can post new messages and respond to messages other users post. You can read messages at any time on the Web. If you would like to have new messages from a particular forum e-mailed to you, click the Subscribe to this Forum icon by the forum name in the forum listing.

For more information about how to use the Wrox P2P, be sure to read the P2P FAQs for answers to questions about how the forum software works as well as many common questions specific to P2P and Wrox books. To read the FAQs, click the FAQ link on any P2P page.

1

About InfoPath

In the spring and summer of 2002, Microsoft started showing pre-alpha versions of what was then called XDocs to selected corporate customers. Something interesting was on the way. XDocs was far from finished, and it wasn't certain how what is now InfoPath would be positioned or how it would fit into the rest of the Office product line. Some limited XML features were already present in the existing Office applications, and it was reasonable to expect enhancements in that area in the next major release. It was also clear, even then, that InfoPath was going to be something of a departure.

If InfoPath joined the Office application suite, it would be the only product without a considerable pre-XML legacy, and there was an opportunity to make a fresh start in introducing XML compatibility to part of the product line. It also seemed, as is still evident, that InfoPath would initially be much more dependent on developer skills than anything else in Microsoft Office 2003.

As time passed we learned that support for XML in the 2003 versions of Access, Excel, and Word would be expanded considerably from what was initially available in Office XP. The missing piece was the fit for InfoPath. In retrospect it seems obvious. InfoPath would be a new information-gathering program using XML as its native file format.

But why does Office need yet another XML processor? With the new features in Word, we can create custom XML documents. And Access 2003 and Excel 2003 will now do a good job of capturing regular data structures in any schema we choose. The answer lies in *forms*, possibly the last arena in office systems that is pretty much untouched by XML technology.

Initially, because of its inheritance from SGML, XML was seen as an enhancement that would benefit online document-oriented applications. Then XML was adopted, some think hijacked, by developers who wanted it as an interoperable format to oil the wheels of e-commerce, and there's no doubt that data-oriented XML has recently been the primary driver of Internet standards. Forms sit somewhere between the two poles of document and data orientation. Whereas documents can have extremely complex information structures, including features such as repeating elements and recursion, regular structures like database tables and spreadsheets are simple and straightforward. Office forms can combine the two features. They are usually quite short but often take a semistructured form, combining simple field lists with optional sections and repeating elements—for example, the dates and details in an expense claim.

XML Forms

Consider first the very general example of the expense or travel claim. Suppose Human Resources has given you an electronic copy of an Excel sheet that will work everything out for you. You fill in the blanks and print it out. Then you put it on your manager's desk so she can sign it. Eventually, it gets to Payroll, where someone else enters some or all of the data again.

Now you perform the same task, this time using InfoPath. Instead of a spreadsheet, you download a form template to complete. It also does the necessary calculations. You e-mail it to your manager, who approves it with a digital signature and routes the form to anyone else who needs to sign. The XML data is harvested by the payroll system, and the repayment gets added to your pay slip in time for the big weekend you have planned. This by itself is probably a sufficient motive for any developer to learn InfoPath and implement a new staff expenses system.

From a less selfish perspective, think of the thoroughly forms-intensive business processes where data is still bound up in paper-based systems. If you have ever worked for an insurance company, a financial services firm, a hospital, or a government department, you'll see the huge potential in unlocking the data carried in office forms.

But without a doubt the most attractive feature of InfoPath is that you can hide the complexities of XML from end users. Even if you understand XML, it can get in the way. A while ago, one of us explored the idea of introducing XML capture for a large group of developers working on a complex API. It would have made the creation of an HTML reference easy, but while everyone saw the validity of the business case, they rebelled at the thought of using a traditional XML editor. If InfoPath had been available then, no doubt they would have been more supportive.

Microsoft isn't the first, let alone the only, vendor to spot the opportunity for forms tools, and there will be plenty of competition for this very large market segment. Microsoft may have an advantage, however, because of its dominant position in the office market.

To put InfoPath in context, we suggest you take a few moments to look at the alternatives there are to the approach that Microsoft has taken. Several observers and commentators have compared InfoPath to XForms, a recent W3C Draft Recommendation intended to be integrated into other markup languages, such as XHTML or SVG. See, for example, Michael Dubinko's *XForms and Microsoft InfoPath* at `www.xml.com/pub/a/2003/10/29/infopath.html`.

Perhaps the comparison is made because there is an implied expectation that forms processing should mainly follow the Web processing model. You may or may not agree that the Web is the natural home for forms, but in any case a direct comparison just isn't productive. As Dubinko points out, that's because InfoPath is an application, whereas XForms, together with a number of other interface markup languages, is an XML vocabulary.

It may be more helpful to look at points of similarity and difference adopted by developers of XML forms applications, including XForms.

Common Features in XML Forms

When it comes down to it, XML forms processors have more in common than you might think. Essentially, they are there to convert user input into new or modified XML data, which can then be routed through a series of business process, possibly on multiple platforms in different organizations.

A central design concept is a "package" of files with distinct functions: a template document with a structure definition from a fixed, industry-standard or custom XML schema; an XML file to contain default data; and form data in an XML file that can be routed to points in a workflow. At each point, the data is loaded into a form, which provides a view into editing all or parts of the form. This process can be repeated as many times as necessary, with any number of participants.

Some approaches, like XForms, use fixed element names for controls and encourage implementers to define the purpose of the data-gathering controls. This makes it easier to generate the related structures automatically, for example, creating different interface objects for PDA and desktop browsers. Others are more focused on providing a rich user interface (UI). However, most have a wide range of display properties that include showing or hiding parts of forms and repeating sections where elements can be added or removed by users.

Points of Difference

Probably the first distinction to note is between Web-based XML forms and rich client systems. Web-based applications have their attractions, and on office intranets they have become a common way to collect some kinds of information from employees. They are easy to deploy and inexpensive to support. But thus far they have not been good candidates for workflow processing. That will soon change as XForms-based tools appear.

Rich client applications are relatively expensive to deploy and maintain, but they are often more robust and can be more readily integrated with other desktop client systems. They can be operated when users are disconnected from the network, and there is some evidence that users prefer them to Web-based tools when they have a choice.

Another distinction is between declarative and scripting approaches. A goal of the XForms specification was to limit the need for scripting; it therefore makes use of XPath-based calculation and validation, and includes XML `action` elements that specify responses to events like setting focus or changing a data value. In contrast, InfoPath, although it makes some use of declarative programming, including XPath expressions, encourages the use of script more often.

InfoPath Features in Outline

Later in the book we'll discuss InfoPath features in greater detail, but for now, here's a summary of some of the key XML technologies and development approaches.

XML from the Ground Up

InfoPath applies a range of XML technologies recommended by W3C that we noted in the Introduction. This is a first for Microsoft, and thus a first for you as an Office developer. Additionally, InfoPath makes use of XML processing instructions and namespaces. There are also methods for accessing the XML document using the InfoPath Object Model (OM).

The following table outlines the use of some XML standards applied in InfoPath.

Name	Description
XML	XML is the format that underlies an InfoPath form.
XSLT	XSLT is a specification for transforming XML files. It is the format of the View files that are produced when a form is designed. The transform creates an XHTML document that is displayed in the user interface.
XML Schema	XML schemas provide the underlying structure of the XML form and are the primary means of data validation. XML Schema is used to define the structure of the form definition. See Appendix A.
XHTML	XHTML is the XML-conformant version of HTML. In InfoPath it is used to display formatted text in rich text controls.
XPath	XPath expressions are used to bind controls to forms. XPath is also used in data validation, conditional formatting, and expression controls.
DOM	The Document Object Model is primarily used in scripts to access the contents of the form document, but it can be used with any XML document in the InfoPath environment.
XML Signature	XML signatures are used to digitally sign InfoPath forms created by. Forms can contain multiple signatures.

Some Constraints

Although InfoPath supports a wide range of XML features, there are some limitations or other constraints in this release that you should note. InfoPath 2003 does not support the following:

❑   XML Schema constructs `xs:any, xs:anyAttribute`

❑   `abstract` and `substitutionGroup` attributes on elements and types

❑   XSL Formatting Objects (XSL-FO) for the presentation of XML data

❑   Import or inclusion of arbitrary XSL files

❑   XML-Data Reduced (XDR) or Document Type Definition (DTD) for defining schemas

❑   Digital signing of parts of a form

❑   XML processor versions earlier than Microsoft XML Core Services (MSXML) 5.0

About Form Development

We've already noted a bit of a bias on the part of Microsoft toward code to extend the functionality of forms. This shouldn't be surprising, because Microsoft and therefore many developers of Microsoft applications have come to XML quite recently and have come from a code-based programming background. The structures found in XSLT, for example, can often seem obscure and foreign. As XML becomes a more prominent component in Office applications, we may come to see that declarative programming approaches are increasingly common.

When you modify InfoPath forms, by setting values in design mode or by editing values in the form files with a text editor, you are customizing the form *declaratively*. When you alter a form *programmatically*, you are writing code using JScript or VBScript following the InfoPath Object Model.

As we've mentioned already, there are often two or three ways to achieve the results that you want.

Declarative Development

Declarative development involves modifying one or more XML files, including:

❑   XML Schema that defines the structure of the form

❑   XSLT files that define the views on a form

❑   XML form definition file or *manifest* that specifies the overall structure of a form

Why might you want to use the declarative approach? Well, one reason might be that you prefer it to programmatic development in certain cases, but there are times when InfoPath leaves you few options. Here are just some occasions when declarative programming is either recommended or necessary:

❑   Custom form merging

❑   New menus and toolbars

❑   Schema and other upgrade modifications

❑   Custom transform templates

❑   Adding processing instructions to XML data files

❑   Exporting form data to custom Excel schemas

❑   Creating custom task panes and their associated files

Programmatic Development

You can customize a form programmatically by writing scripting code to perform a variety of functions. The main components that involve programmatic interaction are listed in the following table.

Component	Description
Object model	Type library composed of collections, objects, properties, methods, and events that give you programmatic control of the environment.
Data validation	XML schemas, expressions, and scripting code used to validate and constrain the data that users are allowed to enter in a form.
Event handling	Event handlers that respond to form loading, changes to content, view switching, and implement custom form submission.
User interface	Customizable interface components including menus and toolbars with related buttons, command bars, and a task pane.
Editing controls	Controls that include collections, optional items, text lists, and fields.

Table continued on following page

Component	Description
Error handling	Event handlers, OM calls, and form definition file entries used to handle errors.
Security	Security levels that restrict access to the OM and system resources.
Data submission	Predefined functions that can be used to implement custom posting and submission.
Business logic	Scripts to implement editing behavior, data validation, event handlers, and control of data flow. The logic can also access external COM components.
Form integration	Integration with other Office applications and SQL Server, SharePoint, or XML Web services.

Microsoft Script Editor

InfoPath includes the Microsoft Script Editor IDE (Integrated Development Environment) creating and debugging code, together with programming languages that you can use to extend your applications. However, while other Office applications use Visual Basic for Applications (VBA) as their primary programming language, InfoPath uses two scripting languages—JScript and VBScript.

JScript is an interpreted, object-based language that is the Microsoft implementation of the ECMA 262 language specification. VBScript is a subset of the Microsoft Visual Basic. However, while you have a choice of languages, you cannot mix the two languages in a single form.

You can set the default language for a form in the design mode interface. When you open Microsoft Script Editor (MSE) from InfoPath in design mode, the MSE code editor appears and the form's default scripting file opens in the code editing window.

In debug mode, you can use all of the debugging features that MSE provides, including using breakpoints, stepping through program statements, and viewing any of the debugging windows.

Introducing the Design User Interface

InfoPath has separate modes for the two distinct tasks of filling out and designing forms. Design mode is the environment in which you create or modify a form template.

Before getting into the details of form architecture in the next chapter, we'd like you to take a quick look at the InfoPath user interface, with an emphasis on the design mode features. So if you haven't already done so, why not start InfoPath and take a short tour with us?

Start by opening the form template called Absence Request that comes with InfoPath. To open the form, click the More Forms button on the Fill Out a Form task pane, and choose the form on the Sample Forms tab of the dialog box. The usual path of the form template files is C:\Program Files\Microsoft Office\OFFICE11\1033\INFFORMS\1033\.

The workspace is divided into two main areas: the form area and the task pane area. The form area appears on the left side of the screen, and the task pane area by default appears on the right, regardless of whether you are designing a form or filling it out. Figure 1-1 shows the Absence Request form with the Help task pane.

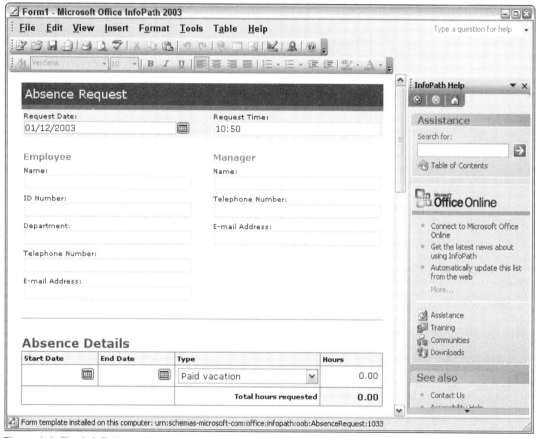

Figure 1-1: The InfoPath workspace.

The Form Area

The form area is where you enter your form data. When you fill out a form, the form template's location is displayed at the bottom left of the form area.

In design mode, a form appears in the same position, but you can access the form controls, set their properties, and define other form options. To switch between fill-out and design modes, you can either choose an option from the drop-down menu at the top of the task pane, click a toolbar button, or choose File⮕Fill Out a Form or Design a Form. Figure 1-2 illustrates the form area in design mode.

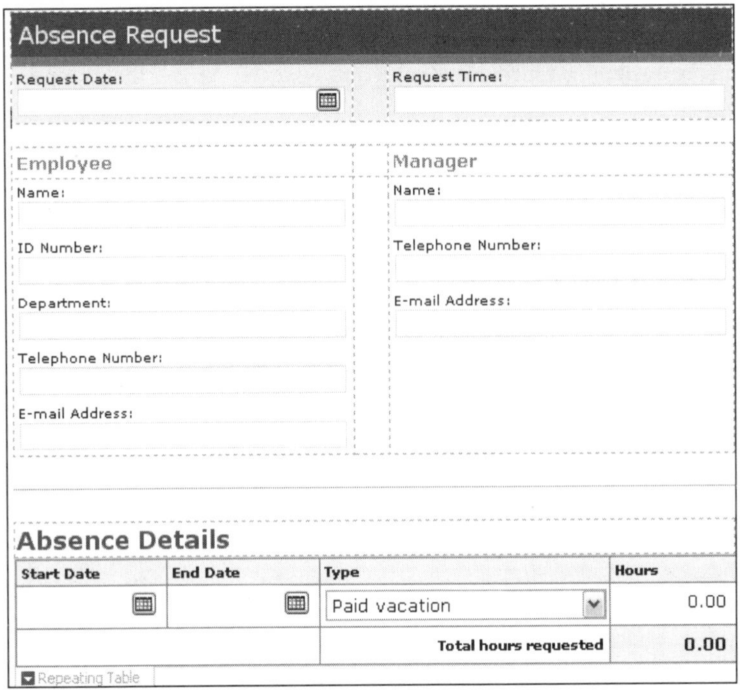

Figure 1-2: The form area in design mode.

The Task Pane Area

You can locate the task pane anywhere you like; it can be moved, resized, docked or floated, opened or closed, just like other Office applications. Depending on the context, task panes can contain commands for switching views, formatting options, and inserting form controls. They can also contain, help text, hyperlinks, or clip art.

When you design a form, you can create custom task panes that will be available to your users when they fill out your form. Custom task panes consist of an HTML file and can also contain form-specific content, such as command buttons and data catalogs.

When you design a form, your options include choosing between creating a new form or modifying a sample. New forms can be built from scratch, starting with a blank form and adding controls. If you create a new form from a data source, you have the option to base the form on an XML schema, a database, or a Web service. See Figure 1-3.

Design Tasks

The design mode task pane, shown in Figure 1-4, provides several options, three of which you'll review here:

❑ Layout

❑ Controls

❑ Data Source

Figure 1-3: The task pane in design mode.

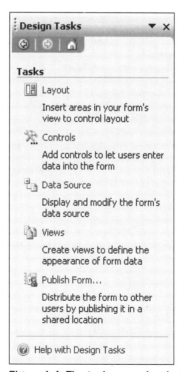

Figure 1-4: The task pane showing design tasks.

Layout

InfoPath provides for several tabular layout options, with four useful commonly used layouts that can be modified and one for a custom table. When you insert a table layout, InfoPath draws a dotted line around the table cells.

There are commands or task pane buttons to merge and split cells, add and remove columns and rows, and so on. Figure 1-5 shows part of the Layout task pane.

Figure 1-5: The Layout task pane showing table options.

Controls

When you click the Controls button, you can choose from a rich set of form controls (see Figure 1-6). Any control can be dragged onto a form. If you are using a blank form, InfoPath gives the control a default name and creates a related form field to which the control is bound. It also creates an element with that name in the form schema.

You'll learn more about the available controls and how to use them as you read through the book, especially in Chapter 8.

Data Source

When you click the Data Source button, InfoPath displays a hierarchical list of the fields to which the form controls are bound. Fields store the data that you enter into controls. Figure 1-7 shows part of the list from the Absence Request form.

You can set or view the properties of a data source field by right-clicking the field in the data source list and choosing Properties from the context menu. The Properties dialog box is displayed automatically if you have created a form from a schema, and you drag a new control onto the form.

Figure 1-6: The controls list.

Figure 1-7: The form data source list.

Figure 1-8 illustrates the properties of the XHTML `notes` element in the Absence Request form. Note that most controls in the dialog box are disabled. This is because the XML schema for the form predetermines the properties, such as name and data type, and you can't change them unless you modify the schema itself.

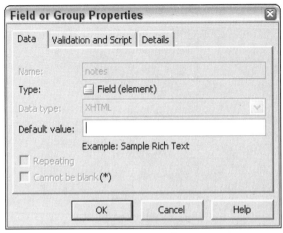

Figure 1-8: The form data source list.

Design Mode Icons

InfoPath makes extensive use of icons to give you feedback on objects in the design interface. It is worth spending a few minutes reviewing them, because it will help you understand the relationships between the form objects and the underlying XML document.

Data Source Icons

A field represents an XML element or an element attribute. If a field represents an element, it can contain attributes fields. The data source list also shows groups, which can contain fields and other groups. Groups typically contain controls like repeating tables and sections.

The table shows the three basic icons and their meanings, together with the decorations that are added for repeating, locked, and required properties.

Icon	Name	Meaning
	Group	An element in the data source that can contain fields and other groups.
	Element field	Stores the data entered into controls. This field can contain attribute fields.
	Attribute field	Stores the data entered into controls. Other fields cannot be added to it.
	Repeating field	May occur more than once. Lists, repeating sections, and repeating tables can be bound to repeating fields.
	Locked field	Cannot be moved or deleted.
	Required field	Cannot be left blank.

Binding Icons

In design mode you can tell if a form control is correctly bound to an element or attribute in the data source. Icons are displayed in the top right corner of the control if a control is not bound to a field or there is a duplicate binding. If the binding is correct, the icon shows only when you mouse over the control. The following table shows the icons and their meanings.

Icon	Meaning
title ⊖	The binding is correct.
ⓘ title (Control stores duplicate data)	The control may not function as expected because more than one control is bound.
Unbound (Control cannot store data) ❶	The control will not function correctly because it is unbound.

Summary

In this introduction to InfoPath, you looked at how InfoPath fits into the new developments in XML forms processing and saw how desktop applications compare and contrast with those designed around declarative approaches like XForms. You also reviewed the use of XML standards in InfoPath and some of the constraints that exist, and followed an outline of the programming environment. As a prelude to the overview of InfoPath architecture in Chapter 2, you dipped into some of the interesting features of the design mode user interface.

Now it's time to start working.

2

Form Template Architecture

This chapter provides an overview of the architecture of an InfoPath form template and gives you insight into the purpose of the various form files that may be combined in a template to meet business requirements. Here, you'll crack open your first template file and examine an annotated form definition file, along with a related XML instance.

You'll learn how XML schemas are associated with InfoPath depending on the data source that you choose. Then, as a prelude to the following chapter, you'll review some of the basic elements and attributes of XML Schema and look at the schema diagram conventions we use throughout the book.

Package Structure

When you open a template in InfoPath, the interface displays a single template file. This is a compressed file format that packages all the form files into one file. To quickly see how a package is made up, open any of the samples that come with InfoPath in design mode. Choose File⇨ `Extract Form Files`, and save them to a convenient folder. What you see in the extract folder will vary with the file you have selected.

When designing a form, you can work with these individual form files. For example, you can make manual changes to the form definition file or edit the XML schema. One reason you might need to make such a change is that it is the only available method. Also, if you are working with a form based on an existing schema, you must modify it outside of InfoPath with a text or XML editor.

InfoPath templates can vary in complexity, depending on the requirement they are addressing, so you won't necessarily need to use all these file types in a given application.

Form Template

The form template is the compressed file format that packages all the form files into one file. If you've extracted some form files from the compressed format as suggested, you can use any text or XML editor to examine them. The file extension is .xsn.

Form Definition

A form definition file is automatically generated by InfoPath when a new template is created and saved in design mode. It contains information about the form as a whole, together with all of the other files and components used in a form. As its name implies, the file serves as the manifest for the template. As you modify the template or add new features to it, InfoPath updates the manifest. The file extension is .xsf.

You can also modify this file directly. Indeed, there are several features that you can't add to the form definition file, such as custom toolbars, in design mode. However, you should take care in making changes, as you might leave the form template in an unusable state.

Because it is so central to form architecture, we've devoted Chapters 3 and 4 to a more detailed analysis of structure of the XSF file. The full XSF schema and a complete InfoPath XSF Reference are contained in Appendixes A and B.

XML Schema

The XML Schema files, referred to in a form's XML data file and that define its structure, are listed in the form definition. For simple forms you'll probably only want to reference a single schema document, but InfoPath supports multiple schemas if you need to use elements from more than one namespace. The file extension is .xsd.

If you use a modular schema and refer to modules using the `xsd:include` or `xsd:import` XML Schema elements, these module files also need to be included in the template. However, only the main schema file should be listed in the form definition.

View

InfoPath supports multiple views of form data. The view files contain the XSLT style sheets that InfoPath uses to build the primary user interface from the underlying XML data file. Each view listed in the form definition contains a reference to the related transform. The file extension is .xsl.

XML Template

The XML template file contains any default data that is displayed in a view when a new form is created by a user. This is just one way of providing default information. You can, for example, create scripts that automate the production of default values. The file extension is .xml.

XML Component Template

The component template contains XML representations of the editing controls that are used when creating and filling out a form. The file extension is .xct.

Presentation

This category includes the files used in conjunction with a view to create a custom user interface. Examples include HTML and image data files, and CSS style sheets.

Business Logic

Any JavaScript, JScript, or VBScript files used to program editing behaviors, data validation, event handlers, and other logic are contained in a scripts section of the form definition. Multiple script files are supported.

InfoPath combines all the listed files into a single scripting environment. Therefore, you should use only one of the supported languages in all the scripts for a form and ensure that script files have unique names and that there will be no name clashes in identifiers.

Binary Data

You can also include custom Component Object Model (COM) components to provide additional business logic.

Repackaging a Template

Often you can design a form without recourse to editing the individual files, because InfoPath will make a wide range of changes in the background, depending on what you choose to modify and the nature of the form's data source.

Our purpose in getting you to extract the form files in this chapter is to let you see the overall makeup of a template and get an overview of the structure of a form definition file. Extracting the form file leaves the original template intact, so you won't need to rebuild the files you've been examining.

However, if you have occasion to modify any of the form files belonging to a template, you can repackage the template by simply right-clicking the XSF file and choosing `Design` to open it. Then, choose `Save As` from the `File` menu, and click the `Save` button to save the template.

You'll read more about modifying form files throughout the book, and you can follow a detailed discussion of upgrading and related issues in Chapter 9.

Resource Manager

To make sure that all your users have access to the various resource files that support the functionality of a form, you can use the Resource Manager interface to add or remove them. For example, you may have decided to include an XML data file to populate a drop-down list and to provide HTML pages and CSS style sheets for a custom task pane. In general, you should plan to include this sort of material in the form as resources.

To access the Resource Manager, open a form template in design mode and choose `Tools⇨Resource Manager`. Figure 2-1 shows a listing of the resource files from the InfoPath developer sample on User Interface, uibasics.xsn.

Figure 2-1: The Resource Manager dialog box.

Form Definition Example

Following is an annotated example of a form definition file to give you an initial impression of XSF structure and content and to help you relate that to the form schema and instance. The XSF file is also from uibasic.xsn. The usual path of the sample files is c:\program files\microsoft office\office11\ samples\infopath\. To follow the examples, from Windows Explorer, you should open the form in design mode by right-clicking the file and choosing Design.

The User Interface sample form allows you to enter the artist, title, track names, and optionally the label of items in a collection of CDs. A custom task pane contains buttons that switch views, sorts the listing, and imports selected CDs from an XML file. Figure 2-2 shows the form interface.

Figure 2-2: Part of the User Interface sample form in design mode.

First, here's the XML schema for the form:

```xml
<?xml version="1.0" encoding="UTF-8" standalone="no"?>
<xsd:schema xmlns:xhtml="http://www.w3.org/1999/xhtml"
xmlns:xsd="http://www.w3.org/2001/XMLSchema">
    <xsd:element name="CustomUISample">
        <xsd:complexType>
            <xsd:sequence>
                <xsd:element ref="CDCollection"/>
            </xsd:sequence>
            <xsd:anyAttribute processContents="lax"
                namespace="http://www.w3.org/XML/1998/namespace"/>
        </xsd:complexType>
    </xsd:element>
    <xsd:element name="CDCollection">
        <xsd:complexType>
            <xsd:sequence>
                <xsd:element ref="CD" minOccurs="1" maxOccurs="unbounded"/>
            </xsd:sequence>
        </xsd:complexType>
    </xsd:element>
    <xsd:element name="CD">
        <xsd:complexType>
            <xsd:sequence>
                <xsd:element ref="Title"/>
                <xsd:element ref="Artist"/>
                <xsd:element ref="Tracks"/>
                <xsd:element ref="Label" minOccurs="0"/>
            </xsd:sequence>
        </xsd:complexType>
    </xsd:element>
    <xsd:element name="Title" type="xsd:string"/>
    <xsd:element name="Artist" type="xsd:string"/>
    <xsd:element name="Tracks">
        <xsd:complexType>
            <xsd:sequence>
                <xsd:element ref="Track" minOccurs="1" maxOccurs="unbounded"/>
            </xsd:sequence>
        </xsd:complexType>
    </xsd:element>
    <xsd:element name="Track" type="xsd:string"/>
    <xsd:element name="Label">
        <xsd:complexType mixed="true">
            <xsd:sequence>
                <xsd:any minOccurs="0" maxOccurs="unbounded"
                    namespace="http://www.w3.org/1999/xhtml" processContents="lax"/>
            </xsd:sequence>
        </xsd:complexType>
    </xsd:element>
</xsd:schema>
```

An XML instance, also in the samples folder, is named cdlist.xml. This file is intended to be used as an example to import. You can also view it in design mode by choosing `File⇨Preview Form⇨With Data File`. It looks like this:

```xml
<?xml version="1.0" encoding="utf-8"?>
<CustomUISample>
    <CDCollection>
        <CD>
            <Title>Meisner Darrell</Title>
            <Artist>Meisner Darrell</Artist>
            <Tracks>
                <Track>When The Saints Go Marching In</Track>
                <Track>On The Sunny Side Of The Street</Track>
                <Track>Ain't Misbehavin'</Track>
            </Tracks>
            <Label></Label>
        </CD>
        <CD>
            <Title>Abbas Syed</Title>
            <Artist>Abbas Syed</Artist>
            <Tracks>
                <Track>Dreams</Track>
                <Track>5150</Track>
            </Tracks>
        </CD>
        .
        .
        .
        <CD>
            <Title>Zimmerman Marc</Title>
            <Artist>Zimmerman Marc</Artist>
            <Tracks>
                <Track>via Medina</Track>
                <Track>Evviva 'o Rre'</Track>
                <Track>Tempo di cambiare</Track>
            </Tracks>
            <Label>Proseware Inc.</Label>
        </CD>
    </CDCollection>
</CustomUISample>
```

Finally, here's the form definition file generated by InfoPath, with some annotations:

```xml
<?xml version="1.0" encoding="UTF-8"?>
<!--
This file is automatically created and modified by Microsoft Office InfoPath.
-->

<!--Top level element with namespace declarations-->

<xsf:xDocumentClass
solutionVersion="1.0.0.2"
productVersion="11.0.5531"
solutionFormatVersion="1.0.0.0"
xmlns:xsf="http://schemas.microsoft.com/office/infopath/2003/solutionDefinition"
xmlns:msxsl="urn:schemas-microsoft-com:xslt"
```

```
xmlns:xd="http://schemas.microsoft.com/office/infopath/2003"
xmlns:xsi="http://www.w3.org/2001/XMLSchema-instance"
xmlns:xhtml="http://www.w3.org/1999/xhtml">

<!--Files in the package and their properties detailed-->

    <xsf:package>
      <xsf:files>
        <xsf:file name="schema.xsd">
          <xsf:fileProperties>
            <xsf:property name="editability" type="string"
              value="none"></xsf:property>
            <xsf:property name="rootElement" type="string"
              value="CustomUISample"></xsf:property>
          </xsf:fileProperties>
        </xsf:file>
        <xsf:file name="template.xml"></xsf:file>
        <xsf:file name="sampledata.xml">
          <xsf:fileProperties>
            <xsf:property name="fileType" type="string"
              value="sampleData"></xsf:property>
          </xsf:fileProperties>
        </xsf:file>
        <xsf:file name="view1.xsl">
          <xsf:fileProperties>
            <xsf:property name="viewWidth" type="string"
              value="542px"></xsf:property>
            <xsf:property name="mode" type="string" value="2"></xsf:property>
            <xsf:property name="componentId" type="string" value="13">
            </xsf:property>
            <xsf:property name="lang" type="string" value="1033"></xsf:property>
            <xsf:property name="xmlToEditName" type="string"
              value="7"></xsf:property>
          </xsf:fileProperties>
        </xsf:file>
        <xsf:file name="AllTracks.xsl">
          <xsf:fileProperties>
            <xsf:property name="viewWidth" type="string"
              value="542px"></xsf:property>
            <xsf:property name="componentId" type="string"
              value="3"></xsf:property>
            <xsf:property name="xmlToEditName" type="string"
              value="1"></xsf:property>
            <xsf:property name="lang" type="string" value="0"></xsf:property>
          </xsf:fileProperties>
        </xsf:file>
        <xsf:file name="internal.js">
          <xsf:fileProperties>
            <xsf:property name="scriptType" type="string"
              value="internal"></xsf:property>
          </xsf:fileProperties>
        </xsf:file>
        <xsf:file name="Import.htm">
          <xsf:fileProperties>
            <xsf:property name="fileType" type="string"
```

```
                    value="resource"></xsf:property>
            </xsf:fileProperties>
        </xsf:file>
        <xsf:file name="taskpane.htm">
            <xsf:fileProperties>
                <xsf:property name="fileType" type="string"
                    value="resource"></xsf:property>
            </xsf:fileProperties>
        </xsf:file>
        <xsf:file name="taskpane.css">
            <xsf:fileProperties>
                <xsf:property name="fileType" type="string"
                    value="resource"></xsf:property>
            </xsf:fileProperties>
        </xsf:file>
        <xsf:file name="script.js">
            <xsf:fileProperties>
                <xsf:property name="scriptType" type="string"
                    value="userEvents"></xsf:property>
            </xsf:fileProperties>
        </xsf:file>
    </xsf:files>
  </xsf:package>

<!--Form metadata-->

    <xsf:importParameters enabled="no"></xsf:importParameters>

<!--Views start here-->

    <!--Name, caption and transform for default view-->

    <xsf:views default="CD Collection">
        <xsf:view name="CD Collection" caption="CD Collection">
            <xsf:mainpane transform="view1.xsl"></xsf:mainpane>

<!--Mainpane editing components-->

        <xsf:editing>

<!--Repeating CD group-->

            <xsf:xmlToEdit name="CD_10" item="/CustomUISample/CDCollection/CD"
                container="/CustomUISample">
                <xsf:editWith caption="CD" xd:autogeneration="template"
                    component="xCollection">
                    <xsf:fragmentToInsert>
                        <xsf:chooseFragment parent="CDCollection">
                            <CD>
                                <Title></Title>
                                <Artist></Artist>
                                <Tracks>
                                    <Track></Track>
                                    <Track></Track>
                                </Tracks>
```

```
                    </CD>
                  </xsf:chooseFragment>
                </xsf:fragmentToInsert>
              </xsf:editWith>
            </xsf:xmlToEdit>

<!--Repeating tracks group-->

            <xsf:xmlToEdit name="Track_14"
               item="/CustomUISample/CDCollection/CD/Tracks/Track"
               container="/CustomUISample/CDCollection/CD">
               <xsf:editWith caption="Track" xd:autogeneration="template"
                  component="xCollection">
                  <xsf:fragmentToInsert>
                     <xsf:chooseFragment parent="Tracks">
                        <Track></Track>
                     </xsf:chooseFragment>
                  </xsf:fragmentToInsert>
               </xsf:editWith>
            </xsf:xmlToEdit>

<!--Optional label with rich text control-->

            <xsf:xmlToEdit name="Label_16"
               item="/CustomUISample/CDCollection/CD/Label"
               container="/CustomUISample/CDCollection/CD">
               <xsf:editWith caption="Label" xd:autogeneration="template"
                  component="xOptional">
                  <xsf:fragmentToInsert>
                     <xsf:chooseFragment>
                        <Label></Label>
                     </xsf:chooseFragment>
                  </xsf:fragmentToInsert>
               </xsf:editWith>
            </xsf:xmlToEdit>
            <xsf:xmlToEdit name="Label_4"
               item="/CustomUISample/CDCollection/CD/Label">
               <xsf:editWith type="rich" autoComplete="no"
                  component="xField"></xsf:editWith>
            </xsf:xmlToEdit>

<!--Artist, track and title-->

            <xsf:xmlToEdit name="Artist_5"
               item="/CustomUISample/CDCollection/CD/Artist">
               <xsf:editWith component="xField" autoComplete="no"></xsf:editWith>
            </xsf:xmlToEdit>
            <xsf:xmlToEdit name="Track_6"
               item="/CustomUISample/CDCollection/CD/Tracks/Track">
               <xsf:editWith component="xField" autoComplete="no"></xsf:editWith>
            </xsf:xmlToEdit>
            <xsf:xmlToEdit name="Title_7"
               item="/CustomUISample/CDCollection/CD/Title">
               <xsf:editWith component="xField" autoComplete="no"></xsf:editWith>
            </xsf:xmlToEdit>
```

```
            </xsf:editing>

<!--Toolbar with buttons to insert/remove objects-->

        <xsf:toolbar caption="CD Collection Toolbar" name="CD Collection Toolbar">
            <xsf:button action="xCollection::insert" xmlToEdit="CD_10"
               caption="New CD" showIf="always"></xsf:button>
            <xsf:button action="xCollection::insert" xmlToEdit="Track_14"
               caption="New Track" showIf="always"></xsf:button>
            <xsf:button action="xOptional::insert" xmlToEdit="Label_16"
               caption="New Label" showIf="always"></xsf:button>
            <xsf:menu caption="Remove">
               <xsf:button action="xCollection::remove" xmlToEdit="CD_10"
                  caption="CD" showIf="always"></xsf:button>
               <xsf:button action="xCollection::remove" xmlToEdit="Track_14"
                  caption="Track" showIf="always"></xsf:button>
               <xsf:button action="xOptional::remove" xmlToEdit="Label_16"
                  caption="Label" showIf="always"></xsf:button>
            </xsf:menu>
        </xsf:toolbar>

<!--Table, Insert and View menu definitions-->

        <xsf:menuArea name="msoTableMenu">
            <xsf:menu caption="Insert Tracks">
               <xsf:button action="xCollection::insertBefore" xmlToEdit="Track_14"
                  caption="Above" showIf="always"></xsf:button>
               <xsf:button action="xCollection::insertAfter" xmlToEdit="Track_14"
                  caption="Below" showIf="always"></xsf:button>
            </xsf:menu>
            <xsf:menu caption="Remove Tracks">
               <xsf:button action="xCollection::remove" xmlToEdit="Track_14"
                  caption="Remove Current Row" showIf="always"></xsf:button>
            </xsf:menu>
        </xsf:menuArea>
        <xsf:menuArea name="msoViewMenu">
            <xsf:button caption="CD Collection" name="SwitchToView0"></xsf:button>
            <xsf:button caption="All Tracks" name="SwitchToView1"></xsf:button>
        </xsf:menuArea>
        <xsf:menuArea name="msoInsertMenu">
            <xsf:menu caption="&amp;Section">
               <xsf:button action="xCollection::insert" xmlToEdit="CD_10"
                  caption="CD" showIf="always"></xsf:button>
               <xsf:button action="xCollection::insert" xmlToEdit="Track_14"
                  caption="Track" showIf="always"></xsf:button>
               <xsf:button action="xOptional::insert" xmlToEdit="Label_16"
                  caption="Label"></xsf:button>
            </xsf:menu>
        </xsf:menuArea>

<!--Context menu-->

        <xsf:menuArea name="msoStructuralEditingContextMenu">
            <xsf:button action="xCollection::insertBefore"
```

```
xmlToEdit="CD_10" caption="Insert CD above" showIf="immediate"></xsf:button>
          <xsf:button action="xCollection::insertBefore"
xmlToEdit="Track_14" caption="Insert Track above" showIf="immediate"></xsf:button>
          <xsf:button action="xCollection::insertAfter" xmlToEdit="CD_10"
caption="Insert CD below" showIf="immediate"></xsf:button>
          <xsf:button action="xCollection::insertAfter"
xmlToEdit="Track_14" caption="Insert Track below" showIf="immediate"></xsf:button>
          <xsf:button action="xCollection::remove"
xmlToEdit="CD_10" caption="Remove CD" showIf="immediate"></xsf:button>
          <xsf:button action="xCollection::remove"
xmlToEdit="Track_14" caption="Remove Track" showIf="immediate"></xsf:button>
          <xsf:button action="xOptional::remove"
xmlToEdit="Label_16" caption="Remove Label" showIf="immediate"></xsf:button>
          <xsf:button action="xCollection::insert"
xmlToEdit="CD_10" caption="Insert CD" showIf="immediate"></xsf:button>
          <xsf:button action="xCollection::insert"
xmlToEdit="Track_14" caption="Insert Track" showIf="immediate"></xsf:button>
          <xsf:button action="xOptional::insert"
xmlToEdit="Label_16" caption="Insert Label" showIf="immediate"></xsf:button>
        </xsf:menuArea>

<!--Print settings-->

        <xsf:printSettings orientation="portrait"></xsf:printSettings>
      </xsf:view>

<!--All tracks view-->

      <xsf:view name="All Tracks" caption="All Tracks">
        <xsf:menuArea name="msoViewMenu">
          <xsf:button caption="CD Collection" name="SwitchToView0"></xsf:button>
          <xsf:button caption="All Tracks" name="SwitchToView1"></xsf:button>
        </xsf:menuArea>
        <xsf:mainpane transform="AllTracks.xsl"></xsf:mainpane>
      </xsf:view>
    </xsf:views>

<!--More metadata-->

    <xsf:applicationParameters application="InfoPath Design Mode">
      <xsf:solutionProperties automaticallyCreateNodes="no"
        scriptLanguage="jscript" lastOpenView="view1.xsl"
        lastVersionNeedingTransform="1.0.0.0">
      </xsf:solutionProperties>
    </xsf:applicationParameters>

<!--Schema reference-->

    <xsf:documentSchemas>
      <xsf:documentSchema rootSchema="yes"
        location="schema.xsd">
      </xsf:documentSchema>
    </xsf:documentSchemas>
```

```
   <xsf:fileNew>
      <xsf:initialXmlDocument caption="User Interface Developer Sample Form"
         href="template.xml">
      </xsf:initialXmlDocument>
   </xsf:fileNew>

<!--Scripts-->

   <xsf:scripts language="jscript">
      <xsf:script src="internal.js"></xsf:script>
      <xsf:script src="script.js"></xsf:script>
   </xsf:scripts>

<!--Taskpane-->

   <xsf:taskpane caption="Custom Task Pane" href="taskpane.htm"></xsf:taskpane>

</xsf:xDocumentClass>
```

Form Schemas

When you create a new blank form and add elements to the data source by using the Add button at the bottom of the task pane or you drag controls onto the form, you are creating an XML schema in the background. Each group in the data source is an XML element that can contain other elements and attributes, and each element field in the data source is an XML element that can contain attributes and data. Each attribute field is an XML attribute.

Existing XML Schemas and Other Data Sources

When you design a form for an existing industry-specific or custom schema, InfoPath creates a data source using the schema definition in the XSD file. Because an existing schema is externally defined, InfoPath doesn't allow you to modify existing fields or groups in the data source. Depending on how restrictive the original schema is, you may not be able to add fields or groups to it either. If this is the case, you'll have to make changes to the schema itself before you proceed.

If you design a form based on an XML document instance, InfoPath creates a schema and the data source, using the content of your document as an example. If you decide to work this way, perhaps because there is no schema available, make sure that you use an example representing as many XML elements and attributes as possible. This will ensure that InfoPath builds a form definition that is close to your needs.

When you use a database or Web service as a primary data source, InfoPath structures the form using the database schema or the description of the operations of the Web service. Again, you won't be able to modify that part of form structure, because the data source must match the database or Web service specifications. However, you will be able to add elements and attributes to the root of the data source.

You can view some schema details by right-clicking an object in the data source and choosing Properties from the context menu. In Figure 2-3, the Details tab of the dialog box shows the properties of a group.

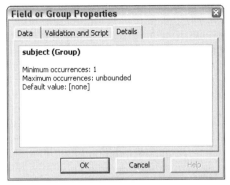

Figure 2-3: The Properties dialog box showing schema detail.

Schema Elements and Attributes

Throughout the book, we present diagrams for the XSF file and other XML schemas. Before you tackle the form definition structure, we'd like to include a short explanation of the symbols you'll see in the diagrams. In case you aren't familiar with XML Schema specification, we'll also briefly review some key parts of schema language.

The root element of a schema is `xsd:schema`, including the `namespace` and other attributes.

```
<xsd:schema xmlns:xsd="http://www.w3.org/2001/XMLSchema">
    .
    .
</xsd:schema>
```

You will see both `xs` and `xsd` used as the namespace prefixes in various sources. Technically it doesn't matter what the prefix is, as long as it is consistent in an individual schema document. In this book we use the `xsd` prefix to be consistent with the convention in Microsoft documentation.

The most common elements are `xsd:element` and `xsd:attribute`. You will also see groups and types, used to build block definitions that can be reused in more complex schemas. Common attributes of elements are `minOccurs` and `maxOccurs` that define the cardinality of an element. The default value for both attributes is 1.

An element containing attributes or other elements is defined as `xsd:complexType`. Within that element the structure is usually an `xsd:sequence` or an `xsd:choice`. Often you'll see `xsd:element` with a `name` attribute, but when an element is a child, it is usually declared separately using `name`. It is then referred to from the containing element using the `ref` attribute, as the following example shows:

```
<xsd:element name="scripts">
    <xsd:complexType>
        <xsd:sequence>
            <xsd:element ref="xsf:script" minOccurs="0" maxOccurs="unbounded" />
        </xsd:sequence>
        <xsd:attribute name="language" type="xsf:xdScriptLanguage" use="required" />
    </xsd:complexType>
</xsd:element>
```

Schema Diagrams

Content model is a term used to describe the set of elements and attributes contained inside another XML element. Although the XML Schema specification is explicit about how schemas should be presented in XML, there is no commonly agreed-upon format for symbols representing information in schema diagrams. Each software product has a different approach to diagramming. For these examples, we've used diagrams made with XMLSpy.

The diagrams show the structure and cardinality of the elements used in these structures. Attributes are not shown.

Sequence

In Figure 2-4, the symbol in the center, with the horizontal dotted line, indicates a sequence. This diagram says the element package consists of the sequence of files elements. Both elements are defined in the InfoPath namespace, whose prefix is xsf. The box with a plus (+) at the right indicates that there is hidden content not shown in the diagram. An arrow at the bottom left of an element indicates that it refers to a declaration elsewhere in the schema. The solid line around the elements indicates they are required elements.

Figure 2-4: The sequence model.

Choice or All

The switchlike symbol in Figure 2-5 indicates a choice; in this case, a choice between adoAdapter, webServiceAdapter and xmlFileAdapter. Only one may occur.

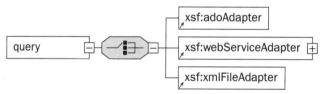

Figure 2-5: The choice model.

Another way of providing a choice is to use the structure diagrammed in Figure 2-6. The symbol is for the xsd:all element that allows the contained elements to occur in any order, either once only or not at all.

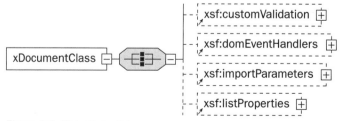

Figure 2-6: The all model.

Cardinality

Cardinality expresses constraints about the minimum and maximum occurrences of elements. A dashed line around an element indicates that it is optional. The number of times it may appear is given by the text below it. In this case, 0..∞ means the `minOccurs` attribute has a value of zero and `maxOccurs` is unbounded (infinity). If there is no such text, the diagram is showing that it can occur only once.

Figure 2-7 shows some additional information. The row of bars at the top left of the `errorMessage` element indicates that only text content is allowed.

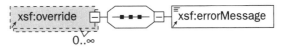

Figure 2-7: Cardinality.

Summary

In this chapter you learned about the architecture of a form definition file and seen how it serves as a manifest for all the form files needed for an application. You also reviewed an XSF example, along with the related schema, and an XML data instance.

We also introduced some basic elements in the XML Schema vocabulary and the symbols used in schema diagrams throughout the book.

In Chapter 3, you begin a detailed exploration of the key form definition elements that stucture the user interface.

3

Key Form Elements

In Chapter 2 you reviewed an example illustrating the overall structure of a form definition file, without going into the structure in depth. Here you dig into the details by looking at the key XML element groups that shape the InfoPath user interface:

❑ Views

❑ Mainpane

❑ Print settings

❑ Editing components

❑ Secondary user interface

Using standard InfoPath features in design mode, you can build a form interface using menus or objects on the task pane. This chapter shows how these controls relate to sets of XML tags in the XSF schema, expanding somewhat on the form definition example you've seen already.

As a basis for these examples, you'll work with a simple schema, based on the Dublin Core Metadata Initiative (DCMI) recommendations. If you want to look at the recommendations in depth, consult the extensive material at `http://dublincore.org`.

When you get to the case study later on in the book, you'll formalize the schema and develop it to include elements from other meta data vocabularies. First, we'll introduce some concepts around resource meta data and Dublin Core elements and look at an example.

Resource Meta Data

Before you begin your analysis of the key form elements, we'd like to introduce the concept of resource meta data. It underlies the examples in this chapter, where you'll work with a simple schema, based on the DCMI recommendations. When you get to the case study later on in the book, you'll formalize the schema and develop it to include elements from other meta data vocabularies.

What do we mean by resource meta data? Meta data means data about data. *Resource meta data* describes a set of properties about information resources and, specifically, about addressable resources. By *addressable resources*, we mean those that we can access on the Internet, using Uniform Resource Identifiers (URIs). Typically, the meta data describes the title and content of a resource, when it was published, and so on. It represents a Web page or a music download, rather than the HTML or MP3 file itself. If you've used a news feed or a Web portal, you've worked with meta data.

The object of defining this meta data is to make it easier to retrieve useful information about Web resources by being specific about their properties. In an ideal meta data world, if you specified a search with `publisher=wrox & title contains asp.net & type=book` as query parameters, you'd probably just get hits from Wrox Press, Amazon, and other book vendors' Web sites. You shouldn't, however, get articles from the MSDN site or ASP Resource Index, because you didn't want articles or either of these publishers.

Meta Data Vocabularies

Several XML vocabularies have been proposed for resource meta data. Nearly all of them use the DCMI recommended core set of 15 elements in some respect or another. You won't use every one of the elements here—just enough to get you started shaping an InfoPath form.

One of the reasons that the DCMI recommendations are widely accepted is that they focus on achieving interoperability. The specification is extremely simple and straightforward to implement. The International Standards organization has recently approved the core elements as an international standard: ISO 15836:2003.

DCMI advocates the *1:1 principle*, whereby one meta data record describes a single resource. So different editions, translations, and formats get separate descriptions. Thus, an image of a famous painting on a Web site is distinct from the physical object it represents, just as it is distinct from a stock negative in the picture library, or the audio guide that comments on the painting. Possibly the only common factor will be the title, but they can easily be related to one another.

Meta Data Example

Suppose you work for an imaginary online information service, NewsLine Inc., that handles a range of media and syndicates it to customers. You have to design an InfoPath form that will handle the creation of meta data about news, features, reviews, and other information categories. The meta data describes the content of the stories that the service publishes. Users of the form will save each instance of the meta data as a separate XML file.

Here's an example of the sort of meta data instance you might need to capture when a story is created, in this case a book review by a staff writer:

```
<meta>
    <identifier>http://newsline.net/reviews/0261.xml</identifier>
    <creator>Maria Grant</creator>
    <title>Stealing Time by Alec Klein</title>
    <description>The downfall of AOL Time Warner was a sensational tale of
dotcom boom and bust. Here is the full story by Washington Post reporter
Alec Klein, the man who exposed the scandals, and has now documented them in
```

```
a book published this month by Simon and Schuster.</description>
    <type>Book review</type>
    <format>text/xml</format>
    <date>2003-06-24</date>
    <subjects>
        <subject>AOL Time Warner</subject>
        <subject>Washington Post</subject>
        <subject>Klein, Alec</subject>
    </subjects>
</meta>
```

Most of the element names are self-explanatory.

The `identifier` gives the URL of the review itself, using a fictitious Web site. An identifier could use other formats, for example, an industry-standard serial identifier like an ISSN (International Standard Serial Number).

`creator` is the generic DCMI name for the person responsible for the intellectual creation of the resource, so it covers roles like composer, photographer, and artist, as well as author. (Secondary roles like editor, translator, and so on are relegated to the `contributor` element.)

DCMI `type` defines either the genre—that is, the intellectual type—of the resource or its presentation (there will be scope to clarify this somewhat ambiguous property in the case study).

The `format` states the Internet Media Type (IMT) of the file. You can read about IMT at `www.isi.edu/in-notes/iana/assignments/media-types/media-types`.

`date` means the date of publication or availability of the review. The recommended format of the date is yyyy-mm-dd, where dates (and times) are encoded with the W3C Encoding rules—a profile based on ISO 8601. See *Date and Time Formats,* W3C Note, `www.w3.org/TR/NOTE-datetime`.

Note the repeating `subject` element. The DCMI recommendation allows for the use of repeating elements in any order. This example puts subjects in a `subjects` wrapper element for convenience. These subjects are simple text labels. In the case study you'll enhance the design to use a consistent vocabulary of terms.

The XSF Root Element

Before you start your review of the key form definition elements, there's quite a bit of detail to absorb about the root element itself, and this seems to be the best place to do it.

xDocumentClass

The `xDocumentClass` element is the root element of the form definition schema. Only two child elements are required: `package` and `views`. Everything else is optional, though in practice most forms will contain a good proportion of the element set, depending on the functionality you've added. Figure 3-1 shows the top-level content model.

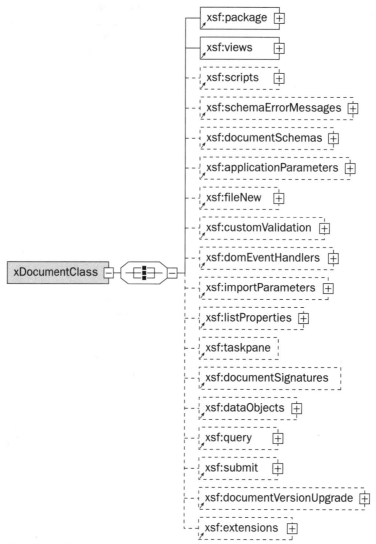

Figure 3-1: The xDocumentClass **content model.**

Root Element Attributes

The author attribute names the author of the form definition.

dataformSolution specifies that the form is based on an ADO or Web service data sources. Allowed attribute values are "yes" and "no" (default). You should set the value to "yes" for forms with a "query" view in order for them to work correctly.

The optional description attribute contains a brief description of the form.

The `name` attribute provides a unique URN for the form. If this attribute is missing, InfoPath uses either the URL or the filename in the processing instruction of the XML document or template. The default value is `"manifest.xsf`, as the `href` attribute in the example shows:

```
<?mso-infoPathSolution solutionVersion="1.0.0.2" href="manifest.xsf"
productVersion="11.0.5329" PIVersion="1.0.0.0" ?>
```

The InfoPath build number with which a form is created is contained in the `productVersion` attribute. The format of this number is nnnn.nnnn.nnnn (major.minor.build).

`publishUrl` is set automatically when a form is published or deployed using InfoPath design mode. When you open a form, InfoPath checks this value against its original location and prevents new forms being created if the template was moved. To enable the template again, you need to set the attribute to the current location.

`requireFullTrust` specifies that the form is a fully trusted URN form. Possible values are `"yes"` and `"no"` (default). If this attribute is set to `"yes"`, the form will get full trust security privileges and a URN in the `name` attribute must identify the form. You'll read more about trusted form and InfoPath form security in Chapter 10.

`solutionFormatVersion` gives the version number of the form definition file. It allows InfoPath to find if the current form is compatible with the product version. `solutionVersion` contains the version number of the form. The format of these two version numbers is nnnn.nnnn.nnnn.nnnn (major.minor.revision.build).

The required `xmlns` attribute declares all the global namespaces. Elements in the XSF schema are from the namespace `http://schemas.microsoft.com/office/InfoPath/2003/ solutionDefinition`.

```
<xsf:xDocumentClass
    author="Ian Williams"
    description="Metadata entry form"
    dataFormSolution="yes"
    name="urn:newsline.net:meta_input"
    productVersion="11.0.5106"
    solutionVersion="1.0.0.1"
    solutionFormatVersion="1.0.0.0"
    requireFullTrust="yes"
    xmlns:xsf="http://schemas.microsoft.com/office/infopath/2003/solutionDefinition"
    xmlns:msxsl="urn:schemas-microsoft-com:xslt"
    xmlns:xhtml="http://www.w3.org/1999/xhtml"
    xmlns:xd="http://schemas.microsoft.com/office/infopath/2003"
    xmlns:xsi="http://www.w3.org/2001/XMLSchema-instance">
    .
    .
    .
</xsf:xDocumentClass>
```

About Views

Each InfoPath form may have several views associated with it. For example, you might want to have separate views for different groups of users and others for printed output. A `view` element defines each view. A required single, top-level `views` tag contains all the views in a form. Figure 3-2 shows the content model for the `views` element.

The `default` attribute of the `views` element contains the name of the default view. In forms that use ADO or a Web service as their primary data source, InfoPath sets the default view using the `initialView` attribute in the processing instruction of the form's XML template file. You cannot alter this attribute in design mode.

```
<?mso-infoPathSolution solutionVersion="1.0.0.1" href="manifest.xsf"
initialView="Query" productVersion="11.0.5531" PIVersion="1.0.0.0" ?>
```

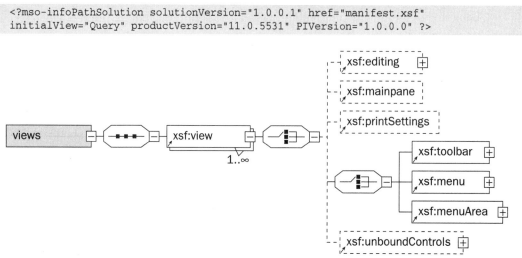

Figure 3-2: The views element and its content model.

The `view` element acts as a container for all the user interface elements for that view: the menus, toolbars, editing components, and so on.

In this application you create two views: an input view, used by writers when they file a story, and a print view, used to print summary information.

view

There must be at least one `view` element in a form, and each view must have a unique identity, specified using the required `name` attribute. If the optional `default` attribute in the parent `views` element contains a reference to a view name, InfoPath will use this view when a user first opens the form. Otherwise, the first listed `view` element will be opened.

You should also define a user-friendly `caption`, which will display in the view list. At this time, you can also choose to name the `printView` for the view, though you have yet to define it. Your input view example will look like this:

```
<xsf:xDocumentClass>
    .
    .
    <xsf:views default="meta_input">
        <xsf:view
            name="meta_input"
            caption="Story details"
```

```
            printView="meta_summary"/>
    </xsf:views>
    .
    .
    .
</xsf:xDocumentClass>
```

mainpane

Within a view, the required `mainpane` element represents the main form area, as distinct from secondary user interface areas such as the menus and toolbars. InfoPath builds the mainpane interface from the underlying XML data, using the XSLT style sheet file defined in the required `transform` attribute. By default, InfoPath names the views in a numbered sequence, "view1," "view2," and so on.

```
<xsf:view name="meta_input" caption="Story details" printView="meta_summary"/>
    <xsf:mainpane transform="view1.xsl"/>
    .
    .
    .
</xsf:view>
```

printSettings

The `printSettings` element specifies the printer settings used when printing a view.

All the attributes are optional. `header` and `footer` are text strings. Allowed values for orientation are `"portrait"` and `"landscape"`. These values correspond to those in the `Print Settings` tab of the design mode View Properties dialog box. `marginUnitsType` gives the unit of measurement for the following four margin values, but you must set all these values by editing the XSF file.

Now you'll define the summary view and apply some values to it:

```
<xsf:view name="meta_summary" caption="Story summary">
    .
    .
    .
    <xsf:printSettings
        header="Story summary"
        orientation="landscape"
        marginUnitsType="in"
        topMargin="1"
        leftMargin="1"
        rightMargin="1"
        bottomMargin="1"/>
</xsf:view>
```

Before you move on from views to editing components, here's a summary example of the elements you've seen so far, not forgetting a `mainpane` element for the summary view:

```
<xsf:xDocumentClass>
    <xsf:views default="meta_input">
        <xsf:view name="meta_input"
            caption="Story details" printView="meta_summary">
            <mainpane transform="view1.xsl"/>
```

```
        <xsf:/view>
        <xsf:view name="meta_summary" caption="Story summary">
            <xsf:mainpane transform="view2.xsl"/>
            <xsf:printSettings
                header="Story summary" orientation="landscape"
                marginUnitsType="in" topMargin="1" leftMargin="1"
                rightMargin="1" bottomMargin="1"/>
        </xsf:view>
    </xsf:views>
</xsf:xDocumentClass>
```

About Editing Components

What are editing components? In a form definition file, an *editing component* provides actions that allow form users to edit XML nodes, and exposes those actions in interface objects such as menus and toolbar buttons. These components are associated with the different XML *editing controls* that you can add to a form in design mode. Figure 3-3 shows the content model.

For example, the xCollection component has actions to insert and remove items from a list. In a form definition file, you can specify how to use a component with a particular XML node, such as one containing a meta data reference to a subject. As a result, you expose the user interface for inserting or removing subjects from the list.

Figure 3-3: The editing element content model.

editing

The editing components section of the form definition file specifies how and when users are able to edit nodes of the underlying XML document. A single editing element, the child of a view, contains information about zero or more xmlToEdit elements:

```
    <xsf:view name="meta_input" caption="Story details" printView="meta_summary">
            <xsf:mainpane transform="view1.xsl"/>
            <xsf:editing>
            .

            .
            </xsf:editing>
    </xsf:view>
```

xmlToEdit

Each time you insert a design mode control, you create a corresponding xmlToEdit node in the XSF. The tag specifies where the control is in the form view.

The required `name` attribute identifies the contained editing component as the target for button actions. There should be no more than one `xmlToEdit` element with the same name in a given view.

The `item`, `container`, and `viewContext` attributes identify the logical location of the control in the view.

`item` is an XPath pattern that specifies the XML nodes to be edited using components in the contained `editWith` elements.

`container` also corresponds to an XPath pattern; it determines the context in which the control can be selected and its actions enabled.

In design mode, InfoPath generates the full XPath expressions from the root element of the form for `item` and `container`. If you edit the form definition manually, you can use relative paths and predicates in your expressions.

The optional `viewContext` attribute is a string that identifies an HTML element in the view. It must have the attribute `xd:CtrlId` set to that string. So `viewContext="myID"` in the form corresponds to `xd:CtrlId="myID"` in the HTML.

```
<xsf:editing>
    <xsf:xmlToEdit name="subject" item="meta/subjects/subject"
            container="meta/subject">
        .
        .
    </xsf:xmlToEdit>
</xsf:editing>
```

editWith

`xmlToEdit` contains zero or one `editWith` elements. While the `xmlToEdit` tag specifies where a control is in the view, `editWith` defines the behavior of a control and specifies the use of a given component. It also provides the parameters to determine the component behavior (see Figure 3-4).

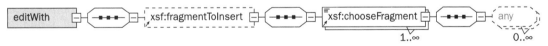

Figure 3-4: The `editWith` content model.

```
<xsf:xmlToEdit name="subject" item="meta/subjects/subject"
    container="meta/subject">
    <xsf:editWith component="xCollection">
        .
        .
    </ xsf:editWith>
</ xsf:xmlToEdit>
```

The principal `editWith` attributes are `component` and `caption`. `component` is the name of the editing component, referenced by the `action` attribute of a `button` element. `caption` is an optional identifier for alternate forms of XML data used in an `xCollection` control.

The table shows possible values for the `component` attribute with the associated design mode controls. You'll find more details about these components in Chapter 8.

Component Attribute	Design Mode Controls
xCollection	Repeating section and repeating table
xOptional	Optional section
xTextList	Bulleted, numbered, and plain lists
xField	Text and rich text boxes
xReplace	Replaces one XML fragment with another
xImage	Picture

All other `editWith` attributes set the parameters of an editing component.

`autoComplete` switches the auto-completion of controls on or off, and proofing does the same with proofng features such as the spelling checker. Allowed values are `"yes"` (default) and `"no"` in both cases.

`removeAncestors` specifies the number of ancestor (parent) elements to be removed when the last item is removed. The value must be a nonnegative integer. The default is `"0"`.

The `field` attribute specifies a relative XPath expression from the `item` attribute of the `xmlToEdit` element.

The following values are allowed for the type attribute: `"plain"` (default), `"plainMultiline"`, `"formatted"`, `"formattedMultiline"`, and `"rich"`.

fragmentToInsert

The `xCollection`, `xOptional`, and `xReplace` editing components can contain the `fragmentToInsert` element. In turn, it contains one or more `chooseFragment` elements in order to supply alternate versions of the fragment.

```
<xsf:editWith component="xCollection">
   <xsf:fragmentToInsert>
      <xsf:chooseFragment>
         <subject></subject>
      </xsf:chooseFragment>
   </xsf:fragmentToInsert>
</xsf:editWith>
```

chooseFragment

The `chooseFragment` element has an open-content model. It may contain text, one or more element nodes, or mixed content. In addition to, or instead of, XML data, it can contain one or more `attributeData` child elements that are each used to specify setting an attribute value.

chooseFragment has two attributes that give a relative XPath. parent gives a path from the container node. It refers to the XML node under which this fragment should be inserted. The default is to insert directly as a child of the parent node, prior to any nodes specified by the followingSiblings attribute.

The followingSiblings attribute is only used during an insert when the current context is not in an item. The behavior is to append to the content of the parent node, unless the followingSiblings attribute is specified, in which case the insertion is still within the content of the parent, but prior to any followingSiblings nodes.

chooseFragment elements are typically ordered in increasing size. The first will be the data fragment to be inserted by the insertBefore and insertAfter actions, when there is already at least one item in the collection. The insert action, on the other hand, can be invoked when there is currently a node in the XML tree corresponding to container, but no node corresponding to item (i.e., it can be used to insert the first "item").

Any element content within the XML fragment, other than attribute data, should be in the appropriate namespace.

attributeData

The attributeData element sets the name and value of an attribute that will be inserted (or modified if it already exists) by the insert action of an xCollection or xOptional component.

The attributes attribute and value set the name and values, respectively.

Secondary UI

By secondary UI, we mean areas of the interface other than the main pane: the built-in menu areas, custom menus and toolbars, and custom task pane.

menuArea

The menuArea element corresponds to the top-level menus found in InfoPath when you are filling out a form. Multiple buttons or menus can be declared within a menuArea. Each button element adds a menu item to the built-in menu and has an action (or command) associated with it. A menu element contained in a menuArea creates a cascading menu. Figure 3-5 shows the content model.

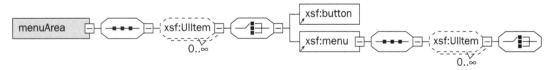

Figure 3-5: The menuArea content model.

The name attribute must be one of the built-in InfoPath named menu areas:

- ❑ msoFileMenu

- ❑ msoEditMenu

- ❑ msoInsertMenu

- ❑ msoViewMenu

- ❑ msoFormatMenu

- ❑ msoToolsMenu

- ❑ msoTableMenu

- ❑ msoHelpMenu

- ❑ msoStructuralEditingContextMenu

```
<xsf:view name="meta_input" caption="Story details" printView="meta_summary">
    .
    .
    .
    xsf:<menuArea name="msoInsertMenu">
    .
    .
    </xsf:menuArea>
    .
    .
</xsf:view>
```

menu

In addition to appending menu items to a menuArea, you can add entirely new menus, again using the menu element directly under the view element. InfoPath places these menus between the built-in Table and Help menus, in the order you declare them in the form definition. In addition, menus can contain both buttons and nested menus.

The required caption attribute contains the title for a menu. If a form-defined menu contains no visible menu items and has no visible submenus, InfoPath hides the caption.

```
<xsf:menuArea name="msoInsertMenu">
    <xsf:menu caption="Insert Subject">
        <xsf:button action="xCollection::insertBefore"
xmlToEdit="Subj_2" caption="Above" showIf="always"/>
        <xsf:button action="xCollection::insertAfter"
xmlToEdit="Subj_2" caption="Below" showIf="always"/>
    </xsf:menu>
    <xsf:menu caption="Remove Subject">
        <xsf:button action="xCollection::remove" xmlToEdit="Subj_2"
caption="Remove Current Subject" showIf="always"/>
        <xsf:button action="xCollection::removeAll"
xmlToEdit="Subj_2" caption="Remove All Subjects" showIf="always"/>
    </xsf:menu>
</xsf:menuArea>
```

toolbar

The `toolbar` element is an optional element of the `view` element. There can be multiple toolbars declared for a view, and each toolbar can have multiple `menu` or `button` elements.

You declare toolbars in much the same way as menus, using the `toolbar` element. Toolbars each contain zero or more `button` elements, with nesting providing for drop-down menus. InfoPath hides toolbar buttons if there are no visible menu items or submenus.

The menu in a toolbar is implemented as a button, displaying the caption together with a downward triangle to the right. Clicking the button displays a drop-down menu. Figure 3-6 shows an example displaying the caption and drop-down menus. When a toolbar is undocked, InfoPath uses the required `caption` attribute as the title of the toolbar.

Figure 3-6: An undocked custom toolbar.

The `name` attribute must be unique within a given view. If two views contain toolbars with identical names, unique naming makes it possible for InfoPath to maintain their location when you are switching between views.

```
<xsf:toolbar caption="Story Summary Toolbar" name=" Story Summary Toolbar">
   <xsf:menu caption="Insert Subject">
    .

    .
   </xsf:menu>
   <xsf:menu caption="Remove Subject">
    .

    .
   </xsf:menu>
</xsf:toolbar>
```

unboundControls

The `unboundControls` element contains the main pane buttons that you can drag from the Controls task pane onto the view in design mode (see Figure 3-7).

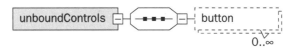

Figure 3-7: The unboundControls content model.

```
<xsf:view>
    .
    .
    .
    <xsf:unboundControls>
        <xsf:button caption="File Story" name="file_meta"></button>
    </xsf:unboundControls>
    .
    .
    .
</xsf:view>
```

button

The button element defines a button and an associated action. Each element corresponds to a button in a toobar, a menu item in a menu, or an unbound object on a form. These buttons or menu items can be dynamically enabled, disabled, or hidden, based on the user's selection in the view. The element also specifies either an associated editing component action or an associated script.

If the caption attribute is not specified, the value defaults to the caption provided by the related editWith element, which itself defaults to the empty string.

You can attach an icon to a button with the icon attribute by specifying a URL for a BMP or GIF image. You may also access a system resource by using its integer identifier. Remember to add any icon files to the form using the Resource Manager. If you omit the icon attribute, the caption alone will be used, and vice versa. If both caption and icon are specified, both will be displayed. If neither is specified, a blank button is shown.

If you use the OnClick event for the button to fire an editing component action, you should use the action and showIf attributes. showIf only applies to buttons used with editing components. Allowed values are as follows:

❏ always (default)

❏ enabled—Shows the button only if the action is contextually enabled

❏ immediate—Shows the button only if the action is contextually immediate

The name attribute associates the OnClick event handler of the button with a scripting function. Although name is optional, it is needed for buttons that use scripting code.

The tooltip attribute provides a pop-up text for toolbar buttons. InfoPath does not display ToolTips on menu items.

The xmlToEdit attribute is optional, but it is necessary for buttons that associate editing components to the OnClick event.

```
<xsf:menuArea name="msoInsertMenu">
    <xsf:menu caption="Insert Subject">
        <xsf:button action="xCollection::insertBefore"
xmlToEdit="Subj_2" caption="Above" showIf="always"/>
        <xsf:button action="xCollection::insertAfter"
xmlToEdit="Subj_2" caption="Below" showIf="always"/>
```

```
        </xsf:menu>
        <xsf:menu caption="Remove Subject">
            <xsf:button action="xCollection::remove" xmlToEdit="Subj_2"
    caption="Remove Current Subject" showIf="always"/>
            <xsf:button action="xCollection::removeAll" xmlToEdit="Subj_2"
    caption="Remove All Subjects" showIf="always"/>
        </xsf:menu>
    </xsf:menuArea>
```

taskpane

The optional `taskpane` element defines a custom task pane. It is a child of `xDocumentClass` and may occur only once.

The required `caption` attribute provides a display caption, used in the task pane's drop-down list box. The required `href` attribute specifies the URL of an HTML file. This file can provide help for users, as well as commands relating to tasks for a form.

To display additional task panes, you can include multiple HTML files in the form template and use the `Navigate` method of the `HTMLTaskPane` object in the InfoPath Object Model.

You can add a custom task pane file directly to your form template, so users can work with the form and task pane while offline, or you can link the custom task pane to the form from another location. Linking creates an absolute path to the custom task pane. Make sure the location of your custom task pane is available to all the users who fill out the form.

```
<xsf:xDocumentClass>
    .
    .

    <xsf:taskpane
        caption="Metadata Help"
        href="meta_help.html"/>
</xsf:xDocumentClass>
```

To complete this chapter, let's recap the key form definition file elements by putting them together in a final example:

```
<xsf:xDocumentClass>
    .
    .

    <xsf:views default="meta_input">
        <xsf:view name="meta_input"
            caption="Story details" printView="meta_summary">
            <xsf:mainpane transform="view1.xsl"/>
            <xsf:editing>
                <xsf:xmlToEdit item="meta/creator">
                    <xsf:editWith component="xField" type="plain" proofing="no"
                    autoComplete="no"/>
                </xsf:xmlToEdit>
                <xsf:xmlToEdit name="subject" item="meta/subjects/subject"
                 container="meta/subject">
                    <xsf:editWith component="xCollection">
```

```
                          <xsf:fragmentToInsert>
                             <xsf:chooseFragment>
                                 <xsf:subject></subject>
                             </xsf:chooseFragment>
                          </xsf:fragmentToInsert>
                      </xsf:editWith>
                  </xsf:xmlToEdit>
              </xsf:editing>
              <xsf:toolbar caption="Story Summary Toolbar" name=" Story Summary
     Toolbar">
                  <xsf:menu caption="Insert Subject">
                     <xsf:button action="xCollection::insertBefore" xmlToEdit="Subj_2"
                      caption="Above" showIf="always"/>
                     <xsf:button action="xCollection::insertAfter" xmlToEdit=" Subj_2"
                      caption="Below" showIf="always"/>
                   <xsf:menu caption="Remove Subject">
                     <xsf:button action="xCollection::remove" xmlToEdit=" Subj_2"
                      caption="Remove Current Subject" showIf="always"/>
                     <xsf:button action="xCollection::removeAll" xmlToEdit=" Subj_2"
                      caption="Remove All Subjects" showIf="always"/>
                   </xsf:menu>
                  </xsf:toolbar>
                  <xsf:menuArea name="msoInsertMenu">
                     <xsf:menu caption="Insert Subject">
                     <xsf:button action="xCollection::insertBefore" xmlToEdit="Subj_2"
                      caption="Above" showIf="always"/>
                     <xsf:button action="xCollection::insertAfter" xmlToEdit=" Subj_2"
                      caption="Below" showIf="always"/>
                     <xsf:menu caption="Remove Subject">
                        <xsf:button action="xCollection::remove" xmlToEdit=" Subj_2"
                         caption="Remove Current Subject" showIf="always"/>
                        <xsf:button action="xCollection::removeAll" xmlToEdit=" Subj_2"
                         caption="Remove All Subjects" showIf="always"/>
                     </xsf:menu>
                  </xsf:menuArea>
                  <xsf:unboundControls>
                     <xsf:button caption="File Story" name="file_meta"></button>
                  </xsf:unboundControls>
              </xsf:view>
              <xsf:view name="meta_summary" caption="Story summary">
                  <xsf:mainpane transform="view2.xsl"/>
                  <xsf:printSettings
                     header="Story summary" orientation="landscape"
                     marginUnitsType="in" topMargin="1" leftMargin="1"
                     rightMargin="1" bottomMargin="1"/>
              <xsf:/view>
          </xsf:views>
          <xsf:taskpane
             caption="Metadata Help"
             href="meta_help.html"/>
     </xsf:xDocumentClass>
```

The example isn't the complete XSF relating to our original form instance. However, Figure 3-8 shows how the complete default view might look.

Figure 3-8: The default form view.

Summary

In this chapter, you looked in detail at the structure of the xDocumentClass element and other key interface elements in the InfoPath form definition file. You were also introduced to some basic concepts relating to resource meta data and have seen how a simple meta data form is constructed using some elements from the Dublin Core standard.

In Chapter 4, you continue your review of XSF element structure by looking at InfoPath form meta data.

Meta Data Elements

In Chapter 3 you reviewed the key interface elements in the InfoPath XSF schema. Here you develop your knowledge in greater depth, by looking at a number of element sets that contain information about the form as a whole. Namely:

- ❑ Form initialization
- ❑ Schemas
- ❑ Files
- ❑ Scripts
- ❑ Event handlers
- ❑ External data sources
- ❑ Submitting data
- ❑ Merging forms
- ❑ Schema errors validation
- ❑ Custom validation
- ❑ Design mode properties
- ❑ Form selection

We deal with document upgrade and InfoPath extension elements in Chapter 9 and with document signature in Chapter 10.

Form Initialization

This section contains information used to initialize the form data when a user opens a new form instance.

fileNew

`fileNew` contains information used when the user creates a form based on a template. It contains a single `initialXMLDocument` element. Figure 4-1 shows the content model.

Figure 4-1: The `fileNew` content model.

initialXMLDocument

`initialXMLDocument` contains a reference to an XML file containing sample data to populate the new form.

The required `href` attribute specifies the URL of the XML sample data to be used by the File⇨New command. The default name is template.xml.

`caption` defines the text string to be used as the name of the form in the Template Gallery and in the most recently used list.

```
<xsf:fileNew>
    <xsf:initialXMLDocument caption="Travel Report
    href=http://server/folder/TravelReportTemplate.xml" />
</xsf:fileNew>
```

Schemas

The XML schema files that define the structure of a form's XML data file are listed in this part of the form definition. For simple forms, a single schema document is usually sufficient. However, InfoPath supports multiple schemas if required.

documentSchemas

The `documentSchemas` element is a container for one or more required `documentSchema` elements. It should contain only the main schema reference and any other declared schemas that are independently referred to in XML instance documents. Figure 4-2 shows the content model.

If you use a modular schema and refer to the modules using the `xsd:include` or `xsd:import` XML Schema elements, these module files also need to be included in the template. However, only the main schema file should be listed in the form definition.

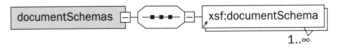

Figure 4-2: The `documentSchemas` content model.

```
<xsf:xDocumentClass>
   <xsf:documentSchemas>
      .
      .
      .
   </xsf:documentSchemas>
</xsf:xDocumentClass>
```

documentSchema

The documentSchema element defines an XML schema for a form. You should include one element for each declared schema in the form, and you should set the rootSchema attribute of the top-level schema entry to "yes".

The required location attribute contains the namespace URI and location URL, relative to the form definition file, and delimited by a space, the filename of the schema. Schemas without a namespace are listed with just the schema filename.

```
<xsf:documentSchemas>
      <xsf:documentSchema
         location="meta1.2.xsd"
         rootSchema="yes"/>
</xsf:documentSchemas>
```

Files

The files section of the form definition contains information about the full range of files in a form. These include default data, schemas, XSLT transforms, images, scripts, and custom task pane files.

package

The required package element is a container for information about all of the files in an InfoPath form. The content model is illustrated in Figure 4-3.

Figure 4-3: The package **element content model.**

```
<xsf:xDocumentClass>
   <xsf:package>
      .
      .
      .
   </xsf:package>
</xsf:xDocumentClass>
```

files

The required files element lists the set of files that are used in a form.

```
<xsf:package>
    <xsf:files>
       .
       .
       .
    </xsf:files>
</xsf:package>
```

file

The `file` element identifies an individual file. The required `name` attribute specifies the filename.

```
<xsf:files>
    <xsf:file name="myschema.xsd">
       .
       .
       .
    <xsf:/file>
</xsf:files>
```

fileProperties

`fileProperties` provides a wrapper for all file properties defined for the current file. See Figure 4-4.

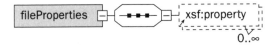

Figure 4-4: The `fileProperties` **content model.**

The number and naming of properties varies for each type of file, but their purpose and allowable values are not documented. You can, however, infer quite a lot by examining the XSF file for a complex form.

property

The optional `property` element defines one property for the containing `file` element. All the attributes are required. `name` gives the property name, and the `type` attribute defines its XML Schema data type.

For simple properties, `value` is included in the attribute. For complex (and multivalued) properties, value is defined in a container node using an open-content model.

```
<xsf:file name="myschema.xsd">
    <xsf:fileProperties>
        <xsf:property name="namespace" type="string"
            value="http://schemas.microsoft.com/office/infopath/2003/myXSD/2003-12-
            15T16:23:22"/>
        <xsf:property name="editability" type="string" value="full"/>
        <xsf:property name="rootElement" type="string" value="meta"/>
    <xsf:fileProperties>
</xsf:file>
```

Scripts

This section of the form definition contains any JavaScript, JScript, or VBScript files used to program editing behaviors, data validation, event handlers, and other logic. Multiple script files are supported.

scripts

The `scripts` element contains all the business logic scripts used in the form. Figure 4-5 shows the content model.

There can be more than one script element, all of which should be written in the same script language declared in the `language` attribute.

InfoPath concatenates script sources and loads the result into a single environment. Duplicate function and property names are resolved to a single object. So you should use unique names across scripts.

All script files must be included in the form template.

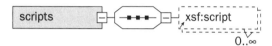

Figure 4-5: The `scripts` **content model.**

script

The `script` element identifies a single script file. The required `src` attribute is the relative URL of the file.

```
<xsf:scripts language="jscript">
   <xsf:script src="internal.js"/>
   <xsf:script src="script.js"/>
</xsf:scripts>
```

Event Handlers

The event handlers section specifies the handlers that are triggered by form or data validation events, as XML nodes in the underlying document are filled out or edited.

domEventHandlers

The `domEventHandlers` element is an optional, top-level child of the `XDocumentClass` element. It contains a collection of pointers to script-based handlers. Figure 4-6 illustrates the content model.

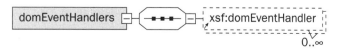

Figure 4-6: The `domEventHandlers` **content model.**

domEventHandler

`domEventHandler` defines an event handler for one or more XML nodes.

Both attributes are required. `match` contains an XPath expression to the node. The expression may not contain predicates. `handlerObject` identifies the unique name of the handler object in the script. For example, a script may contain functions such as `TravelExpenses::OnValidate` and `TravelExpenses::OnAfterChange` that are called whenever the specified events occur at the matching XML DOM node.

```
<xsf:domEventHandlers>
   <xsf:domEventHandler
      match="TravelReport/Expenses"
      handlerObject="TravelExpenses"/>
</xsf:domEventHandlers>
```

External Data Sources

InfoPath uses three kinds of data adapters to access external data sources, often called secondary sources. A *data adapter* is an object used to send data to and retrieve data from sources such as

❑   XML data files

❑   Databases

❑   Web services

This section of the form definition contains the data source references to any sources you define for a form.

dataObjects

The optional `dataObject` element defines all secondary data objects used in a form template. It is a top-level child of the `xDocumentCLass` element and contains a collection of `dataObject` elements that are used to populate the form from external data sources. See Figure 4-7.

Figure 4-7: The `dataObjects` content model.

dataObject

You can include multiple `dataObject` elements in a form. Each one is a node set that you can populate with external data.

The required `name` attribute is the unique name for a `dataObject`. You can use this name to access the object from XSLT view code and any form scripts.

In design mode, InfoPath packages the schema for each data object. An entry is made for the schema files under the `files` element, and this filename is identified in the `schema` attribute in the `dataObject`.

The optional `initOnLoad` attribute specifies whether the data object should be initialized on document load, using the query method for the object. Allowed values are `"yes"` and `"no"` (default).

```
<xsf:dataObjects>
   <xsf:dataObject
   name="topics"
   schema="topics.xsd"
   initOnLoad="yes">

       .
       .

   </xsf:dataObject>
<xsf:dataObjects>
```

query

The `query` element associates a data adapter with a data object or a form's underlying XML document. Only one data adapter definition is allowed in a query. There are no attributes. Figure 4-8 shows the content model.

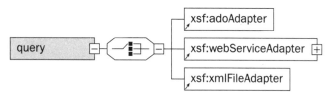

Figure 4-8: The `query` **content model.**

The `query` element can also be the child of `XDocumentClass`, in which case the main data source for the form is, for example, an ActiveX Data Objects (ADO) object. In this context InfoPath provides a form interface to add to or edit the data source.

```
<xsf:dataObject name="Currency" schema="currency.xsd" initOnLoad="yes">
   <xsf:query>
   .

   .
   </xsf:query>
</xsf:dataObject>
```

adoAdapter

The `adoAdapter` element defines an ADO data adapter to be used to access the data from an ADO data source.

The required `connectionString` attribute contains all the parameter values needed to connect to the data source. The required `commandText` attribute contains the SQL command for querying the data source.

queryAllowed is an optional attribute that specifies whether data can be retrieved using the query method of the data adapter object. Allowed values are "yes" and "no" (default). submitAllowed specifies the same options for the submit method.

```
<xsf:query>
    <xsf:adoAdapter
        connectionString="Provider=Microsoft.Jet.OLEDB.4.0;
            Password=&quot;&quot;;;User ID=Admin;
            Data Source=infnwind.mdb;Mode=Share Deny None;
            Extended Properties=&quot;&quot;;;..."
        commandText="select [EmployeeID],[LastName],[FirstName]
            from [Employees] as [Employees]"
        queryAllowed="yes"
        submitAllowed="yes">
    </xsf:adoAdapter>
</xsf:query>
```

webServiceAdapter

The webServiceAdapter element specifies a Web service data adapter to be used to retrieve the data from a Web service for the specified data object. You can also use it to define an adapter used to submit the main form data. The content model is illustrated in Figure 4-9.

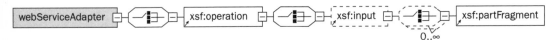

Figure 4-9: The webServiceAdapter **content model.**

The wsdlURL attribute contains the URL of the Web Service Definition Language (WSDL) file describing the Web service. The attributes submitAllowed and queryAllowed have the same purpose as in the adoAdapter element.

WSDL is an XML vocabulary used to describe a Web service. It specifies the location of the service and the operations (or methods) the service exposes. There are network protocol bindings for SOAP, HTTP GET/POST, and MIME. You can read the latest W3C Working Draft of the core specification at www.w3.org/TR/wsdl12/.

```
<xsf:query>
    <xsf:webServiceAdapter
    wsdlUrl="http://server1/bvtService/Service1.asmx?wsdl"
    queryAllowed="yes"
    submitAllowed="yes">
        .
        .
        .
    </xsf:webServiceAdapter>
</xsf:query>
```

operation

The required operation element defines a method on a Web service.

The `name` attribute is the unique name of the method. `serviceUrl` attribute contains the Web service URL to which the request should be sent. The required `soapAction` attribute contains the value of the identically named attribute in the SOAP request message. For example:

```
<soap:operation soapAction="http://xChange.com/getOrders"/>

<xsf:webServiceAdapter
    wsdlUrl="http://server1/bvtService/Service1.asmx?wsdl"
    queryAllowed="yes"
    submitAllowed="yes">
    <xsf:operation
       name="getOrders"
       soapAction="http://tempuri.org/getOrders"
       serviceUrl="http://localhost/infopathwebservicesample.asmx">
       .
       .
       .
    </xsf:operation>
</xsf:webServiceAdapter>
```

input

The optional `input` element contains the substitution information for parts of the input SOAP message to the Web service.

The required `source` attribute contains the name of the resource file in the form template that contains the XML Schema for the input SOAP message of the selected operation of the Web service.

partFragment

The `partFragment` element describes a specific part of the `input` element SOAP message. Multiple `partFragment` elements are allowed.

Both attributes are required and contain XPath expressions. `match` identifies nodes in the input SOAP message schema to be substituted/replaced. `replaceWith` points to the nodes in the XML form data that replace the input.

```
<xsf:input source="Submit.xml">
    <xsf:partFragment
       match="/dfs:myFields/dfs:dataFields/s0:IsPrime/s0:inValue"
       replaceWith="/dfs:myFields/dfs:dataFields/s0:IsPrime"/>
</xsf:input>
```

xmlFileAdapter

The `xmlFileAdapter` element defines a data adapter for retrieving information from an XML data source.

The required `fileUrl` attribute contains the URL of the file.

You can use this adapter to access relatively small amounts of static data, as opposed to a more dynamic source such as a database. In the case study, you'll see an example used to access a list of subject categories.

Another way that you can use an XML source is to populate drop-down lists in a form. This makes it possible to modify the choices from such a list from a single source, without having to make changes to a form template and redeploy it.

```
<xsf:query>
    <xsf:xmlFileAdapter fileUrl="currencies.xml" />
</xsf:query>
```

Submitting Data

This section contains information about submit functions for a form's data. As with data sources, you can submit data in several ways. You've already seen the definition for a `webServiceAdapter`, so we won't cover it again here.

submit

The optional submit element is a top-level child of the XDocumentClass element. Figure 4-10 shows the content model.

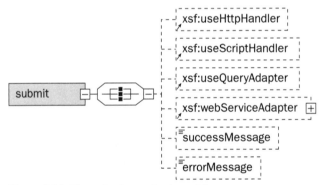

Figure 4-10: The `submit` content model.

The optional `caption` attribute defines the name of the submit button and corresponding menu item that will appear on the File menu. You can include a keyboard shortcut by inserting `&amp;` before the key. If you don't provide a caption, InfoPath uses `"Submit"` as the value. `disableMenuItem` specifies whether the menu item for the submit operation should be disabled.

`onAfterSubmit` specifies the action after a submission was successful. Allowed values are `"Close"`, `"KeepOpen"` (default), or `"OpenNew"`. If the submit operation is not successful, the `onAfterSubmit` attribute is ignored and the form is kept open.

`showSignatureReminder` specifies whether a dialog box should be displayed to prompt the user to digitally sign the form before submitting it.

showStatusDialog specifies whether the status dialog box should be shown after the submit operation. Values include "yes" (default) and "no". If the attribute is set to "yes", and no custom messages are defined, InfoPath displays default messages.

```
<xsf:xDocumentClass>
    <xsf:submit
    caption="Su&amp;bmit"
    disableMenuItem="no"
    onAfterSubmit="KeepOpen"
    showStatusDialog="yes"
    showSignatureReminder="yes">
    .
    .
    </xsf:submit>
</xsf:xDocumentClass>
```

useHTTPHandler

The useHTTPHandler element has two required attributes. The href attribute specifies the URL to which the form should be submitted. method specifies the HTTP method to use for the submit operation.

```
<xsf:submit>
    <xsf:useHttpHandler
    href="http://MyServer/InfoPathScripts/MyScript.asp"
    method="POST"/>
    .
    .
</xsf:submit>
```

useQueryAdapter

When you read about the query element earlier in this chapter, you saw that it could be a top-level element in a form with a database as a primary data source. useQueryAdapter is used to submit data to the ADO adapter contained in that query element. Note that this *not* the query element that is the child of a dataObject.

The useQueryAdapter element is an empty element with no attributes.

```
<xsf:submit>
    <xsf:useQueryAdapter/>
    .
    .
</xsf:submit>
```

useScriptHandler

When used with the submit element, useScriptHandler specifies that the form data will be processed by code in the associated script file. Submit code must be written in the OnSubmitRequest function in the script file.

`useScripthandler` has no attributes or child elements.

```
<xsf:submit>
   <xsf:useScriptHandler/>
   .
   .
   .
</xsf:submit>
```

successMessage

The optional `successMessage` element specifies the text to be used to notify the user that the submission was successful.

If the `onAfterSubmit` attribute of the `submit` element contains `"KeepOpen"`, InfoPath displays the message; otherwise, it is ignored.

errorMessage

`submit` may also contain an `errorMessage` element. The details of the `errorMessage` structure are covered later in the chapter, under *Custom Validation*.

```
<xsf:submit>
   .
   .
   .

   <xsf:successMessage>Submit was successful.</xsf:successMessage>
   <xsf:errorMessage>Submit failed for some reason, possibly a network
problem. Please contact your system administrator
   </xsf:errorMessage>
   .
   .
   .
</xsf:submit>
```

Merging Forms

If you have multiple forms that are either created from the same form template or are designed to work together, you can merge them into a single form. You'll see an example in the case study, where desk editors merge forms from several contributors into a single story list for later processing.

The form template specifies whether the Merge Forms feature is enabled for a given form, the appearance of the merged form, and the data to be merged into the new form.

importParameters

The `importParameters` element contains values that define how merging works for a form. If no importParameters section is present, merging is disabled. Figure 4-11 shows the content model.

If no contained `importSource` element is defined, the default XSLT file is used for all transformations during a merge operation.

The required `enabled` attribute specifies if form merging is enabled. Allowed values are `"yes"` (default) and `"no"`.

Figure 4-11: The `importParameters` **content model.**

importSource

The `importSource` element specifies all the parameters to be used when you are merging a form of a specific schema into the form.

The `name` attribute gives the URL of the source form as defined in its processing instruction.

The `schema` attribute identifies a schema URN. If the source form belongs to the schema, the XSLT specified in the `transform` attribute is used for merging into the current form.

```
<xsf:importParameters enabled="yes">
   <xsf:importSource name="" schema="meta1.2.xsd" transform="merge.xsl"/>
</xsf:importParameters>
```

Schema Errors

In this section and the next one, you learn about customizing schema error messages and custom validation using the XSF file. For more on business logic, schema validation, validation in design mode, and using the InfoPath Object Model (OM), see Chapter 6.

The default schema error messages returned by InfoPath, which simply match the XML Schema data type of an element, are not very helpful to users. Unfortunately, there is no way to change the defaults in design mode.

schemaErrorMessages

However, you can use the `schemaErrorMessage` element to specify your own messages for data type errors in the form definition file. See Figure 4-12.

Figure 4-12: The `schemaErrors` **content model.**

```
<xsf:xDocumentCLass>
   <xsf:schemaErrorMessages>
      .
      .
      .
   </xsf:schemaErrorMessages>
</xDocumentCLass>
```

override

You specify these messages by adding a set of overrides matching the errors you want to report. Each `override` element defines one overriding error message for schema data type errors for an individual XML node. So you can be very specific on message content. The nested `errorMessage` element is covered in the next section.

The `match` attribute contains a relative XPath to the node for which the override is defined.

```
<xsf:schemaErrorMessages>
   <xsf:override match="/meta/releaseTime">
      <xsf:errorMessage shortMessage="Embargo value is invalid">
         You must specify a complete date-time for an embargoed story
      </xsf:errorMessage>
</xsf:schemaErrorMessages>
```

Custom Validation

You use a very similar technique to apply custom validation to your forms. Figure 4-13 shows the `customValidation` content model.

Figure 4-13: The `customValidation` **content model.**

customValidation

The `customValidation` element is an optional child of `xDocumentClass`. It defines rule-based validation in addition to the validation enforced by the XML schema. You can enter a single validation rule using the design mode interface, but for multiple error conditions, you'll need to edit the form definition.

When you create additional error conditions on a field by entering `errorCondition` elements in the XSF file, they will not appear in the Data Validation dialog box when you are working in design mode.

```
<xsf:xDocumentCLass>
   <xsf:customValidation>
      .
      .
      .
   </xsf:customValidation>
<xsf:xDocumentCLass>
```

errorCondition

The optional `errorCondition` element defines a custom validation or error condition for a XML node in a form.

The required `expression` attribute contains an XPath expression (relative to the `expressionContext` attribute, if specified) that must be evaluated to validate the XML node specified in the `match` attribute. If the specified expression evaluates to `true`, it is considered to be an error condition and the specified error message is displayed.

`expressionContext` is a relative XPath expression that identifies the node on which the expression is rooted and therefore should be evaluated. The default value is `"."`. This is the same as the matched node.

The required `match` attribute identifies the XML nodes on which this custom validation is declared.

`showErrorOn` contains an XPath expression relative to `expressionContext` node. It defines the nodes on which the error should be displayed when the form is filled out.

```
<xsf:customValidation>
    <xsf:errorCondition
        match="/exp:expenseReport"
        expressionContext="exp:reportDate"
        expression="msxsl:string-compare(., ../exp:startDate) < 0
and ../exp:startDate != """
        showErrorOn=".">
        .
        .
        .
    </xsf:errorCondition>
</xsf:customValidation>
```

errorMessage

The `errorMessage` element is a required child element of the `errorCondition`, `override`, and `submit` elements. It specifies two types of error message to be returned if the value of an XML node is invalid.

You can supply both long and short error messages as values. The long error message is the content for this element. Its maximum length is 1,023 characters. The short message is contained in the `shortMessage` attribute and is limited to 127 characters.

If the error message `type` attribute is set to `"modal"`, the long error message is displayed when the user right-clicks `Full error description` on the shortcut menu. The short message value is ignored. If the attribute is set to `"modeless"` (default), the short message is displayed as a ToolTip. The attribute corresponds to the `Dialog box alert"` and `Inline alert` values in the `Error alert type` options in the Data Validation dialog box.

When the dialog box is closed, the form field is marked with a dashed red border to indicate that the value is invalid. If the field is invalid as a result of scripting code or because it was invalid to begin with, but has not been edited, it is marked with a red underline.

```
<xsf:errorCondition
    match="/exp:expenseReport"
    expressionContext="exp:reportDate"
    expression="msxsl:string-compare(., ../exp:startDate) < 0
and ../exp:startDate != """
    showErrorOn=".">
    <xsf:errorMessage
        type="modeless"
        shortMessage="The report date occurs before the end of the
expense period.">
        The report date occurs before the end of the expense period.
Verify that this is correct.
    </xsf:errorMessage>
</xsf:errorCondition>
```

Design Mode Properties

This section of the XSF file contains optional design mode properties.

applicationParameters

The `applicationParameters` element is an optional child of `xDocumentClass`. It contains the optional `solutionProperties` element. See Figure 4-14.

Figure 4-14: The `applicationParameters` **content model.**

The required `application` attribute identifies the name of the application used to design the InfoPath form. The value must be `"InfoPath Design Mode"`.

```
<xsf:xDocumentClass>
    <xsf:applicationParameters application="InfoPath Design Mode">
        .
        .
        .
    </xsf:applicationParameters>
</xsf:xDocumentClass>
```

solutionProperties

The optional `solutionProperties` element specifies how a form should be used in design mode. All the attributes are optional.

`allowCustomization` indicates whether the form can be modified or customized. Allowed values are `"yes"` (default) and `"no"`. If it is set to `"no"`, the `Design the Form` toolbar button is disabled. If the user tries to modify the form template, a warning message is displayed. This attribute corresponds to the `Enable Protection` option on the `General` tab of the Form Options dialog box.

automaticallyCreateNodes indicates whether XML nodes will be automatically generated when controls are inserted in the view in design mode. It corresponds to the Automatically create data source option on the Controls task pane. If you are customizing a sample form or have specified an existing schema, this option is disabled in the user interface.

fullyEditableNamespace contains the namespace URI and location URL of the schema in the form template that can be entirely modified in design mode.

lastOpenView gives the name of the view that was open when the form was last in design mode.

If a script is used to upgrade form instances to conform to a new version of the template, the lastVersion NeedingTransform attribute is used to store the value contained in the maxToVersionUpgrade attribute in the useTransform element.

scriptLanguage contains the name of the scripting language of the form.

```
<xsf:applicationParameters application="InfoPath Design Mode">
    <xsf:solutionProperties
        allowCustomization="no"
        automaticallyCreateNodes="no"
        fullyEditableNamespace="urn:names?pace1:mynames"/>
        lastOpenView="view1"
        lastVersionNeedingTransform="1.1.0.10"
        scriptLanguage="JScript"
</xsf:applicationParameters>
```

Form Selection

This optional section is used to identify properties for a list view of all forms belonging to a form template. XML documents belonging to a form can be placed in a single folder or library. Depending on the underlying support in the file system or server, this information can be used to create meaningful list views on a set of forms.

For example, when InfoPath forms are saved into a Sharepoint Services form library that is based on an InfoPath form as a template, the form properties specified in this section are automatically promoted and made available to the default view of the form library.

listProperties

The optional listProperties element is a top-level child of xDocumentClass. It is the container for the properties that appear in a list view in a form library. Figure 4-15 shows the content model.

Figure 4-15: The listProperties **content model.**

fields

The `fields` element contains one or more fields for form library columns.

field

The `field` element defines a single field for form library columns. It specifies a relative XPath expression from the `item` attribute of an `xmlToEdit` element.

The required `node` attribute contains an XPath expression that identifies the XML node or nodes in the form from which the data is read for list display.

The required `name` attribute is the label to be used on the list header.

The `type` attribute contains the XML Schema data type.

`columnName` identifies the column name in the SQL table containing the list view.

`maxlength` gives the maximum size of the field in bytes.

`required` indicates if NULL values are allowed. Allowed values are `"yes"` and `"no"` (default).

`viewable` indicates whether the field should be added to the default list view. Allowed values are `"yes"` and `"no"` (default).

The `aggregation` attribute specifies how form property data should be processed to obtain a single value for a form library report. It can either be an aggregation action or an indication of the particular element in the collection.

```
<xsf:listProperties>
    <xsf:fields>
        <xsf:field
            type="xsd:date"
            name="TravelDate"
            columnName="TravelDate"
            required="yes"
            viewable="yes"
            node="TravelReport/Header/travelDate"
            aggregation="first"/>
    </xsf:fields>
</xsf:listProperties>
```

Summary

Phew! That's it. If you've followed us through both Chapters 3 and 4, you should have learned much of what you need to know about the XML structures in the form definition file.

In this chapter you reviewed the structure of a wide range of element sets, most of which can be described under the general heading of form meta data. In other words, they are elements that specify properties about the form as a whole, rather than the user interface to XML data.

Now you're in a position to start using the declarative approach to form design. By combining it with working with InfoPath in design mode, you'll understand what lies under the design mode interface.

Before you move on, we suggest you work through the design mode interface again. See if you can relate the XSF elements and attributes to design objects, and try to identify areas where you may find it convenient to use XSF editing as part of your design methods.

You may want to revisit these sections again as you continue through the book. Remember, too, that there's a complete XSF reference in Appendix B.

In the next three chapters you begin to get up to speed on InfoPath scripting code features, starting with integrating secondary data sources.

5

Integrating Secondary Data Sources

Data gathering is normally a task that requires fast tools so that end users don't become bogged down in user interface inefficiency. For this reason, you can find a lot of mainframe applications where you have to input fields representing product codes, category codes, area codes, and so on. This allows experienced people to fill out application forms very quickly, since they already know all the company codes. The other side of the coin is when you have new employees who don't know any codes and must search each time for individual items in large lists.

In this chapter you see how to solve this kind of problem while maintaining a high level of flexibility and usability within the application.

Make It Simple, but Not Simpler

Today, data gathering solutions are varied. In generally, Internet-based application forms are simple and directed to people without much computer experience. These kinds of forms are also inefficient, since they present a lot of documentation, many views, and few fields per view. They are perfect for their target, commercial market, but they aren't appropriate for the internal use of enterprises.

Consider a help desk operator who must wait for 30 seconds for each view switch just because the network is busy. To alleviate the problem, mainframe-style applications could be used. Such systems are fast; however, because these kinds of applications are governed by codes the operators must memorize, the operators need to be experienced. After several months (or years), an operator might become proficient, but what about new employees? Because of this learning curve, mainframe-style applications become inefficient too.

The solution is to get the best from both scenarios. InfoPath provides the ability to create templates that work internally with codes, but also lets the user see clear descriptions. You can create a form that accepts input, clear text, and code, in order to satisfy all needs.

Basically, the feature is provided through secondary data sources that can be fed by XML data files, Web Services, database objects (tables, views, or stored procedures), and other applications or services.

Lookups

Consider the scenario where you have a data source field containing a product code, but you want to provide a clear list of product names when the user uses your template. You need something to improve the usability of your form.

The basic idea is to have a field in the data source that is populated by a value selected by a drop-down list, which contains the list of all products available to sell. The main difference from mainframe applications is that the visualized content is different from the field content. For this reason, you'll set two different properties: `Value` and `Display name`. The former will be bound to the data source field, whereas the latter will be bound to the drop-down list box control.

In a simpler way, you can add entries to the drop-down list box control from InfoPath by just selecting the control properties, as shown in Figure 5-1.

Figure 5-1: Drop-down list box control entries.

As Figure 5-1 suggests, the data source field is an integer named `Product`, while the display value is a string containing the name of the product. The final effect is shown in Figure 5-2, where a list of products are selected from a drop down list box containing only clear product descriptions.

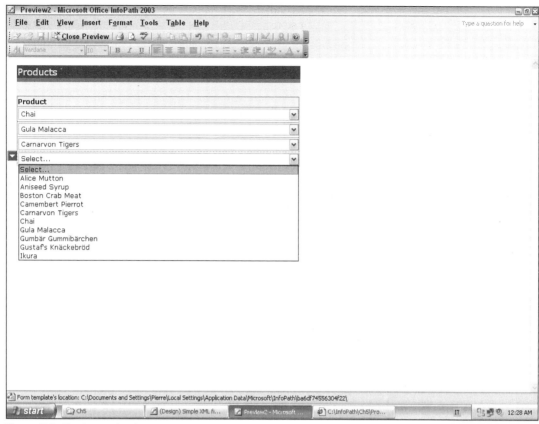

Figure 5-2: Product selection.

The resulting InfoPath document contains only product codes, as follows:

```
<?xml version="1.0" encoding="UTF-8"?>
<?mso-infoPathSolution solutionVersion="1.0.0.6"
productVersion="11.0.5531" PIVersion="1.0.0.0"
ref="file:///C:\InfoPath\Ch5\Simple%20XML%20file%20Lookup.xsn" ?>
<?mso-application progid="InfoPath.Document"?>
<my:myFields
 xmlns:my="http://schemas.microsoft.com/office/infopath/2003/myXSD/2003-09-
 29T22:20:07" xml:lang="en-us">
<my:Products>
 <my:Product>
  <my:ProductID>1</my:ProductID>
 </my:Product>
 <my:Product>
  <my:ProductID>44</my:ProductID>
 </my:Product>
 <my:Product>
  <my:ProductID>18</my:ProductID>
 </my:Product>
```

```
    <my:Product>
     <my:ProductID>10</my:ProductID>
    </my:Product>
   </my:Products>
  </my:myFields>
```

Even if the previous sample works in many static scenarios, the list of products generally comes from external data sources (usually back-end services). InfoPath provides a way for getting the data from an external data source such as an XML file, Web service, or database, as you'll see throughout the chapter.

Lookup to an XML File

In the previous sample, the lookup XML file was embedded in the InfoPath form. While this type of link can work for all situations when the list of products is static, this doesn't work in all scenarios. Suppose, for example, your company needs to update the list of products periodically—for example, every week. Embedding the XML file into the form, you have to update your InfoPath form weekly, making it unmanageable. A better solution is to maintain the XML products file externally and then link to it from the form.

The file content is pretty simple. It's an XML file containing product codes and descriptions:

```xml
<?xml version="1.0" encoding="utf-8" ?>
<Products>
 <Product>
  <ProductID>17</ProductID>
  <ProductName>Alice Mutton</ProductName>
 </Product>
 <Product>
  <ProductID>3</ProductID>
  <ProductName>Aniseed Syrup</ProductName>
 </Product>
 <Product>
  <ProductID>40</ProductID>
  <ProductName>Boston Crab Meat</ProductName>
 </Product>
 <Product>
  <ProductID>60</ProductID>
  <ProductName>Camembert Pierrot</ProductName>
 </Product>
 <Product>
  <ProductID>18</ProductID>
  <ProductName>Carnarvon Tigers</ProductName>
 </Product>
</Products>
```

Figure 5-1 shows a second option in the list box entries section: Look up in a database, Web service, or file. When you select this option, you have to create a secondary data source if it's not already present (see Figure 5-3).

Figure 5-3: Lookup to external data.

For adding a new data source, the wizard offers you three data source types:

❑   XML data file

❑   Database (SQL Server or Microsoft Office Access only)

❑   Web service

If you choose the first one (for others see later in this chapter), you have to enter the location of the XML data file (see Figure 5-4).

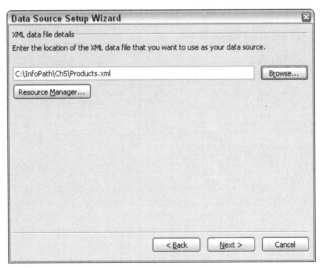

Figure 5-4: Link to external XML data file.

Since you can create resources with InfoPath (as seen in Chapter 2), you can also use one of these resources as an XML data file by selecting it from the `Resource Manager. . .` button. Continuing with the wizard, you have to define the data source name (that name must be unique with regard to other secondary data sources) and set the loading time (see Figure 5-5).

Figure 5-5: Secondary data source name and loading time.

By default, the data source is loaded when the form is opened, but you can choose to load from the script at a later time and then uncheck this option. When you click the `Finish` button you are warned about the data accessibility (see Figure 5-6).

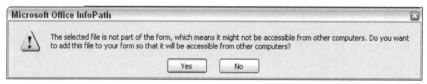

Figure 5-6: XML data accessibility.

If you click `Yes`, the XML data file will be embedded in the template so that you don't have to deploy it with the form. Otherwise, the file will be maintained externally. The advantage of maintaining it externally is that you can modify the XML file content, and all changes will be reflected in the drop-down list box content. If you consider the scenario we showed earlier, this is the right choice. Obviously, this can generate some deployment problems, since the XML data file is linked to the template with its full file system path, as demonstrated by this XSF template source fragment:

```
<xsf:dataObjects>
  <xsf:dataObject name="Products" schema="Products1.xsd" initOnLoad="yes">
    <xsf:query>
      <xsf:xmlFileAdapter fileUrl="C:\InfoPath\Ch5\Products.xml"></xsf:xmlFileAdapter>
    </xsf:query>
  </xsf:dataObject>
</xsf:dataObjects>
```

That issue can be solved easily, as you will see later in this section. Once you add the secondary data source, you have to set the `Value` and `Display name` elements by getting them from the XML document (see Figure 5-7).

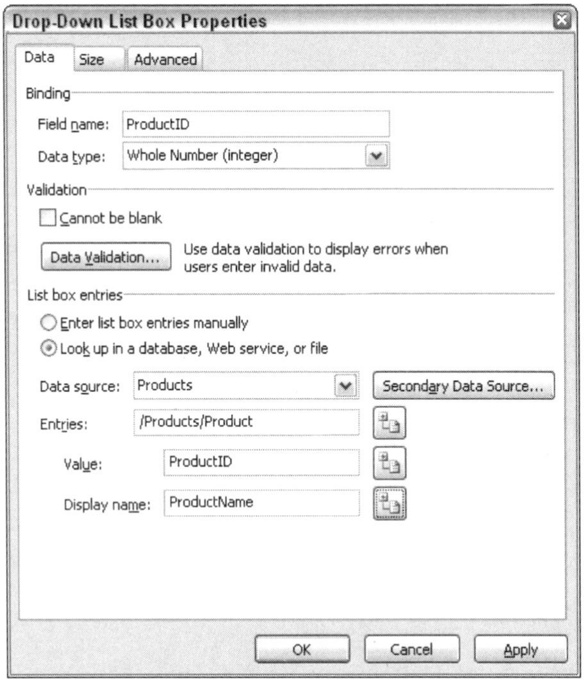

Figure 5-7: Value and display name binding.

The final effect is exactly the same as shown in Figure 5-2, but when you change some items in Product.xml, these are reflected in the drop-down list box.

> *If you want to set a default value, such as "Select . . . ", you can add the item in the XML file with a default code e.g., 0) and then define the default value for the data source field. When InfoPath opens, it will assign the default value to the field and show the new item just added.*

So, what happens if you change the XML data filename? Or its file system location? You get an exception opening the InfoPath template informing you that it can't open the document since it doesn't find the secondary data source. A workaround to this problem is to implement the `OnLoad` event handler and set the `FileURL` property of the secondary data source:

```
function XDocument::OnLoad(eventObj)
{
 try
 {
  XDocument.DataObjects["Products"].QueryAdapter.FileURL =
        "C:\\InfoPath\\Ch5\\Products2003.xml";
  XDocument.DataObjects["Products"].Query();
  eventObj.ReturnStatus = true;
 }
 catch(ex)
```

```
    {
      XDocument.UI.Alert("Unable to load the lookup file.");
      eventObj.ReturnStatus = false;
    }
}
```

The filename here is hard-coded, but you can save its path in a configuration file or prompt a dialog box when the user opens the form or uses an alternative strategy. After setting the filename, you have to force the secondary data source to load again, invoking the Query method of DataObject (see Appendix C for the InfoPath Object Model Reference).

Lookup to a Web Service

The lookup list isn't always available locally, and you may need to get it from a Web site. You have many ways to get data from a Web site, but since InfoPath is natively built over XML standards, the optimal method is to use a Web service, which is built on XML standards too.

Suppose you have to get the product list from a Web service. The Web service would be implemented in ASP.NET as follows:

```
[WebService(Namespace="http://www.peway.com/book")]
public class Products : System.Web.Services.WebService
{
  [WebMethod]
  public Product[] GetProductList()
  {
    ArrayList products = new ArrayList();
    SqlConnection cn = new SqlConnection(
      "Integrated Security=SSPI;Persist Security Info=False;Initial" +
      "Catalog=Northwind;Data Source=.");

    try
    {
      SqlCommand cmd = new SqlCommand(
        "SELECT ProductID, ProductName, UnitPrice FROM Products", cn);

      cn.Open();
      SqlDataReader reader = cmd.ExecuteReader();

      while(reader.Read())
      {
        products.Add(new Product(
          Convert.ToInt32(reader["ProductID"]),
          reader["ProductName"].ToString(),
          Convert.ToDouble(reader["UnitPrice"])));
      }

      reader.Close();
    }
    catch(Exception ex)
    {
      throw ex;
    }
    finally
```

```
    {
      if(cn.State == ConnectionState.Open)
        cn.Close();
    }

    return (Product[])products.ToArray(typeof(Product));
  }
}

public class Product
{
  public int ID;
  public string ProductName;
  public double UnitPrice;

  public Product() {}

  public Product(int id, string productName, double unitPrice)
  {
    ID    = id;
    ProductName = productName;
    UnitPrice = unitPrice;
  }
}
```

Then, the Web service returns a list of products with an ID, product name, and unit price from the Northwind SQL Server database. The Web method opens a connection to the Northwind database and selects the products items from the Products table. It then fills an array with all the products found in the table. Finally, it returns the array of products to the caller (InfoPath).

This is the classic scenario where you can't access a database table directly, since you are requesting the product list from the Internet. When you run the secondary data source wizard (see Figure 5-1) and choose Web Service, you have to enter the WSDL path so that InfoPath will recognize the methods available from the Web service (see Figures 5-8 and 5-9).

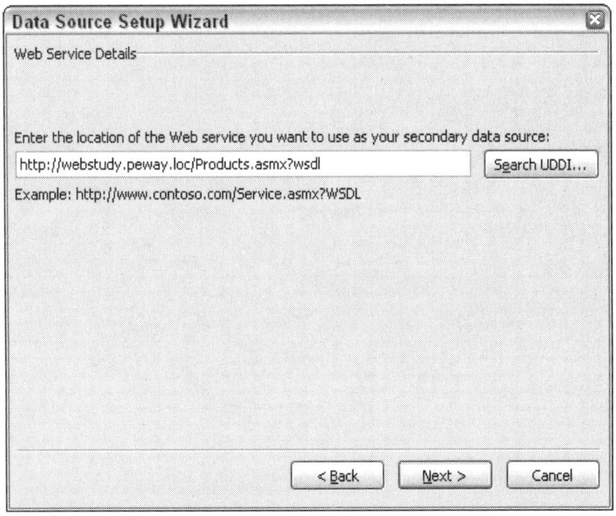

Figure 5-8: Web service details.

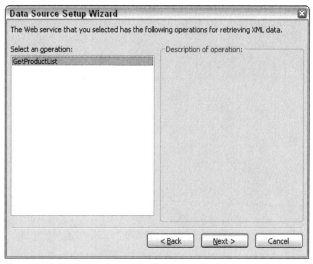

Figure 5-9: Web service operations.

Although our sample, shown in Figure 5-5, doesn't have parameters, if you need to set some parameters with the Web method, you can do so on the next screen. Finally, you need to define the value and display fields, as shown in Figure 5-7.

As you have seen, InfoPath provides the same secondary data source building process as for XML files. Nevertheless, we added a new feature in this last scenario, the unit price. When the user downloads a product catalog, he or she should be given as much pertinent information as possible. In this case, when the user selects a product, you could automatically provide its unit price.

To do that, you have to implement the `OnAfterChange` event from the drop-down control list containing the list of products:

```
function msoxd_my_ProductID::OnAfterChange(eventObj)
{
 var product;

 if(eventObj.Operation == "Insert")
 {
   XDocument.GetDOM("GetProductList").setProperty("SelectionNamespaces",
     'xmlns:my="http://schemas.microsoft.com/office/infopath/2003/myXSD/2003-10-
     13T19:57:58" xmlns:s0=http://www.peway.com/book
   xmlns:dfs="http://schemas.microsoft.com/office/infopath/2003/dataFormSolution"');
   product =
   XDocument.GetDOM("GetProductList").selectSingleNode("//s0:Product/s0:ID[text()='"
   + eventObj.Site.nodeTypedValue + "']/../s0:UnitPrice");

   XDocument.DOM.selectSingleNode("/my:myFields/my:UnitPrice").text = product.text;
 }
}
```

First, you have to define the namespaces used by the secondary data source and then select the node from which the ID is selected from the drop-down list. The ID is the value present in the `Site` node of `eventObj`, as you can see in the InfoPath Object Model Reference in Appendix C. Once you have the unit price, you can assign it to the `UnitPrice` field in the form.

This is an example of how to get additional information from the secondary data source. If the drop-down list contains too many items (more than 100), creating a drop-down list is impractical because InfoPath becomes very slow during the editing phase. You could solve the problem by devising an alternative way of getting lookup information from a large list of data. This is covered in the next section.

Lookup from a Task Pane

Suppose you have an order form with a product list of more than 1,000 products. In that case you can't use a drop-down list because it would be too slow to use. A possible alternative is to create your own task pane resource that contains a simple search engine for products (see Figure 5-10). The query will provide a smaller result list of items that will be used to fill the order form.

This sample came from the Samples directory in InfoPath.

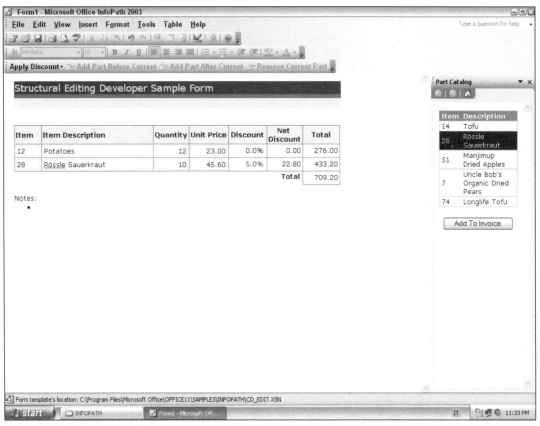

Figure 5-10: Task pane lookup sample.

The task pane contains an HTML form with a method that interacts with the InfoPath Object Model (see Chapter 3 for details about task panes):

```html
<html>
<head>
<script language="jscript" type="text/javascript">
 var gobjCurrentPartSelected = null;

  function SelectPart(objPart)
  {
  // Enable the Add Part button now that one of the parts is selected.
  if (gobjCurrentPartSelected == null)
   btnAddPart.disabled = false;

   // If this is not the currently selected part, mark the new part as selected
   // by switching it's
   // CSS class.  Unselect the currently selected part, if any.
   if (objPart != gobjCurrentPartSelected)
   {
    if (gobjCurrentPartSelected)
     gobjCurrentPartSelected.className = "";
    gobjCurrentPartSelected = objPart;
    gobjCurrentPartSelected.className = "selected";
   }
  }

  function AddPartToInvoice(objPart)
  {
  // Call the insertPartFromCatalog function in the business logic, passing
  // the details for the part.
  window.external.Window.XDocument.Extension.InsertPartFromCatalog(
     objPart.PartNumber, objPart.PartDescription, objPart.UnitCost);
  }
</script>
<style type="text/css">
 body, table, td, th
 {
  font-family: Verdana;
  font-size: 10pt;
 }
 table#partList
 {
  border-collapse:collapse;
  word-wrap:break-word;
  border-top: "1px #a9b6cb solid";
  border-left: "1px #a9b6cb solid";
  border-right: "1px #a9b6cb solid";
 }
 #partlist thead
 {
  text-align: left;
  background-color:#7389af;
  color: white;
 }
```

```
    #partList tr td, #partList tr th
    {
     border-bottom: "1px #a9b6cb solid";
    }
    table#partlist tr td, table#partlist tr th
    {
     padding: 1px 4px 1px 4px;
    }
    table#partlist tr.selected
    {
     background-color: #0000A0;
     color: white;
    }
    </style>
    </head>
    <body>
     <table id="partList" cellspacing="0" width="100%">
      <thead>
       <tr>
        <th>Item</th>
        <th>Description</th>
       </tr>
      </thead>
      <tbody>
       <tr id="part1"
         PartNumber="14"
         PartDescription="Tofu"
         UnitCost="23.25"
         onClick="SelectPart(this)"
         onDblClick="AddPartToInvoice(this)">
        <td unselectable="on">14</td>
        <td unselectable="on">Tofu</td>
       </tr>
       <tr id="part2"
         PartNumber="28"
         PartDescription="R&ouml;ssle Sauerkraut"
         UnitCost="45.60"
         onClick="SelectPart(this)"
         onDblClick="AddPartToInvoice(this)">
        <td unselectable="on">28</td>
        <td unselectable="on">R&ouml;ssle Sauerkraut</td>
       </tr>
       <tr id="part3"
         PartNumber="51"
         PartDescription="Manjimup Dried Apples"
         UnitCost="53.00"
         onClick="SelectPart(this)"
         onDblClick="AddPartToInvoice(this)">
        <td unselectable="on">51</td>
        <td unselectable="on">Manjimup Dried Apples</td>
       </tr>
       <tr id="part4"
         PartNumber="7"
         PartDescription="Uncle Bob's Organic Dried Pears"
```

```
      UnitCost="30.00"
      onClick="SelectPart(this)"
      onDblClick="AddPartToInvoice(this)">
     <td unselectable="on">7</td>
     <td unselectable="on">Uncle Bob's Organic Dried Pears</td>
    </tr>
    <tr id="part5"
      PartNumber="74"
      PartDescription="Longlife Tofu"
      UnitCost="10.00"
      onClick="SelectPart(this)"
      onDblClick="AddPartToInvoice(this)">
     <td unselectable="on">74</td>
     <td unselectable="on">Longlife Tofu</td>
    </tr>
   </tbody>
  </table>
  <p style="text-align: center">
   <button id=btnAddPart onClick=
     "AddPartToInvoice(gobjCurrentPartSelected)" disabled>Add To Invoice
   </button>
  </p>
 </body>
 </html>
```

AddPartToInvoice is a function that gets the selected values and submits them to InfoPath through the InsertPartFromCatalog InfoPath function. AddPartToInvoice is invoked by the btnAddPart button or the double-click event button of each item available in the HTML table.

This code shows how you can interact with the InfoPath Object Model from an external script code. This can be extended to the Web resources used inside the InfoPath task pane.

Lookup to a Database

In this chapter you saw several ways to get data from an XML file, a Web service, or hard-coded inside the form source. The last method InfoPath provides to look up information is through a database link. Actually, InfoPath provides two kind of data provider link: Microsoft Access and Microsoft SQL Server.

Suppose you have direct access to the enterprise database of your company. You can create a secondary data source (see Figure 5-3) by selecting the database as the data source type. Then you have to link to a database getting it from your local data sources available under your Windows account (see Figure 5-11).

In the sample, say that you want to get the list of products available on Northwind database of SQL Server (installed by default in SQL Server). You select the Northwind Products.odc data source from the list and proceed to the next step, clicking the Open button. InfoPath provides the list of the fields available in the selected table. You can choose which fields you need to fill the lookup, which are normally ProductID and ProductName (see Figure 5-12).

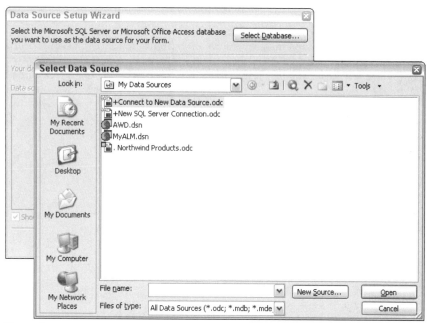

Figure 5-11: Data source connection form.

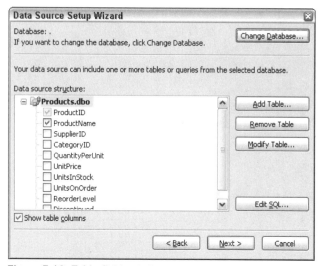

Figure 5-12: Table fields choice.

From this screen you can then define the secondary data source name (see Figure 5-5) and, finally, the drop-down list box properties (see Figure 5-7).

Summary

When you need to retrieve complementary information from secondary data sources, InfoPath provides many new ways to collect this data. The standard way is to create a simple secondary data source from an XML file, a Web service, or a database and use it as a standard XML document. If the data source is heavy, you need to consider implementing your own task pane in order to filter the result before you load it.

Adding Business Logic

Any datasheet form you have to fill in a real-world application must follow some predefined rules. For example, you could have a section where you have to set the phone number as a sequence like (999) 999-9999, or a valid e-mail address, or your personal Web site URL, and so on. It doesn't make a difference if the form is paper or electronic; the form must be filled with the correct information beforehand to be processed.

Microsoft InfoPath 2003, as a data gathering authoring tool, provides rich support for business logic definitions. This characteristic makes InfoPath an ideal application for creating complex forms for business.

In this chapter you see how you can enforce business rules with InfoPath to create real-world form applications.

Data Validation

Data validation is the common way to enforce one or more business rules. InfoPath provides three different, and complementary, mechanisms to validate a document instance, as shown in Figure 6-1.

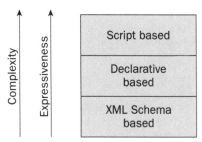

Figure 6-1: Data validation layers.

The first layer is represented by the XML Schema. As you have seen in Chapter 1, the primary source of the InfoPath document template is an XML schema. The XML Schema defines several rules (principally based on the type system and data structure), and the document instance must always conform to the assigned schema.

The second layer is represented by a declarative set of business rules. The developer can define one or more validation rules for each element of the document, either data source element or control. The declarative way permits you, among other things, to define a behavior when the business rule isn't respected during the data input. This provides a better level of flexibility while maintaining a reasonable level of complexity.

The last layer available is also the most complex, since it requires development skill. It is the script-based validation rules where you can, by programming either in JScript or VBScript, apply all business rules over each node or set of nodes of the document. As you will see later in this chapter, the basic principle is that you implement one or more event handlers attached to events of the DOM document updates.

The schema validation is always applied when you update a single field of the form, and this kind of validation cannot be disabled. Even if you have an invalid form, InfoPath permits you to save the form to your file system, but prevents you from submitting the data to the back-end system. In that way you can fill the form in several steps (consider the scenario when you don't have all information available at the same time) and then send it only when the form is correct and complete.

Schema Validation

In Chapter 1 you examined the structure of an InfoPath document. You also noticed that an InfoPath document instance is represented by an XML file with some preprocessing instructions. The structure of that document is contained in the InfoPath template (XSN file), and it is represented by a standard XML schema. The main advantage of using an XML schema instead of a proprietary source is to maintain a high level of standardization of the document meta data. As you have seen, that characteristic permits you to import an XML schema from any data provider (i.e., database or Web service) or application (e.g., Biztalk Server) to build your data gathering form.

Another advantage of using an XML schema as meta data is having a "built-in" and extensible data type system. As you have seen in Chapter 1, InfoPath permits to define your own XML schema by choosing the option of designing a blank document, but this option provides a limited subset of XML Schema type system. For this reason, it is very important to know how to build your own schema externally and then import it into InfoPath.

You have already seen what the XML Schema is. In this chapter you see how to build you own type system, then how to extend the existing one. Note that for a complete overview of the XML Schema specification, please refer to the W3C Web site.

XML Schema Data Types

Part 2 of the XML Schema specification provides a set of built-in types split into two categories: primitive and derived. Primitives are a set of types not derived by others; as the specification states, they exist *ab initio*. Derived types are inherited from other types. The following table lists all built-in types defined by the specification. Note that the third column shows the types available when you implement the data source from InfoPath without importing it from an external provider.

Built-in Data Type	Primitive/ Derived	Implemented inside InfoPath	Sample
String	P	Yes	"Hello World !"
Boolean	P	Yes	True, false
Decimal	P		12.2
Float	P		12.2
Double	P		12.2
Duration	P		P1347Y
dateTime	P	Yes	2000-03-04T23:00:00+03:00
Time	P		13:30:55
Date	P		8/14/2002
gYearMonth	P		2002-02
gYear	P		2002
gMonthDay	P		—03-02
gDay	P		02
gMonth	P		12
hexBinary	P		Any binary data in hexadecimal form
base64Binary	P	Yes	Any binary data in base 64
anyURI	P	Yes	http://www.wrox.com
QName	P		urn:test
NOTATION (only as attribute)	P		
normalizedString	D		
Token	D		
Language	D		
NMTOKEN	D		23DEA67
NMTOKENS	D		23DEA67 GF56
Name	D		
NCName	D		myns
ID	D		12
IDREF	D		21

Table continued on following page

Built-in Data Type	Primitive/ Derived	Implemented inside InfoPath	Sample
IDREFS	D		12 12
ENTITY	D		
ENTITIES	D		
Integer	D		212
nonPositiveInteger	D		-11
negativeInteger	D		-21
Long	D		23
Int	D		2321
Short	D		12
Byte	D		1
nonNegativeInteger	D		32
unsignedLong	D		123
unsignedInt	D		123
unsignedShort	D		21
unsignedByte	D		1
positiveInteger	D		123

It is beyond the scope of this book to explain the meaning of each data type, but it is interesting to note that when you create an InfoPath document without importing an external data source and then define your own inside InfoPath, you have a restricted subset of types defined by the specification.

If you consider that these built-in types are not enough (this assumption is generally true!), you can create your own types. The XML Schema specification provides two categories of types: simple types and complex types. Simple types are just a simple extension or restriction of the built-in types, whereas complex types can define a complex structure of hierarchical elements and attributes applied to elements.

Simple Types

With the primitive types shown in the Table 6-1, you can define a simple XML schema with strongly typed elements so that InfoPath will force the user to fill in the fields with the correct type. For example, the following XML schema represents a single field XML document containing an e-mail address:

```xml
<?xml version="1.0" encoding="utf-8" ?>
<xs:schema targetNamespace="urn:Professional.InfoPath"
 elementFormDefault="qualified" xmlns="urn:Professional.InfoPath"
 xmlns:mstns="urn:Professional.InfoPath"
 xmlns:xs="http://www.w3.org/2001/XMLSchema">
<xs:element name="EMailDocumentValidation">
  <xs:complexType>
   <xs:sequence>
```

```
      <xs:element name="Email" type="xs:string" />
    </xs:sequence>
   </xs:complexType>
  </xs:element>
 </xs:schema>
```

This simple schema will notify InfoPath that the Email field is a string. In a business application, that constraint can't be considered sufficient, since a user could send any kind of character sequence (e.g., "Leonardo Da Vinci") and InfoPath would validate it even if it isn't formally correct. In that case, you have to apply some more restrictions on the string domain.

XML Schema simple types help in that scenario—that is, where you have to change the domain of a built-in type. Simple types are defined by the construct simpleType, and they permit you to modify the domain of the primitive through three different types of derivation: list, restriction, and union.

Derivation by list defines a new data type as a list of another data type, delimited by white spaces. For example, if you want define your own data type as a list of integer numbers, you can write the following fragment of code:

```
<xs:simpleType name="Numbers">
 <xs:list itemType="xs:int" />
</xs:simpleType>
```

Normally, the most common form of derivation used is by restriction, where you define some restrictions (called *simple type facets*) to a valid data type. For example you can create a new data type called "age" with a range of values between 0 and 120 through a couple of facets (minInclusive and maxInclusive), as shown in the following:

```
<xs:simpleType name="age">
   <xs:restriction base="xs:int">
    <xs:minInclusive value="0" />
    <xs:maxInclusive value="120" />
   </xs:restriction>
</xs:simpleType>
```

The XML Schema specification defines a large set of type facets that you can apply more than once for each data type you are defining (see the following table). Note that when you create the data source directly from InfoPath, you have just one facet available: minLength, which is set when you define the field "cannot be blank" from the Field or Group Properties dialog box.

Type	length	min Length	max Length	pattern	enumer- ation	white Space	max Inclusive	max Exclusive	min Exclusive	min Inclusive	total Digit	fraction Digit
String	x	x	X	x	x	x						
Boolean				x		x						
Decimal				x		x	x	x	x	X	x	x
Float				x	x	x	x	x	x	X		
Double				x	x	x	x	x	x	X		
Duration				x	x	x	x	x	x	X		
dateTime				x	x	x	x	x	x	X		
Time				x	x	x	x	x	x	X		
Date				x	x	x	x	x	x	X		
gYearMonth				x	x	x	x	x	x	X		
gYear				x	x	x	x	x	x	X		
gMonthDay				x	x	x	x	x	x	X		
gDay				x	x	x	x	x	x	X		
gMonth				x	x	x	x	x	x	X		
hexBinary	x	x	X	x	x	x						
base64 Binary	x	x	X	x	x	x						
anyURI	x	x	X	x	x	x						
QName	x	x	X	x	x	x						
NOTATION (only as attribute)	x	x	X	x	x	x						
normalized String	x	x	X	x	x	x						
Token	x	x	X	x	x	x						
Language	x	x	X	x	x	x						
NMTOKEN	x	x	X	x	x	x						
NM TOKENS	x	x	X		x	x						
Name	x	x	X	x	x	x						
NCName	x	x	X	x	x	x						
ID	x	x	X	x	x	x						
IDREF	x	x	X	x	x	X						

Type	length	min Length	max Length	pattern	enumer- ation	white Space	max Inclusive	max Exclusive	min Exclusive	min Inclusive	total Digit	fraction Digit
IDREFS	x	x	X		x	x						
ENTITY	x	x	X	x	x	x						
ENTITIES	x	x	X		x	x						
Integer				x	x	x	x	x	x	X	x	x
nonPositive Integer				x	x	x	x	x	x	X	x	x
negative Integer				x	x	x	x	x	x	X	x	x
Long				x	x	x	x	x	x	X	x	x
Int				x	x	x	x	x	x	X	x	x
Short				x	x	x	x	x	x	X	x	x
Byte				x	x	x	x	x	x	X	x	x
nonNegative Integer				x	x	x	x	x	x	X	x	x
unsignedLong				x	x	x	x	x	x	X	x	x
unsignedInt				x	x	x	x	x	x	X	x	x
unsignedShort				x	x	x	x	x	x	X	x	x
unsignedByte				x	x	x	x	x	x	X	x	x
positiveInteger				x	x	x	x	x	x	X	x	x

One of the most interesting facets is the pattern facet, which is really useful for defining a data type that must follow a complex expression rule (regular expression). Consider, for example, the e-mail address type shown previously. You could enforce the domain as shown in the following:

```
<xs:simpleType name="EMailType">
  <xs:restriction base="xs:string">
   <xs:maxLength value="255" />
   <xs:pattern value="\w+([-+.]\w+)*@\w+([-.]\w+)*\.\w+([-.]\w+)*" />
  </xs:restriction>
</xs:simpleType>
```

In this case the user will be forced to enter a valid e-mail address into the field. How? You set the e-mail type with no more than 255 characters and a regular expression pattern for a valid e-mail address string stream. In this way, the user can't fill the field with any sentence without being notified with an error message from InfoPath.

A simple type might not be enough to define a real business type, such as an invoice address, business contact, or whatever else. In fact, simple types can apply rules only to a single field. To enlarge the rules' visibility over a set of XML elements and attributes, you have to create your own complex types.

Complex Types

When you have to create your own structure, composed not only of custom data types but also of child elements, you have to create your own structure. Consider a basic mail address containing the following fields:

❑ Street

❑ Zip code

❑ City

❑ Country

This will be coded as a `complexType`:

```
<xs:complexType name="address">
 <xs:sequence>
  <xs:element name="street" type="xs:string" />
  <xs:element name="zip" type="xs:positiveInteger" />
  <xs:element name="city" type="xs:string" />
  <xs:element name="country" type="xs:string" />
 </xs:sequence>
</xs:complexType>
```

The type address contains a sequence of subelements. Each child element is constrained by another type. In the previous sample these types are all primitives, but you can have your own simple types or other complex types. For example, you can restrict the country element to a predefined list with your own simple type:

```
<xs:complexType name="address">
 <xs:sequence>
  <xs:element name="street" type="xs:string" />
  <xs:element name="zip" type="xs:positiveInteger" />
  <xs:element name="city" type="xs:string" />
  <xs:element name="country" type="countries" />
 </xs:sequence>
</xs:complexType>
<xs:simpleType name="countries">
 <xs:restriction base="xs:string">
  <xs:enumeration value="Italy" />
  ...
  <xs:enumeration value="United Kingdom" />
  ...
  <xs:enumeration value="USA" />
 </xs:restriction>
</xs:simpleType>
```

You do this so that the user can't work with a nonexistent country.

Applying XML Schema inside InfoPath

In the previous section you saw how the XML Schema data type can be personalized. Now you will see how InfoPath uses the rules defined in the XML Schema for form validation.

Consider a simple form where you need to take a census of a personal contact. You open InfoPath and start designing the form, as shown in Figure 6-2.

Figure 6-2: InfoPath contact form design.

Finally you deploy the form to several end users. After some time, you discover some data inconsistency in several fields. Many e-mails are not well formed. As you have seen previously, if the InfoPath designer doesn't provide a rich control over the data type definition, you have to modify the XML Schema outside InfoPath. You can, for example, use the same e-mail type defined in the beginning of this chapter, producing the following schema:

```
<?xml version="1.0" encoding="utf-8" ?>
<xs:schema targetNamespace="http://tempuri.org/XMLSchema.xsd"
elementFormDefault="qualified" xmlns="http://tempuri.org/XMLSchema.xsd"
xmlns:mstns="http://tempuri.org/XMLSchema.xsd"
xmlns:xs="http://www.w3.org/2001/XMLSchema">
 <xs:element name="contact">
  <xs:complexType>
   <xs:sequence>
    <xs:element name="firstname" type="xs:string" />
    <xs:element name="lastname" type="xs:string" />
    <xs:element name="address" type="address" />
    <xs:element name="contacts" type="contacts" />
   </xs:sequence>
  </xs:complexType>
 </xs:element>
 <xs:complexType name="address">
  <xs:sequence>
   <xs:element name="street" type="xs:string" />
   <xs:element name="zip" type="xs:positiveInteger" />
   <xs:element name="city" type="xs:string" />
   <xs:element name="country" type="xs:string" />
  </xs:sequence>
 </xs:complexType>
 <xs:complexType name="contacts">
  <xs:sequence>
   <xs:element name="email" type="email" />
   <xs:element name="phone" type="xs:string" />
  </xs:sequence>
 </xs:complexType>
 <xs:simpleType name="email">
  <xs:restriction base="xs:string">
   <xs:maxLength value="255" />
   <xs:pattern value="\w+([-+.]\w+)*@\w+([-.]\w+)*\.\w+([-.]\w+)*" />
  </xs:restriction>
 </xs:simpleType>
</xs:schema>
```

By importing the schema in InfoPath, you will not be able to input an invalid e-mail address without being notified by InfoPath (see Figure 6-3).

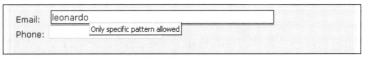

Figure 6-3: Email field notification error.

Unfortunately, the error message isn't really clear, and InfoPath doesn't provide a way to change it at design time. To provide your own schema validation message, you have to edit the XSF file manually. This means you have to add an override to the `schemaErrorMessage` element applied to the e-mail document element, as shown in the following:

```
<xsf:schemaErrorMessages>
    <xsf:override match="/mstns:contact/mstns:contacts/mstns:email">
        <xsf:errorMessage shortMessage="Invalid email format.">
```

```
                    This isn't a valid email address. Please type a valid email,
                    such as test@test.com
                </xsf:errorMessage>
            </xsf:override>
        </xsf:schemaErrorMessages>
```

The xsf:override contains a mandatory attribute match that identifies the element to which you apply the error message. The match attribute contains an XPath query. xsf:override also contains a mandatory element: xsf:errorMessage. This last element has a shortMessage required attribute that is shown as ToolTip and an optional attribute called type. The type attribute can contain two values: "modal" and "modeless" (default). If you set the type attribute to "modeless" or nothing, the error message shown is the value defined in shortMessage, as shown in Figure 6-4.

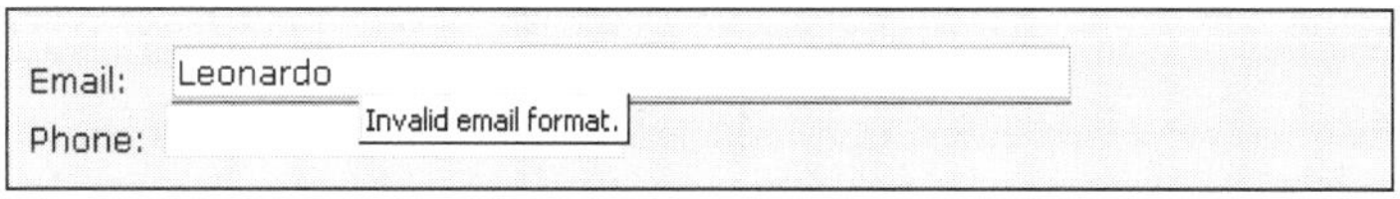

Figure 6-4: Modeless error validation message.

If you set the type attribute to "modal", a dialog box with a validation message will appear (see Figure 6-5).

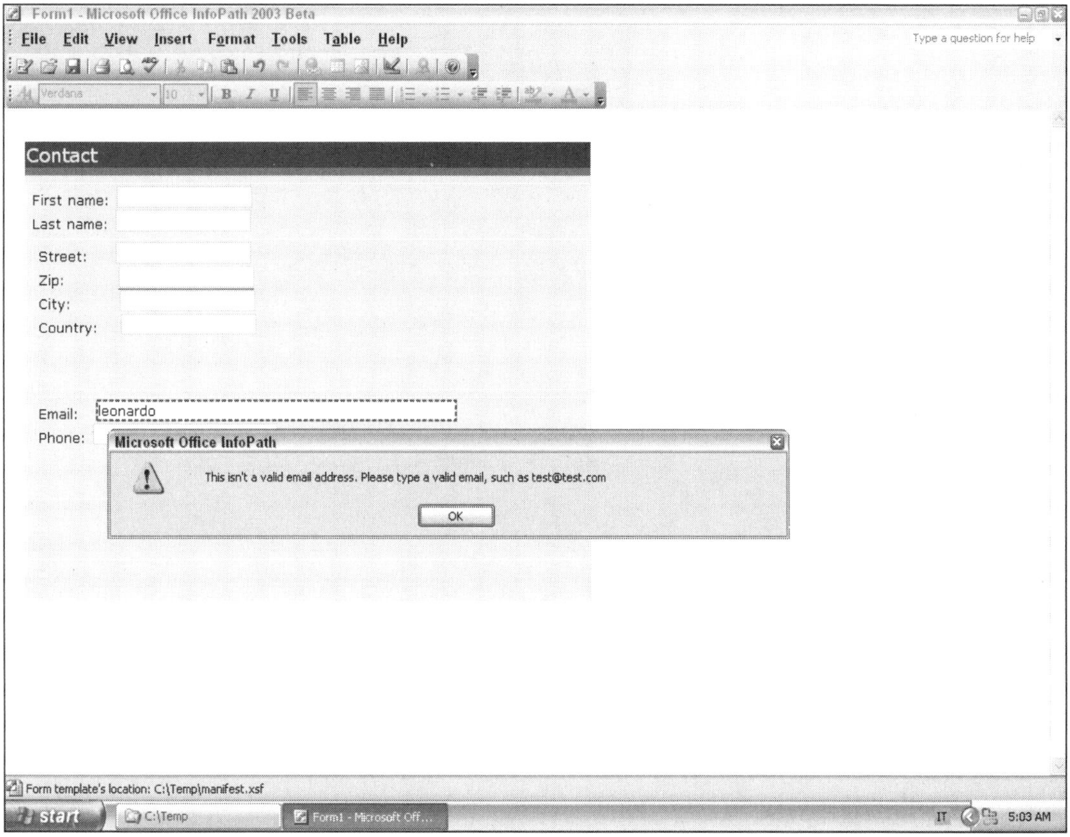

Figure 6-5: Modal error validation message.

When you define a rich type system for your form through an XML Schema, you have generalized support for several kinds of validation errors. In the next section you see how to enforce business rules at design time.

Rule-Based Validation

Defining business rules only by a rich data type system, as you can do with an XML schema, is not enough for a business form because some types of data are context-based. For example, you can have an order form that contains two kinds of addresses: invoice and shipping. You might have a check box item that permits you to say that the shipping address is the same as the invoice address, avoiding making the user fill it in twice. This is a situation where you can't define the element shippingAddress as required at the XML Schema level, but it becomes necessary if the check box is unchecked.

InfoPath provides two levels for defining rule-based validation: data source and single field. If you define a validation to the data source level, that rule is then applied to all controls mapped to that field (consider the multiview scenario), whereas if you define at control level, the rule will be applied only to that control and nowhere else.

To define a validation rule at control level, you have to right-click the control and select the Properties item. Clicking the Data Validation . . . button displays a dialog box appears that provides two options: Validation and Script (see Figure 6-6). You use Validation to define business rules at design time and Script to define business rules when you are developing custom scripts. Scripts are discussed in further detail later in this chapter.

Figure 6-6: Data Validation dialog box.

If you right-click over a data source element to the properties item and click the Validation and Script tab, you get the same result as shown in Figure 6-6. From the dialog box in Figure 6-6, you can click the Add button and another Data Validation dialog box appears (see Figure 6-7).

In this box you can define a set of business rules applied to the selected field or control. The first parameter to set is the field to control. By default, the field is the selected one, but you can choose any field available in the document. This feature permits you to define linked validation rules, where one field depends on another.

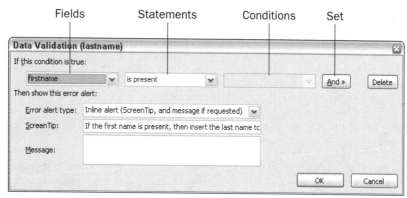

Figure 6-7: Data Validation dialog box.

The second parameter to define is the statement. The following table provides a list of the statements available in InfoPath.

Statement	Sample
Is equal to	Age == 120, FirstName == "Michelangelo"
Is not equal to	Age <> 120, FirstName <> "Michelangelo"
Is less than	Age < 10
Is less than or equal to	Age <= 80
Is greater than	Age > 20
Is greater than or equal to	Age >= 20
Is present	FirstName node is present
Is not present	FirstName node is not present
Is blank	FirstName == ""
Is not blank	FirstName <> ""
Contains	EMail contains ".com"
Does not contain	EMail doesn't contain ".com"
Begins with	FirstName starts with "P"
Does not begin with	FirstName doesn't start with "P"

The third parameter is the condition. This one can vary depending on the field data type and can be either a constant value (e.g., "Michelangelo", 120, etc.) or another field.

You can also define which kind of alert to show: inline or message-box-based. If you choose the former, you have to define the ScreenTip value; otherwise, you have to define the Message value. If you accept the rules (by clicking OK), the rules will be applied every time the data is updated, and then when you move from one control to another.

Note that, as Figure 6-7 states, you can define a set of rules tied by boolean conditions. This feature gives you the chance to create complex rules by adding a set of simple ones.

All these rules are reflected in the XSN file, under the `xsf:customValidation` element. For example, the rule defined in Figure 6-7 will be written as:

```
<xsf:customValidation>
<xsf:errorCondition match="/mstns:contact" expressionContext="mstns:lastname"
  expression="../mstns:firstname">
<xsf:errorMessage type="modeless" shortMessage="If the first name is present,
  then insert the last name too"></xsf:errorMessage>
</xsf:errorCondition>
</xsf:customValidation>
```

If you combine XML Schema validation and design time rules, you have a rich control over the form data. But there are situations where these rules aren't enough. Then, the last choice you have is to develop your own rules with some scripts.

Script-Based Validation

InfoPath 2003 provides a robust object model composed of a collection of objects, properties, methods, and events that give template authors and developers programmatic control over XML source documents and the InfoPath environment (see Appendix C for details). The OM (Object Model) is also used for business rules and validation constraint.

For example, consider an order request, where the user enters all the items he or she wants to order. Adding each item, you could check if you have enough items in stock and eventually calculate the shipping date based on availability. Then, you have several business rules to implement:

❑ Check if the item code exists.

❑ If it exists, then check the quantity.

❑ If it is not in stock, then set the shipping date to 10 days from today.

These rules can't be implemented either by XML Schema or declarative business rules; you have to implement them by yourself. With InfoPath you can write scripts that respond, between others, to node-level events, that is, specific actions that occur within a single field or a whole group (e.g., section or table row). The single action can trigger three kinds of events, in a well-defined sequence:

1. `OnBeforeChange`
2. `OnValidate`
3. `OnAfterChange`

OnBeforeChange is fired after the DOM has been updated but before it has been accepted and then validated by the XML Schema. If the ReturnStatus is set to false or an exception appears in the script, InfoPath rolls back to the previous value. This event is generally used for data validation or updating status before moving forward.

OnValidate is fired after the changes to the DOM have been accepted. Since it occurs after the XML Schema validation, it is normally used for data validation and error reports.

OnAfterChange is fired after OnValidate. This event is often used for document update and calculations.

Depending on the event type, you can then choose which operation to do. Generally you'll use OnBeforeChange and OnValidate for data validation and error management, and OnAfterChange for calculations.

Scripts for Data Validation

The event handlers defined previously can also be used for different purposes. Normally, you implement OnBeforeChange when the control to validate is single and OnValidate when the control to validate is included in a repeating (section or table) control.

Consider a simple document containing a list of items (ItemCode and Quantity). You want to check if the ItemCode exists, and if it exists, you want to verify the quantity available in stock. Then, the quantity that the user will input cannot exceed the quantity available. You can then create your data source with a group named Items and two child elements named ItemCode and Quantity, respectively. Finally, you add a repeating table into the view bounded over the Items group.

To check whether or not the ItemCode is available, you can implement the OnBeforeChange event as shown in Figure 6-8.

As you can see in Figure 6-8 (see Microsoft Script Editor window), OnBeforeChange provides an IDataDOMEvent instance as a parameter (for a detailed description of DataDOMEvent properties, refer to Appendix C), indicating and handling node changes. Since you need to check whether or not the ItemCode is valid, you can control the current node content (field content) of the DataDOMEvent object, as in the following:

```
function msoxd_my_ItemCode::OnBeforeChange(eventObj)
{
 if(!ItemCodeExists(eventObj.Site.nodeTypedValue))
   eventObj.ReturnStatus = false;
}

function ItemCodeExists(itemCode)
{
 // Back-end check
 if(itemCode == "AAA1")
  return true;
 else
  return false;
}
```

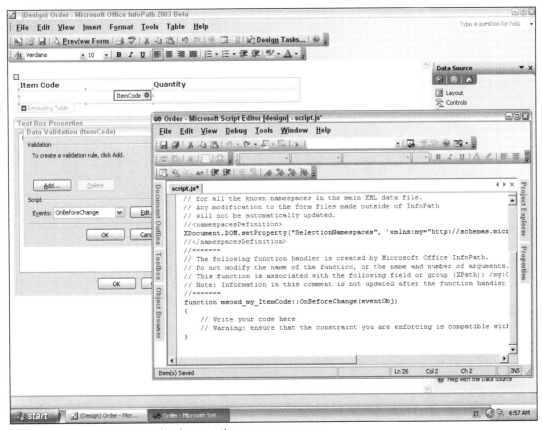

Figure 6-8: Script-based event implementation.

The function `ItemCodeExists` just checks whether or not the code exists. In a real-world scenario, you could check a database, Web service, or in any other back-end system. In this sample we just hard-coded the `ItemCode` for simplification. `eventObj` contains a property, `Site`, which is the `XMLDOMNode` where the event is currently processed. Then the typed value is passed to the checking function. If the `ItemCode` isn't valid or doesn't exist, you have to notify the user of this constraint violation. `ReturnStatus` indicates whether or not an error was detected.

Running the previous code, you get two kinds of problems. First of all, the error message is cryptic: "Invalid update: A custom constraint has been violated." To provide a clearer error message, you can set the `ReturnMessage` property:

```
function msoxd_my_ItemCode::OnBeforeChange(eventObj)
{
  if(!ItemCodeExists(eventObj.Site.nodeTypedValue))
  {
    eventObj.ReturnMessage = "The item code is not valid.";
    eventObj.ReturnStatus = false;
  }
}
```

When the user inputs a wrong item code, he or she gets the error message you defined and the item code will be deleted from the TextBox.

The second problem is caused by the repeating table control. When the control adds a new row with "Insert items above" or "Insert items below" menu commands, InfoPath creates a clone of the node used in each row with empty (or default) values. Doing that, InfoPath fires all events implemented by the fields. This means that the `OnBeforeChange` event handler is fired also. Since you are creating a new row with empty values, `OnBeforeChange` will return `false` and InfoPath will roll back the operation, avoiding creating a new row.

To deceive InfoPath, you can implement `OnValidate` instead of `OnBeforeChange`, because the former doesn't roll back to the previous value:

```
function msoxd_my_ItemCode::OnValidate(eventObj)
{
  if(!ItemCodeExists(eventObj.Site.nodeTypedValue))
  {
    eventObj.ReturnMessage = "The item code is not valid.";
    eventObj.ReturnStatus = false;
  }
}
```

If you want to provide a detailed error message, you can use the method `ReportError` instead of `ReturnMessage`:

```
function msoxd_my_ItemCode::OnValidate(eventObj)
{
  if(!ItemCodeExists(eventObj.Site.nodeTypedValue))
    eventObj.ReportError(eventObj.Site, "The item code is invalid", false);
}
```

`ReportError` is a method of the `DataDOMEvent` object and lets you provide a detailed error message to the user. The first parameter is the XML node with which the error is associated, the second parameter is the short error message (shown as a ToolTip), and the third parameter indicates that this error is associated with this specific XML node or all nodes of the same type. `ReportError` also provides three other parameters (optional): the long description used for dialog box notification, the error code, and the notification type (modal or modeless).

```
function msoxd_my_ItemCode::OnValidate(eventObj)
{
  if(!ItemCodeExists(eventObj.Site.nodeTypedValue))
    eventObj.ReportError(
      eventObj.Site,
      "The item code is invalid",
      false,
      "The item code is not present in our stock. Please insert a new one.",
      100,
      "modal");
}
```

Scripts for Business Calculations

You can implement script code not only for data validation but also to apply business calculations. Consider an order form where the user adds the items' descriptions and prices. You could provide a total box that is updated each time the user changes the price of any items. Since you are working on form data, you must be sure that all information is valid; then you can do it at the last level of the node event chain, `OnAfterChange`:

```
function msoxd_my_Price::OnAfterChange(eventObj)
{
 var total = 0.0;
 var i;
 var prices = XDocument.DOM.selectNodes("/my:Order/my:Items/my:Price");

 for(i = 0; i < prices.length; i++)
   total += parseFloat(prices.item(i).nodeTypedValue);

 XDocument.DOM.selectSingleNode("//my:Total").text = total; (
}
```

The calculation is done over all `Price` elements of the document. You then have to get all `Price` items from the XML document. To get them, you select all `Price` nodes through the `DOMDocument.select Nodes` method, setting the XPath query. If you have a result (list of nodes), you cycle over it and calculate the total. Since, in XML, all element contents are string-based, you have to convert as float in order to add to the total value. Finally, you fill the node `Total` with the calculated value. The `Total` XML element will be reflected automatically in the form field bound to it.

In your script, you can then work over all nodes of the document, creating your business rules as needed. You can also have more complex scripts, such as invoking Web services or COM objects that delegate the calculation to a third-party business logic entity.

Summary

The primary use of a data gathering application is to define business rules so that the user cannot make mistakes and fill the form with wrong data. InfoPath provides a complete solution to this problem at several levels: meta data, design time, and script. Moreover, you can enforce business rule calculations in the form when one or more fields changes by manipulating the XML document directly from your script code. These features make InfoPath a rich data gathering application eliminating a huge number of problems.

It is important to take all possible precautions before submitting to the back-end system in order to prevent incorrect document submission, which consumes network and server resources needlessly. In the next chapter you see how to send the document data to a back-end system.

7

Back-End Services

InfoPath 2003 is a rich client application able to create and edit business forms. As you have seen in the previous chapter, the output of a business form is a structured XML document. XML is the *lingua franca* that is easily interoperable with back-end processes and applications, such as database, Web services, application services, and so on.

This chapter provides you with a general overview of the back-end integration process and the benefits of InfoPath 2003 in regard to this process. When you have finished this chapter, you will have an understanding of how to integrate your business forms with several business scenarios.

Integration Requirements

InfoPath is interoperable with any server and client process that can take an XML message as input. Since it is also programmable, you can implement any script code that interacts with third-party applications using COM objects as your communication model. The programming model also permits you to submit the form data to more than one back-end system for a better integration with your business. Consider, for example, an order confirmation form where you submit some information to the order process application and other information to a data warehouse for marketing analysis.

When you create a new template from a data source, you have three choices:

- ❑   XML schema or XML data file
- ❑   Database (Microsoft SQL Server or Microsoft Access only)
- ❑   Web service

In the first case you have a file-system-based form, in the sense that you can create and read InfoPath documents from the file system (or Web storage such as Microsoft SharePoint Portal Server) that follows (is validated) by the XML schema used during the template design.

If you choose the second option, the meta data (template XML schema) is defined by the selected table or SQL Query statement. Then, the data source that will be available will reflect all information found into the database. By default, any submit is saved directly into the database table selected during the design phase.

The last choice is a Web service. Depending on the Web method signature (if it lets you submit data), you will submit the form data automatically to the Web service without writing any piece of script code. This is the InfoPath behavior default. In business forms, back-end integration is often more complex than the preceding scenarios, and you have to, for example, submit information to different data sources or, in the case of a database, different tables or databases (i.e., either the data warehouse or supply chain database). As explained in the previous chapter, InfoPath is extensible by custom scripts, and you can also control the back-end integration through your script code.

Integrating with SQL Server or Access

In this section, you see the database link in action with InfoPath. When you choose the Database check, InfoPath requires a database connection, represented by an Office Database Connection (.odc) file, which contains connection information, keywords, and descriptions for the data connection. You can also provide a Microsoft Data Link (.udl) file (which is a standard file format created by Microsoft for specifying connection strings). In either case, InfoPath opens the personal My Data Source folder containing all your connections files. If you don't have a connection file, you can create a new one by selecting the item +New SQL Server Connection.odc, as shown in Figure 7-1.

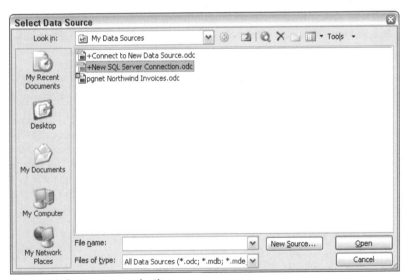

Figure 7-1: Data source selection.

If you want to connect to a Microsoft Access database, you have to select your MDB file. Then InfoPath will provide the list of tables available in the MDB.

When you choose to create a new SQL Server connection, InfoPath starts the Data Connection Wizard, asking you the SQL Server database instance name and authentication data (i.e., username and password) to access to the database. If you have access to the database (you are authenticated), you have to choose the database and (optionally) the table name, as shown in Figure 7-2.

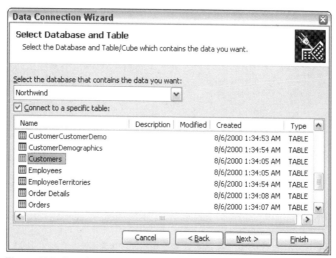

Figure 7-2: Database and table selection.

If you deselect the `Connect to a specific table` check box, your data connection file will be data-table-independent, and then you are free to define the table later during the template design phase. The final box in the wizard is the filename and properties box (see Figure 7-3).

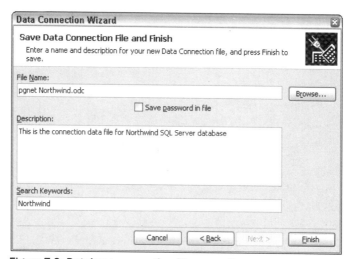

Figure 7-3: Database connection file properties.

Note that if you keep `Save password in file` unchecked, you will always be prompted to insert the password for database connection. Otherwise, if you check it, the password will be saved in a clear form into the ODC file, exposing you to a high security risk. The best solution is to use a trusted connection where the current logged user will be the user logged in to the database.

Going ahead, you have to choose the table you want to bind to your data form (see Figure 7-4).

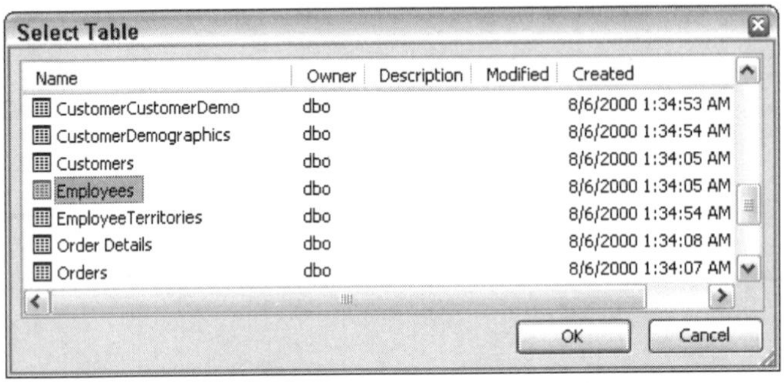

Figure 7-4: Table selection.

If you added the table name during the data file connection, the table selection box will not appear. The next step is to choose the table fields you want to use for the template (see Figure 7-5).

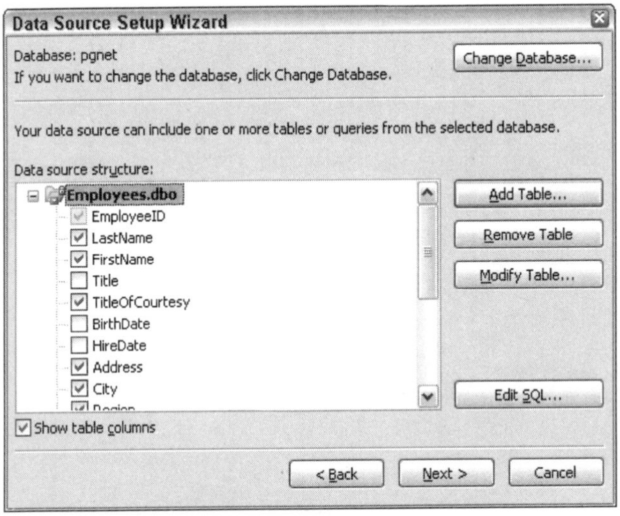

Figure 7-5: Table fields selection.

This table fields box gives you rich support for creating more complex table relations. For example, in Figure 7-5 the Employees table of the Northwind database is selected. You could also ask for all the orders of the employee. This can be done by adding a new table, Orders, and defining the fields relationship, EmployeeID. InfoPath then creates a hierarchy with Employees as parent and Orders as child (see Figure 7-6).

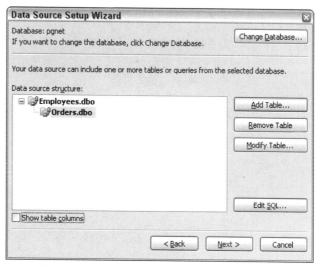

Figure 7-6: Data table relationship.

The last step is to choose whether to display the query view or data view first when the user opens InfoPath for the first time. By default, the query view is filled, while the data view is empty. You can create the data view from the data source, as you have seen in Chapter 1. If you following the preceding steps, the form is automatically linked to the database table chosen, and you can read, create, delete, and update records in the database when you submit the form. InfoPath does everything for you transparently.

There are other scenarios where you have to submit the data in a different way—for example, through a stored procedure. That is a case where you have to implement some script code by yourself.

Programming Database Integration

In the previous section you saw how to link an InfoPath template to database tables. If you want to use stored procedures instead of tables, you lose some ease of use and have to write a little bit of code.

Consider the scenario where you have to add a new employee to the Northwind database through a simple stored procedure:

```
CREATE PROCEDURE AddEmployee
  @LastName nvarchar(20),
  @FirstName nvarchar(10)
AS
  INSERT INTO Employees(LastName, FirstName) VALUES(@LastName, @FirstName)
GO
```

Then create a simple InfoPath template as shown in Figure 7-7.

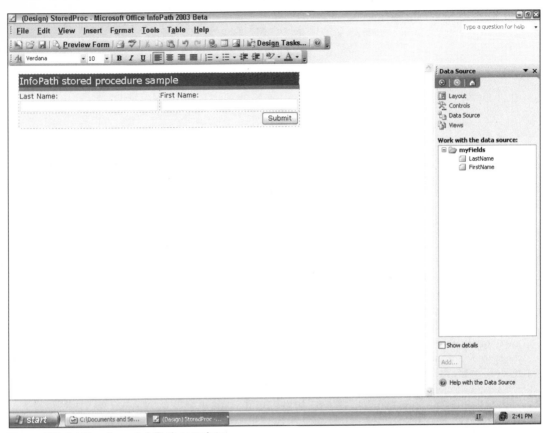

Figure 7-7: AddEmployee InfoPath template.

Select the button properties and define the action as Submit. The Submitting forms box appears, as shown in Figure 7-8, and then you enable the submit to custom script option box.

Figure 7-8: Submitting Forms dialog box.

If you click the OK button, the Microsoft Script Editor opens and makes the OnSubmitRequest handler ready to implement. You should now implement the code to execute the stored procedure through ADO:

```
function XDocument::OnSubmitRequest(eventObj)
{
 var lastName = XDocument.DOM.selectSingleNode("//my:LastName").text;
 var firstName = XDocument.DOM.selectSingleNode("//my:FirstName").text;

 try
 {
  var cn = new ActiveXObject("ADODB.Connection");
  var sqlSP = "EXEC AddEmployee '" + lastName + "', '" + firstName + "'";
  cn.ConnectionString = XDocument.DataObjects("Employees").QueryAdapter.Connection;
  cn.ConnectionTimeout = XDocument.DataObjects("Employees").QueryAdapter.Timeout;

  cn.Open();
  cn.Execute(sqlSP);
  cn.Close();

  eventObj.ReturnStatus = true;
 }
 catch(e)
 {
  XDocument.UI.Alert(e.description);
  eventObj.ReturnStatus = false;
 }
}
```

First, you have to get the fields value from the document. Then you can create a new ADODB.Connection object and build the SQL statement for a new employees database insert. Next, you get the connection string. Finally, you execute the SQL statement command. If you don't have errors, you inform InfoPath that the submission was fine; otherwise, you show the error and return false.

Since you created a template from a blank form, you don't have any DataAdapter available and the sample doesn't work. You have two choices to make it work:

❑ Create a secondary data source, disabling "Connect to the secondary data source when the form is opened," as described in Chapter 5.

❑ Create an InfoPath form from a database data source and a fictitious table.

In both cases you can inherit the connection string from the DataAdapter. In the previous sample, we used a secondary data source named "Employees". If you used the alternative, the code should be as follows:

```
function XDocument::OnSubmitRequest(eventObj)
{
 var lastName = XDocument.DOM.selectSingleNode("//my:LastName").text; ;
 var firstName = XDocument.DOM.selectSingleNode("//my:FirstName").text;

 try
 {
  var cn = new ActiveXObject("ADODB.Connection");
```

```
        var sqlSP = "EXEC AddEmployee '" + lastName + "', '" + firstName + "'";
        cn.ConnectionString = XDocument.QueryAdapter.Connection;
        cn.ConnectionTimeout = XDocument.QueryAdapter.Timeout;

        cn.Open();
        cn.Execute(sqlSP);
        cn.Close();

        eventObj.ReturnStatus = true;
    }
    catch(e)
    {
        XDocument.UI.Alert(e.description);
        eventObj.ReturnStatus = false;
    }
}
```

Integrating with Web Services

There are several scenarios where you don't have direct access to the database. When you are working on extranet and intranet environments, you can't have direct access for security reasons. To solve this problem, you could send and receive data forms to and from the company through one or more Web services. This isn't the only solution available, as you will see later in the chapter, but it's certainly the most flexible, thanks to the flexibility of Web services technology.

As for the database situation, you can design an InfoPath form from a WSDL (Web Service Description Language), which is normally produced by the back-end developers or tools. For example, if you want to use a Microsoft AS.NET Web Service, you can get its WSDL specification referring to the Web Service URL by adding ?WSDL as postfix, such as http://myserver/myservice.asmx?WSDL. The WSDL is important because it contains the XML schema of the data exchanged between the client (InfoPath) and the server.

> WSDL is a specification defined by W3C that describes how a Web service is callable. The document is divided in several sections; one of these is the XML schema of the data sent and received by the Web method.

There are two ways that you can approach Web service integration:

❑ Design a form from a WSDL.

❑ Design the form and attach the data source to the Web service later.

In both cases the data source structure (and data types) must follow the XML schema defined into WSDL. First you'll see how to design an InfoPath form starting from a Web service.

When you select Web Service from the Data Source Setup Wizard (see Figure 7-9), you have to load the WSDL source (see Figure 7-10).

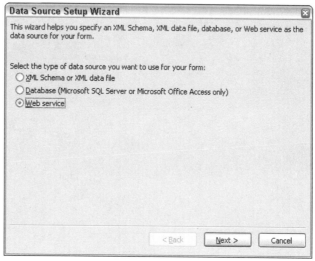

Figure 7-9: Data source selection.

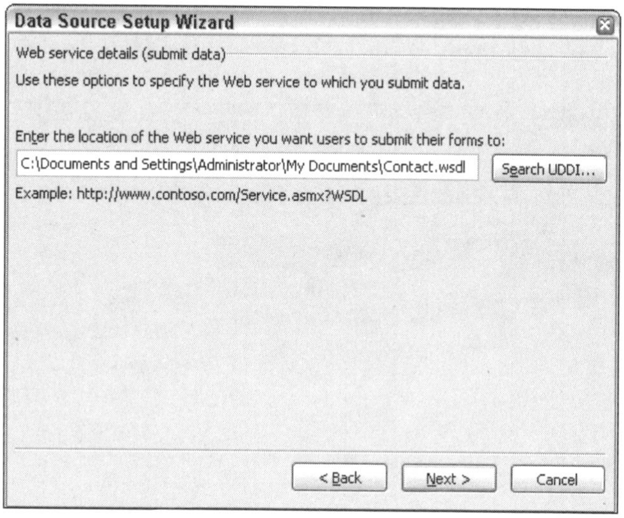

Figure 7-10: WSDL selection.

The WSDL can be loaded from the file system as well as from the Web (HTTP connection). A third possibility is to query a UDDI (Universal Description, Discovery, and Integration) repository. UDDI is something like a yellow pages for Web services.

When you selected the WSDL source, the wizard provides a list of functions (formerly operations) available from the selected Web service, as shown in Figure 7-11.

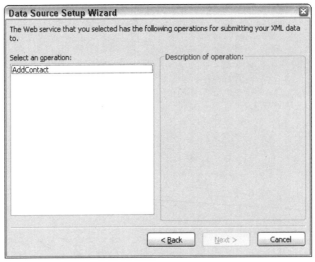

Figure 7-11: Web Service operation selection.

As a last step, the wizard creates the data source based on the parameter list of the operation selected. The design of the form is then similar to that shown in this book (see Figure 7-12).

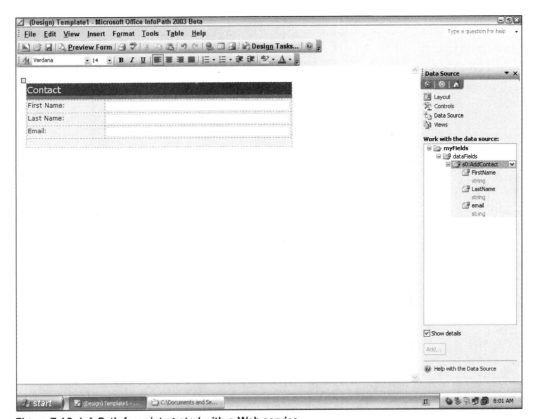

Figure 7-12: InfoPath form integrated with a Web service.

The template is then bound to the Web service, and each time the user submits the data form, it will be sent to the Web service automatically. There are situations where you don't have the WSDL available when you start to design the form; in this case, you need to attach the Web service later. InfoPath provides an easy way to bind an existing template to a Web service. You have to select Tools⇨Submitting Forms . . . . A new dialog box appears (see Figure 7-13).

Figure 7-13: Submitting Forms dialog box.

If you enable Submit and select the Web service item, InfoPath will propose the same Web service wizard as shown in Figure 7-10. There is only one added step in the wizard where you have to map the InfoPath data source fields with the Web service parameters (see Figure 7-14).

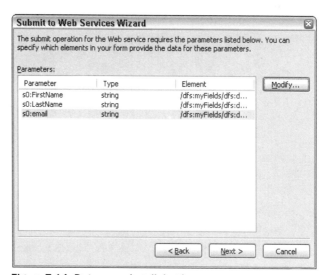

Figure 7-14: Data mapping dialog box.

After that, the template will be bound to the Web service as explained previously. The design process seen in this section is simple, since InfoPath hides all binding complexities needed to attach a general-purpose form to a Web service.

113

Integrating with a File System

File system integration is used in many enterprise scenarios. Consider, for example, a network share where another application picks up all files available every hour for processing. This application could be Microsoft Biztalk Server or another process that connects to that directory though the FTP protocol (it is the standard way for mainframe-based architectures).

This kind of integration is probably the most simple. You only have to save the file in the correct directory. However, this assertion isn't always true. If you remember that InfoPath permits you to save the file even if it is not validated, this could be a serious problem. What happens if you save a wrong or incomplete form on the share and the data is processed? InfoPath advises the user that the form contains errors, but what happens if the user is careless? Depending on the content, that could be a serious issue.

You then have to implement the script code needed to save the file to the right directory. The script should be called during the submit so that InfoPath disables the submission until the form is valid.

If you select `Submit using custom script` from the Submitting Forms dialog box (see Figure 7-13), InfoPath will create the following code:

```
function XDocument::OnSubmitRequest(eventObj)
{
 // If the submit operation is successful, set
 // eventObj.ReturnStatus = true
 // Write your code here
}
```

`OnSubmitRequest` will be invoked every time the user selects the `Submit item` menu command or presses the `Submit` button. The InfoPath Object Model provides a method called `SaveAs` that permits you to save the document into a given directory:

```
function XDocument::OnSubmitRequest(eventObj)
{
 try
 {
  XDocument.SaveAs("D:\Temp\MyForm.xml");
  eventObj.ReturnStatus = true;
 }
 catch(e)
 {
  eventObj.ReturnStatus = false;
 }
}
```

In this way, each time the user submits the form, it is validated before it is saved. As you will see in Appendix C, `SaveAs` works only if the form is fully trusted, as described in Chapter 10.

Integrating with Applications and Services

Previously, you have seen how to integrate with databases, Web services, and file systems. There are scenarios where you have to integrate with applications, such as Microsoft Word, Excel, and Outlook, and services such as MSMQ and IIS. In most of these cases you have to develop some script procedure in order to send data to back-end systems.

In the following section you see how to send an e-mail with an InfoPath document attached to it and how to write into a Microsoft Word document. The last sample integrates InfoPath with the MSMQ (Microsoft Message Queuing) service. As you will see, the samples demonstrate the power of InfoPath when you develop custom scripts in order to interact directly with applications.

Sending the Form by E-mail

When you need to integrate with Microsoft Office 2003, it is easier than with custom applications, since you already have a high level of integration. For example, you can send the document as an attachment to an e-mail in Microsoft Outlook 2003. If you don't have Outlook 2003 available, but a previous version, you should use the CDO (Collaboration Data Objects) model:

```
function XDocument::OnSubmitRequest(eventObj)
{
 try
 {
  XDocument.SaveAs("D:\Temp\document.xml");

  var conf = new ActiveXObject("CDO.Configuration");
  conf.Fields.Item("cdoSendUsingMethod")        = 1; // cdoSendUsingPickup;
  conf.Fields.Item("cdoSMTPServerName")         = "somehost";
  conf.Fields.Item("cdoSMTPConnectionTimeout")  = 10; // quick timeout
  conf.Fields.Item("cdoSMTPAuthenticate")       = 1; //cdoAnonymous;
  conf.Fields.Item("cdoURLGetLatestVersion")    = true;
  conf.Fields.Update();

  var cdo = new ActiveXObject("CDO.Message");
  cdo.To = "to@infopath.com";
  cdo.From = "from@infopath.com";
  cdo.Subject = "InfoPath document";
  cdo.TextBody = "This is the document you are looking for.";
  cdo.AddAttachment("D:\Temp\document.xml");

  cdo.Send();

  eventObj.ReturnStatus = true;
 }
 catch(e)
 {
  XDocument.UI.Alert(e.description);
  eventObj.ReturnStatus = false;
 }
}
```

First, you save the document on the file system. Then you configure the CDO with all parameters needed to send an e-mail (SMTP server, username, password, etc.). Next, you create the message, attaching the document saved. Finally, you send the message. You can delete the file after sending it to keep the local file system clean. The only problem you have is that the form must be fully trusted, since you are using the SaveAs function, which requires higher security privileges.

Updating a Microsoft Word Document

Consider a form where you collect contacts. You need a button in the form that updates a Microsoft Word document. You can create a script code that loads the Word application, fills the document content, saves the document, and closes the application.

This can be done with the Microsoft Word object model as shown in the following sample code:

```
function XDocument::OnSubmitRequest(eventObj)
{
 try
 {
  var name = XDocument.DOM.selectSingleNode("//my:Name").nodeTypedValue;

  var word = new ActiveXObject("Word.Application");
  word.Visible = false;
  word.Documents.Add();

  var range = word.ActiveDocument.Range(0);
  range.InsertAfter("Hello " + name);

  word.ActiveDocument.SaveAs("D:\\Temp\\MyDocument.doc");
  word.ActiveDocument.Close();

  word.Quit();
  word = null;

  eventObj.ReturnStatus = true;
 }
 catch(e)
 {
  XDocument.UI.Alert(e.description);
  eventObj.ReturnStatus = false;
 }
}
```

You have to create a Word application object and then a new document. In the preceding sample, we are getting all defaults from Microsoft Word (normal document), but you can also define all the properties you want, such as the document template to use (.dot). When the document is created, you add the text. As you can see, the text is composed of two parts: one constant value (Hello) and one field content from InfoPath (Name). Finally, you save the document to the file system and close the Word application.

Sending a Document to MSMQ

The previous code listings are samples of integration with applications. You might also need to integrate with operating system services like MSMQ. In the following sample, you send the XML document into a queue of MSMQ:

```
function XDocument::OnSubmitRequest(eventObj)
{
 try
 {
  var strFormatName = "DIRECT=OS:pew-wks1\\private$\\InfoPathQueue";
```

```
    var qinfo = new ActiveXObject("MSMQ.MSMQQueueInfo");
    qinfo.FormatName = strFormatName;
    var qdest = qinfo.Open(2, 0);

    var msg = new ActiveXObject("MSMQ.MSMQMessage");
    msg.Label = "InfoPath document";
    msg.Body = XDocument.DOM.xml;

    msg.Send(qdest);

    qdest.Close();

    eventObj.ReturnStatus = true;
}
catch(e)
{
  XDocument.UI.Alert(e.description);
  eventObj.ReturnStatus = false;
}
}
```

The first parameter is the direct format name of the queue that tells the queue where to send the message. Then you open the queue and create the message with a constant label and the XML document as body. Finally, you send the message to the queue. Note that you can also define a message label depending on some fields content, concatenating the strings.

Summary

Integration with back-end services is the final step of the InfoPath data gathering process. InfoPath provides three built-in bindings for easy back-end integration. If these features aren't enough for your needs, you can implement your script code and have full control over the integration process.

You have learned how to use an existing object model and integrate the InfoPath template with a third-party application. The complexity of this implementation is then proportional to the complexity of the object model with which you integrate.

8

Component Types and Controls

In Chapter 3, you learned something about the different component types supported in the form definition `editing` element. At that point we didn't go into much detail, because we wanted you to get a broad picture of how XML data was represented in the XSF file.

Now it's time to look further into the way InfoPath handles the six editing component types, some of which are rather complex:

- ❑ xField
- ❑ xTextList
- ❑ xCollection
- ❑ xOptional
- ❑ xReplace
- ❑ xImage

When you drag a data source onto a form, you bind the data source to the selected form control. Data binding is what you'll do most of the time. But as you'll see later, not all controls are bound to data. Some can be used to create new values by combining data sources. So you'll also examine the potential of two other InfoPath form controls: hyperlinks and expression boxes.

Types and Related Controls

In the form definition file, component types are defined in the `component` attribute of an `editWith` element. You'll probably recall that `editWith` defines the behavior of an editing control and specifies the use of the component. It also provides the parameters to determine the component behavior.

As a reminder, Figure 8-1 shows the content model.

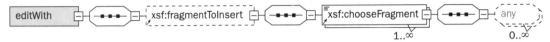

Figure 8-1: The `editWith` **content model.**

Here's a recap on the attributes of `editWith` that you first met in Chapter 3:

- ❏   `caption` is an optional identifier for alternate forms of XML data used in the component.
- ❏   `component` is the name of the editing component, referenced by the `action` attribute of a `button` element.
- ❏   `autoComplete` switches the auto-completion of controls on or off.
- ❏   `proofing` does the same with proofing features, such as the spelling checker.
- ❏   `removeAncestors` specifies the number of ancestor elements to be removed when the last item is removed.
- ❏   `field` specifies a relative XPath expression from the `item` attribute element.
- ❏   `type` specifies the type of editing for the fields that match the XPath expression specified by the `item` attribute of `xmlToEdit`.

xField

The `xField` component allows users to edit XML nodes as text or rich text boxes. There are five possible values for the `type` attribute, but only data that is in a CDATA section, or that corresponds to XHTML, can support values other than `plain`:

- ❏   `plain` (default)—Wrapped or unwrapped text
- ❏   `plainMultiline`—Paragraphs with no formatting
- ❏   `formatted`—Formatting with no paragraphs
- ❏   `formattedMultiline`—Formatting and paragraphs
- ❏   `rich`—Tables, images, and other objects

Plain text is what you'll use most of the time, and it could hardly be more straightforward. For more elaborate formatting, you need a rich text control, and that raises an interesting schema design point.

Suppose you want your users to be able to add features like paragraphs, tables, and emphasis to a meta data `description` element, with an XSF structure like this.

```
<xsf:editing>
    <xsf:xmlToEdit name="description_1" item="/meta/description">
        <xsf:editWith type="rich" autoComplete="no" component="xField"/>
    </xsf:xmlToEdit>
</xsf:editing>
```

You might think that you can just point to the data source and define the field as rich text. Unfortunately, you can't, and the requirements for this component may make it difficult for you to import existing XHTML data to rich text.

If you want to bind an element to a rich text field, you *must* use the following type of declaration in the form schema. The element name defined in the name attribute can be anything you like.

```
<xsd:element name="richText">
   <xsd:complexType mixed="true">
      <xsd:sequence>
         <xsd:any namespace="http://www.w3.org/1999/xhtml"
processContents="lax" minOccurs="0" maxOccurs="unbounded"/>
      </xsd:sequence>
   </xsd:complexType>
</xsd:element>
```

Of course, this structure only gives you just one named element. If you have more than one rich text area, it is better to create a complex type and refer to it, along the following lines. Figure 8-2 illustrates the structure.

Figure 8-2: The content model for the xText component using rich text.

```
<xsd:element name="description" type="richText"/>
      .
      .
<xsd:complexType name="richText" mixed="true">
   <xsd:sequence>
      <xsd:any namespace="http://www.w3.org/1999/xhtml"
processContents="lax" minOccurs="0" maxOccurs="unbounded"/>
   </xsd:sequence>
</xsd:complexType>
```

InfoPath inserts an XHTML fragment in the element content. Note the namespace declaration in the XHTML elements:

```
xmlns="http://www.w3.org/1999/xhtml"
```

Microsoft seems to have decided to use div tags to contain text blocks, rather than paragraph elements, as the following example shows:

```
<description>
   <div xmlns="http://www.w3.org/1999/xhtml">
      <font size="2">
      <div>
         <strong>
```

```
            <font face="Trebuchet MS" color="#969696" size="5">SOAP Version 1.2</font>
            </strong>
        </div>
        <div> </div>
        <div>
            <font size="2">
            <font size="2">
                <div>Simple Object Access Protocol (SOAP) is a lightweight
protocol intended for exchanging structured information in a
decentralized, distributed environment.</div>
                <div> </div>
            </font>
            </font>
        </div>
        <div>
            <em>
            <font color="#008080">
                <strong>Part 1 Messaging Framework</strong>
            </font>
            </em>
            <font size="2">defines the SOAP envelope, an overall framework
for representing the contents of a SOAP message, identifying who should deal
with all or part of it, and whether handling such parts are optional or
mandatory. It also defines a protocol binding framework, which describes
how the specification for a binding of SOAP onto another underlying protocol
may be written.</font>
        </div>
        <div> </div>
        <div>The example shows part of a SOAP envelope header.</div>
        <div> </div>
        <div>
            <font face="Lucida
Console">&lt;env:Header&gt;<br/> &lt;m:reservation</font>
        </div>
        <div>
            <font face="Lucida Console">
xmlns:m="http://travelcompany.example.org/reservation" <br/>
env:role="http://www.w3.org/2003/05/soap-envelope/role/next"<br/>
env:mustUnderstand="true"&gt;<br/> &lt;m:reference&gt;</font>
        </div>
        <div>
            <font face="Lucida Console">     uuid:093a2da1-q345-739r-ba5d-</font>
            <font face="Lucida Console">pqff98fe8j7d</font>
        </div>
        <div>
            <font face="Lucida Console">&lt;/m:reference&gt;<br/>
&lt;m:dateAndTime&gt;2001-11-29T13:35:00.000-05:00&lt;/m:dateAndTime&gt;<br/>
```

```
&lt;/m:reservation&gt;<br/>
&lt;n:passenger xmlns:n="http://mycompany.example.com/employees"<br/>
env:role="http://www.w3.org/2003/05/soap-envelope/role/next"<br/>
env:mustUnderstand="true"&gt;<br/>
&lt;n:name&gt;Mike Smith&lt;/n:name&gt;<br/>
&lt;/n:passenger&gt;<br/>&lt;/env:Header&gt;<br/>
        </font>
    </div>
    </font>
    <div>
    <font size="2">
        <div>
        <font color="#008080">
            <em>
            <strong>Part 2 Adjuncts</strong>
            </em>
        </font>
        <font size="2">defines a data model for SOAP, a particular encoding
scheme for data types which may be used for conveying remote procedure calls
(RPC), as well as one concrete realization of the underlying protocol binding
framework defined in Part 1. This binding allows the exchange of SOAP messages
either as payload of a HTTP POST request and response, or as a SOAP message in
the response to a HTTP GET.</font>
        </div>
        <div> </div>
        <div>
        <strong>Acknowledgement</strong>
        </div>
        <div>This description is adapted from the W3C SOAP tutorial,
 which you can access at:
<a href="http://www.w3.org/TR/2003/REC-soap12-part0-20030624/">
http://www.w3.org/TR/2003/REC-soap12-part0-20030624/</a>
        </div>
    </font>
    </div>
    </div>
</description>
```

However, whatever you may think of the quality of the XHTML code generation, you have to admit that using rich text shows off the InfoPath UI. Figure 8-3 illustrates a little of what is possible, including multiple fonts, highlighting, formatting for style and different colors, and a hyperlink. Notice the spelling checker at work in the code example. (And if you read it carefully, you can learn a bit about SOAP, including where to find a tutorial.)

> ## SOAP Version 1.2
>
> Simple Object Access Protocol (SOAP) is a lightweight protocol intended for exchanging structured information in a decentralized, distributed environment.
>
> *Part 1 Messaging Framework* defines the SOAP envelope, an overall framework for representing the contents of a SOAP message, identifying who should deal with all or part of it, and whether handling such parts are optional or mandatory. It also defines a protocol binding framework, which describes how the specification for a binding of SOAP onto another underlying protocol may be written.
>
> The example shows part of a SOAP envelope header.
>
> ```
> <env:Header>
>   <m:reservation
>       xmlns:m="http://travelcompany.example.org/reservation"
>       env:role="http://www.w3.org/2003/05/soap-envelope/role/next"
>       env:mustUnderstand="true">
>     <m:reference>
>       uuid:093a2da1-q345-739r-ba5d-pqff98fe8j7d
>     </m:reference>
>     <m:dateAndTime>2001-11-29T13:35:00.000-05:00</m:dateAndTime>
>   </m:reservation>
>   <n:passenger xmlns:n="http://mycompany.example.com/employees"
>       env:role="http://www.w3.org/2003/05/soap-envelope/role/next"
>       env:mustUnderstand="true">
>     <n:name>Mike Smith</n:name>
>   </n:passenger>
> </env:Header>
> ```
>
> *Part 2 Adjuncts* defines a data model for SOAP, a particular encoding scheme for data types which may be used for conveying remote procedure calls (RPC), as well as one concrete realization of the underlying protocol binding framework defined in Part 1. This binding allows the exchange of SOAP messages either as payload of a HTTP POST request and response, or as a SOAP message in the response to a HTTP GET.
>
> **Acknowledgement**
> This description is adapted from the W3C SOAP tutorial, which you can access at:
> http://www.w3.org/TR/2003/REC-soap12-part0-20030624/

Figure 8-3: A rich text control.

xTextList

The xTextList component corresponds to bulleted, numbered, or plain lists. The component consists of one or more *identical elements* that are siblings under the node described in the item attribute on the containing xmlToEdit element. The schema for an xTextList element is shown in the following example. Figure 8-4 illustrates the model.

Figure 8-4: The content model for the xTextList **component.**

```
<xsd:element name="subjects">
    <xsd:complexType>
        <xsd:sequence>
            <xsd:element ref="subject" minOccurs="0" maxOccurs="unbounded"/>
        </xsd:sequence>
```

```
      </xsd:complexType>
   </xsd:element>
   <xsd:element name="subject" type="subjectType"/>
```

The XML data looks like this:

```
<subjects>
   <subject>George Bush</subject>
   <subject>World Bank</subject>
   <subject>Matsushita</subject>
</subjects>
```

User actions to split, merge, and remove items are associated with the Enter, and Backspace, or Delete keys, respectively. All three actions require that the insertion point be within a field in the list.

split creates a copy of the current item XML node and inserts it as a sibling after the current one. It fills the field nodes with the content preceding and following the insertion point. Because the split is associated with the Enter key, the fields may not be any of the multiline field types. Only the types plain and formatted are supported.

merge additionally requires that the insertion point be at the beginning of a field node, and there must be another field node before it. If the insertion point is at the beginning of the field, merge deletes the current content and appends it to the content of the preceding field.

remove removes the current node.

xCollection

The xCollection component allows the insertion and removal of repeating sections or tables. This requires *two levels of nesting*: a group within a group and the second group containing the table or other field elements. The schema shows the structure, and the content model diagram is shown in Figure 8-5.

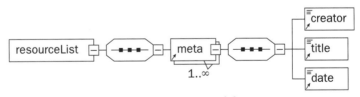

Figure 8-5: The xCollection **content model.**

```
<xsd:element name="resourceList">
   <xsd:complexType>
      <xsd:sequence>
         <xsd:element ref="meta" minOccurs="1" maxOccurs="unbounded"/>
      </xsd:sequence>
   </xsd:complexType>
</xsd:element>
   <xsd:element name="meta">
      <xsd:complexType>
            <xsd:sequence>
```

```
                  <xsd:element ref="creator" minOccurs="1"/>
                  <xsd:element ref="title" minOccurs="1"/>
                  <xsd:element ref="date" minOccurs="1"/>
                    .
                    .
                    .
            </xsd:sequence>
      </xsd:complexType>
</xsd:element>
<xsd:element name="creator" type="xsd:string"/>
<xsd:element name="title" type="xsd:string"/>
<xsd:element name="date" type="xsd:date"/>
```

The form instance data will look like this:

```
<resourceList>
   <meta>
      <creator>Ian Williams, Pierre Greborio</creator>
      <title>Professional InfoPath 2003</title>
      <date>2004</date>
   </meta>
   <meta>
      <creator>Michael Kay</creator>
      <title>XSLT Programmer's Reference, 2nd Edition</title>
      <date>2001</date>
   </meta>
</resourceList>
```

All the following actions require the current context to be within the scope of a container.

With the `insert` action, if the insertion point is within an item, the insertion is equivalent to `insertAfter`. Otherwise, InfoPath inserts the `fragmentToInsert` at the end of the content of the appropriate parent node, and/or add attributes to the parent node. If the current context has a mapping to within some other child node of the parent node, the insert will be after that node, rather than appended to the content. A button entry for this action is in the `msoInsertMenu` and `msoStructural EditingContextMenu` named menu areas.

`insertBefore` and `insertAfter` require that the current context be within a node. These actions insert the `fragmentToInsert` before or after the current node, and/or add attributes to the parent node. Button entries for these actions are in the `msoStructuralEditingContextMenu` named menu area.

`remove` requires that the current context be within a node. The action removes the node. If the `removeAncestors` attribute is not zero, this action also removes the corresponding number of parents/ancestors of the item XML node. Button entries for this action are in the `msoStructural EditingContextMenu` named menu area (for the context menu and the shortcut menu).

`removeAll` requires that the `minOccurs` value for the element in the schema be 0. The action removes all XML nodes that are descendants of the container node and satisfy the `item` XPath pattern. If the `removeAncestors` attribute is not zero, it also removes the corresponding number of parents/ancestors of the item XML node.

xOptional

xOptional applies where the inserted data is an optional item. Only *one instance* of the optional data can be inserted.

```
<xsd:element name="meta">
    <xsd:complexType>
        <xsd:sequence>
            <xsd:element ref="releaseTime" minOccurs="1" maxOccurs="1"/>
        </xsd:sequence>
    </xsd:complexType>
</xsd:element>
```

All insert and remove actions require the current context to be within the scope of a container.

insert requires that the container node does not already have a descendant satisfying the item XPath. It appends the fragmentToInsert at the end of the content of the appropriate parent node, and/or adds attributes to the parent node.

remove requires that the current context be within an item. The action removes the item. If the remove Ancestors attribute is not zero, this action also removes the corresponding number of parents/ancestors of the node.

xReplace

xReplace provides a replace action, allowing different versions of content specified in the schema xsd:choice element to be replaced by one another.

replace is enabled when the current context is an item. The action replaces the current item by the xmlFragment.

```
<xsd:element name="rights">
    <xsd:complexType>
        <xsd:choice>
            <xsd:element ref="rightsAgent"/>
            <xsd:element ref="copyright"/>
        </xsd:choice>
    </xsd:complexType>
</xsd:element>
```

Again, this requires two levels of nesting, with two or more section controls within a group. Figure 8-6 illustrates part of a typical structure.

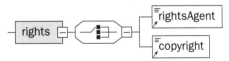

Figure 8-6: The xReplace **content model.**

In the following example from a form definition file, the `rightsAgent` element replaces `copyright`. There is, of course, a comparable entry for the `rightsAgent` element.

```
<xsf:xmlToEdit name="rightsAgent_13" item="/resourceList/meta/rights/copyright"
container="/resourceList/meta/rights">
    <xsf:editWith caption="Rights Agent" xd:autogeneration="template"
component="xReplace">
        <xsf;fragmentToInsert>
            <xsf:chooseFragment>
                <xsf:rightsAgent/>
            </xsf:chooseFragment>
        </xsf:fragmentToInsert>
    </xsf:editWith>
</xsf:xmlToEdit>
```

`xReplace` is intended for simple pairings like this, although in principle, there can be more choices. However, the permutations could become unmanageable as the options increase.

xImage

`xImage` corresponds to an image control and specifies the XML item in which the image data is inserted or referenced.

As a quick reminder, the relevant `xImage` declaration in the form definition file will look something like this:

```
<xsf:editing>
    <xsf:xmlToEdit name="embedded" item="person/thumbnail">
        <xsf:editWith component="xImage"/>
    </xsf:xmlToEdit>
<xsf:editing>
```

Form users can insert images in fields you have specified as an `xImage` component or in rich text fields. For example, you might want users to be able to add a photograph to a personnel record (or possibly a thumbnail that opens a larger linked file). Figure 8-7 shows the user interface for an image field.

**Figure 8-7: An image filed
in the user interface.**

Image Fields

In design mode you can define picture elements as embedded or linked objects. As with other forms of linking and embedding, you have to weigh several options.

On the one hand, embedding an image adds to the size of the form, and any XML processor outside of the InfoPath environment will have to know how to handle the binary data in the element content. On the other hand, with linked information, there are issues regarding ongoing access to the images that users can link to.

In your main form schema, the respective element declarations should have the following data types. Embedded images must be encoded as `xsd:base64Binary` data, and linked image elements as `xsd:anyURI`.

```
<xsd:element name="thumbnail" type="xsd:base64Binary" nillable="true"/>
```

```
<xsd:element name="linked_image" type="xsd:anyURI"/>
```

Images in Rich Text

When a user inserts an image in a rich text field, InfoPath includes it as an inline XHTML `img` element. The embedded binary value of the image is base64 encoded as an attribute of the element.

```
<div>
   <img
   style="WIDTH: 52px; HEIGHT: 29px" tabIndex="-1" height="29"
   src="msoinline/a3baabfb94ed43b8"
   width="52"
   xd:inline="iVBORw0KGgoAAAANSUhEUgAAADQAAAAdBAMAAAAX9VImAAAAMFBMVEUAAADAwMD///
8AAAAAAAAAAAAAAAAAAAAAAAAAAAAAAAAAAAAAAAAAAAAACVom0/AAAACXBIWXMAAA7EAAAOx
AGVKw4bAAAAB3RJTUUH0wkBES4SCIhwFgAAAAd0RVh0QXV0aG9yAKmuzEgAAAAMdEVYdERlc2NyaXB0
aW9uABMJISMAAAAKdEVYdENvcHlyaWdodACsD8w6AAAADnRFWHRDcmVhdGlvbiB0aW1lADX3DwkAAAAJ
dEVYdFNvZnR3YXJlAF1w/zoAAAALdEVYdERpc2NsYWltZXIAt8C0jwAAAAh0RVh0V2FybmluZwAG+aH
AAAAB3RFWHRTb3VyY2UA9f+D6wAAAAh0RVh0Q29tbWVudAD2zJa/AAAABnRFWHRUaXRsZZQCo7tInAAAA
1U1EQVR4AbWRURKEIAxDWW7AnqD2/oc0iRYorF87dkbH+hoSa/HHKo/EX0Jlqhru8rI5S2+E+qBGGoiNK
otESZVHvgRYRXigUP31HdLR/UamG45SVIDjiQhrpHVTfDM66I8UP1WkKmuosprm1sO/y0xiGud9mUtYEW
GURdtfxlkIHSNij6hpf7wcmpFJUxUJlIFCjLrvET5edWL/Z50k4AAAAASUVORK5CYII="
   xmlns:xd="http://schemas.microsoft.com/office/infopath/2003"/>
</div>
```

Persistent Images

By *persistent images* we mean those that appear on every form instance. You might want to include something on every form for a group of users, such as a company logo or an icon associated with the type of form or even the view in use. Persistent images can also be structured as hyperlinks.

You can insert this type of image in design mode by choosing Insert⇨Picture. If you embed the image, InfoPath renames the image file and adds it to the files section of the XSF file. InfoPath then adds an HTML `img` element to the style sheet for the form for both linked and embedded images, with the linked or renamed file in the `src` attribute.

Supported Image Formats

Your users can insert several graphics file formats into forms, either directly or with the use of graphics filters.

File Types That Do Not Require Filters

You don't need a separate graphics filter installed to insert the following file formats:

- ❑ Enhanced Metafile (.emf)
- ❑ Graphics Interchange Format (.gif)
- ❑ Joint Photographic Experts Group (.jpg)
- ❑ Portable Network Graphics (.png)
- ❑ Microsoft Windows Bitmap (.bmp, .rle, .dib)
- ❑ Windows Metafile Graphics (.wmf)
- ❑ Tagged Image File Format (.tiff)
- ❑ Encapsulated PostScript (.eps)

File Types That Require Filters

You will need a graphics filter installed to insert all other graphics file formats. These graphics filters are *not* supplied with the standalone version of InfoPath. To use the filters, you need to install the appropriate Microsoft Office edition or a standalone version of Microsoft. The following list contains common file types and the corresponding graphic filters that are supported. For additional documentation on these formats, see InfoPath Help.

- ❑ Computer Graphics Metafile (.cgm)
- ❑ CorelDRAW (.cdr, .cdt, .cmx, and .pat)
- ❑ FlashPix (.fpx)
- ❑ Encapsulated PostScript (.eps)
- ❑ Hanako (.jsh, .jah, and .jbh)
- ❑ Kodak Photo CD (.pcd)
- ❑ Macintosh PICT (.pct)
- ❑ PC Paintbrush (.pcx)
- ❑ WordPerfect Graphics (.wpg)

Additional Filters

For information on graphics filters that you can download, choose Help⇨Office on Microsoft.com to connect to the Microsoft Office Web site.

Other Controls

InfoPath provides additional controls that don't directly correspond to editing components, though they can make use of them. Here, we briefly describe two of the more interesting controls, Hyperlink and Expression Box.

Hyperlinks

InfoPath allows users to insert a hyperlink into any rich text field. If the field doesn't support rich text, the menu item is disabled. In design mode you can also place a link anywhere on a form. For example, you might want to link your users to a Web site containing procedural instructions for the relevant part of a business process. In both cases, InfoPath will automatically recognize URLs, filenames, and e-mail addresses and format them as links.

Design mode additionally provides a hyperlink control that you can drag onto the form. You can specify a static URL or point to a data source element or attribute containing the URL you want the link to use. You can also specify a separate text for the link object either statically or again using the form data source.

In this example the link takes the value of a data source:

```
<div> Follow this <a class="xdDataBindingUI" xd:disableEditing="yes">
   <xsl:attribute name="href">
      <xsl:value-of select="procedure/@url"/>
   </xsl:attribute>link</a> for assistance with this procedure.
</div>
```

In the case study Contributor view, there's a link from a persistent form image of an e-mail icon. The icon is a hyperlink to a news desk e-mail address in the form header. Figure 8-8 shows the interface control.

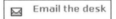

Figure 8-8: The user interface for the e-mail link.

```
<a class="xdDataBindingUI"
   title="Launch Outlook to email the desk" tabIndex="9"
   xd:disableEditing="yes">
   <xsl:attribute name="href">
      <xsl:value-of select="concat(&quot;mailto:&quot;,
../formHeader/@email, &quot;?subject=&quot;, title)"/>
   </xsl:attribute>
   <img title="Email the desk" style="BORDER-RIGHT: #0000ff 1.5pt;
BORDER-TOP: #0000ff 1.5pt; BORDER-LEFT: #0000ff 1.5pt; WIDTH: 24px;
BORDER-BOTTOM: #0000ff 1.5pt; HEIGHT: 24px" height="24" src="EDB78201.png"
width="24"/>@@@AU: Please break lines where appropriate (i.e., no wrap
</a>
```

One other attractive feature of hyperlinks is that you can use XPath to build values using the same techniques as expression box controls. For example, you might want to take a base URL and add to it the local name that identified a given file:

```
concat(baseurl,'/'date,'/',formheadr/@deskID,'/',identifier,'.html')
```

This would give a link value such as `http://newsline.net/20031103/ny0522.html`.

We can hear your mind ticking. There's more to come next.

Expression Boxes

You can use expression boxes to add, subtract, multiply, and divide numeric values, as well as perform other calculations. The values used are relative XPath expressions to the XML nodes containing the information. So an example might be

```
payment/dollarValue div exchangeRate
```

The following table gives the expression syntax for each function.

Function	Expression
Add two fields	field1 + field2
Subtract a field from another	field1 - field2
Multiply two fields	field1 * field2
Divide a field by another	field1 div field2

With repeating fields or parts of a repeating group, you can perform counts sums and averages on columns of figures, for example:

```
count(meta/subjects/subject)
```

Or you can write out a row number next to a row in a repeating table with a simple `position()` statement:

```
position()
```

The form layout in Figure 8-9 shows the use of position in a repeating table. The Order Item column contains an expression box using the `position` function, and a total of the order values below the Value column is calculated using the `sum` function. Before you start filling in the form, the total expression box shows 1.#QNAN (meaning "not a number"). To avoid this, either provide a default value for the field or filter the blanks in the empty field by using a pattern in your xPath expression.

```
sum(orders/value[.!=""])
```

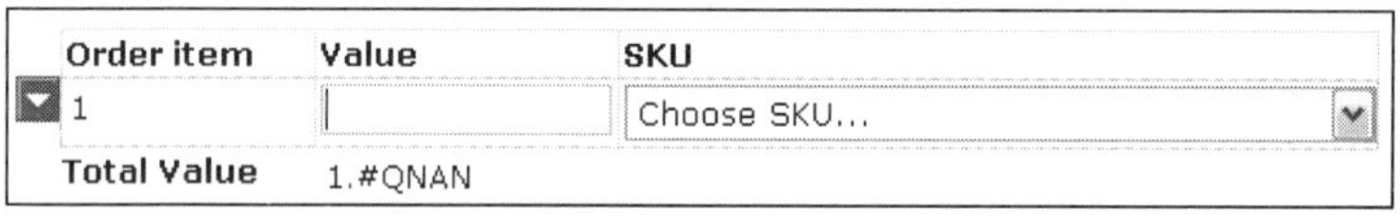

Figure 8-9: The empty form control.

As you fill out the form, the order items are numbered and the total builds. See Figure 8-10.

Order item	Value	SKU	
1	19.99	DG-1923785	˅
2	15.25	SZ-001946	˅
3	44.85	XC-87162	˅
Total Value	£80.09		

Figure 8-10: The filled-out control.

With text fields you can concatenate values using the `concat` expression, as you saw in the section on hyperlinks:

```
concat(formHeader/@deskID,' ',formHeader/@email)
```

This is just like the expressions you are familiar with if you've used XSLT. It's worth experimenting here, as you can create dynamic values very readily. Just remember that you aren't creating data that is bound to a data source and, therefore, to an element or attribute. If you want to preserve the results, you'll have to use a script to assign the value you've created.

Have fun!

Summary

There's a good deal to absorb about the workings of the different component types available in InfoPath and their associated controls. In this chapter you reviewed the six component types and how they are used with XML Schema structures. You also looked into what's possible with hyperlinks and with using concatenation and calculations with expression box controls.

As you've seen, there are some constraints in how controls can be used, but despite these limitations, you have an extensive set of features to explore. There's more to read on controls in Chapter 11 and in the case study.

An important subject comes next: upgrading forms.

9

Upgrading Forms

After you have deployed a form template and users have begun to create a legacy of form data, it is almost certain that before too long, requirements will change. Users will have thought of improvements to the business process, a big customer will have moved the goalposts, or a standards organization will produce a new version of a critical schema. Some (minor) bugs in your design may even have surfaced.

In this chapter you consider the issues around upgrading your InfoPath application, including:

❏ Changes to the main schema

❏ Modifications to external data sources

❏ XSF upgrade parameters

❏ Review of how InfoPath maintains information about form versions

❏ InfoPath extensions

In fact, much of this section also applies to the development and testing cycle, as you'll undoubtedly issue series of prototype upgrades as you iterate through the steps of application building. Even if you have had plenty of experience in developing applications, you will find that InfoPath has some specific requirements.

Handling Template Modifications

Before you make changes to a template, you should to be aware of how your changes will impact the existing forms based on it. Some changes have a more severe impact than others, to the extent that in the worst case, it is sometimes better to start with a clean slate and create an entirely new design. Here are some of the changes that can impact your users:

❑ Renaming elements or attributes in a data source, or adding, removing, or moving them

❑ Renaming or moving a template

❑ Changing repeating items to nonrepeating

❑ Altering the data type of a field

❑ Manually changing the version number of a template

Changes to the Data Source

When you design a form, InfoPath assumes that the data source is completely and correctly defined, and it won't adapt to subsequent changes you make to the underlying form, database, or Web service schema. When you need to change a data source, several form files will be affected to some degree. The table shows the form files you'll need to modify and the type of changes you will have to make.

File	Type of Change
Form definition	`xmlToEdit` elements. ADO or Web service queries.
Template	Element and attributes.
Schema	Element and attributes.
View transform	`xsl:apply-templates` and the `match` attribute of `xsl:template` elements.
Script	XPath statements.

The extent of change will depend on the number of data source elements or attributes that you alter, and the kind of modifications you make. The next table shows the impact of these changes on existing forms and the actions you will need to take. The changes are listed in the order of increasing level of complexity.

Change	Impact on Existing Forms	Action Summary
Rename	Forms become incompatible with schema unless they are updated.	All files require that a corresponding item has to be updated.
Add	All XML forms will open with the new schema unless the new items are required by the schema.	XSF, XSN, and XSD require corresponding items to be added.
Delete	Forms become incompatible with the data source schema unless they are updated. Views may not display content.	All files require that a corresponding item has to be removed.
Move	Forms become incompatible with the data source schema unless they are updated. Views may not display content.	Effectively combines the actions of adding and deleting.

Changes to Trusted Forms

The way you make changes to trusted form depends on whether you are making design mode changes to the form template or to the extracted files. If you change the template, your users can replace the existing templates with the new one. If you alter the extracted files, you have to repackage them and have users reinstall the trusted form. In this case you can use the form registration tool to convert the template to a fully trusted form. Its use is described in Chapter 10.

Updating XML Data

The InfoPath SDK contains a processing instruction update tool that simplifies the task of updating the processing instructions of a form's underlying XML document. This is a command-line utility you can use to update a single form or to handle multiple updates. The filename is pifix.exe, and it is usually located in the tools folder in C:\Program Files\Microsoft Office 2003 Developer Resources\Microsoft Office InfoPath 2003 SDK.

Here's a reminder of how a PI looks:

```
<?mso-infoPathSolution productVersion="11.0.5531" PIVersion="1.0.0.0"
href="file:///D:\infopath\meta2\manifest\manifest.xsf" language="en-us"
solutionVersion="1.0.0.89" ?>
```

To use the utility, open a command prompt and type **pifix** followed by the command-line switches and values described in the table. All the switches are optional except for the filename. The tool updates the PIs and creates a log file.

Switch	Description
/O	Path and name of the output file(s).
/URN	URN is to replace the existing URN.
/URL	URL is to replace the existing URL.
/V	Version number of the form that is to replace the existing version number. If part of the version number is not specified, 0 is used by default.
/IV	Name of the initial view.
/L	Path and name of the XML log file.
/?|/h|/help	Help for the tool.
filename	Required. Full path, which can contain wildcard characters, of the form(s) to update.

Here's a multiple update example:

```
pifix /URN urn:metadata:newsline /V 1.0.0.19 /IV contributor /L updatelog.xml
d:\newsline\stories\week08\*.xml
```

Some Precautions

InfoPath has an automatic upgrade option that helps ensure that your modifications can be made without affecting your users' ability to continue working with existing forms. If the option is enabled (default), InfoPath can reconstruct the form to conform to a new schema. If this option is disabled, the forms won't be upgraded and may not open or function correctly. The third possibility is to upgrade using a script. You see how that works later in this chapter.

In design mode, choose Tools⇨Form Options and go to the Advanced tab. In the On version upgrade drop-down list, select the version upgrade method you want to use. Figure 9-1 shows the interface.

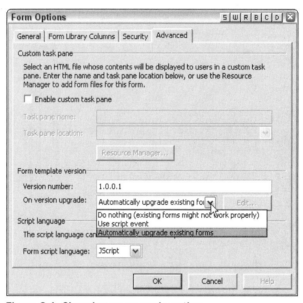

Figure 9-1: Choosing an upgrade option.

Additionally, you can minimize or avoid risk by following some other basic precautions:

- ❑ Make backup copies of the extracted files before you modify them.
- ❑ Add fields or groups to the data source but don't remove them.
- ❑ Don't move data source objects unless the structural change is vital.
- ❑ Don't alter the names of groups or fields after they have been published.
- ❑ Publish modified templates with a new name or location, instead of overwriting the existing ones.

Main Schema

Changes to your main form schema will most likely be needed because of changes to a business process, and a resulting need to review the form data structure. However, modifications can also come from developments in industry standards you are conforming to or because your business partners are requesting new ways of working.

Of course, alterations to a form schema can cascade all the way through your application. But for the moment, let's look at the implications of a main schema change in itself.

Suppose you have to make several changes to the data structure, adding new elements and attributes, and altering or even removing others. Apart from developing and testing the schema design with several new data instance examples, you will need to make changes to the form interface, and possibly to associated scripts, the help text, and so on.

Schema Identifiers

If you haven't already done so, work out a simple version labeling method for your schemas that will identify the major implemented revisions, such as "schemaName_versionNumber_date". Use this identifier in the filename, so that you can always see from the schema `location` attribute exactly which version InfoPath is using.

It is also a good idea to edit and test schemas in a separate folder and copy the tested version to the extract folder before building a new template version. This prevents the possibility of you inadvertently saving a schema file from InfoPath and overwriting your work.

Changing XSF References

InfoPath has stored a reference to the initial schema in the `documentSchemas` section of the XSF file. When you have copied your new schema file to the extract folder, open the form definition file and edit the location attribute of the `documentSchema` element to match your new version:

```
<xsf:documentSchemas>
    <xsf:documentSchema
        location="meta_11.xsd"
        rootSchema="yes"/>
</xsf:documentSchemas>
```

Then, edit the `file` element that refers to the same schema:

```
<xsf:files>
    <xsf:file name="meta_11.xsd">
    .
    .
    <xsf:/file>
</xsf:files>
```

If you try to open the manifest immediately, you may well get a schema validation error. Figure 9-2 shows the error dialog box. Clicking `Show Details` usually helps you identify the problem.

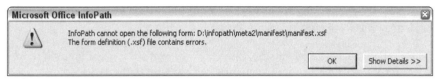

Figure 9-2: Schema error dialog box.

The most probable reason for an error at this time is that InfoPath has found incorrect or missing references to new or changed elements or attributes on the form. If you have added or modified any elements or attributes, you will also need to make appropriate changes to `xmlToEdit` elements in the XSF.

```
<xsf:xmlToEdit name="paymenta_12" item="/meta/payment/@amount">
   <xsf:editWith proofing="no" autoComplete="no" component="xField"/>
</xsf:xmlToEdit>
<xsf:xmlToEdit name="paymentc_13" item="/meta/payment/@currency">
   <xsf:editWith proofing="no" autoComplete="no" component="xField"/>
</xsf:xmlToEdit>
```

External Data Sources

If your organization is responsible for maintaining an external data source, you'll probably have a degree of control about how and when it is modified. However, you may be confronted with changes you must adapt to—for example, new or changed functions in a Web service. For each secondary data source, InfoPath requires entries in the `documentSchemas` section of the XSF file.

In this example, which you'll see again in the case study, a secondary source is used to populate drop-down lists with categorized topics.

```
<?xml version="1.0"?>
<xsd:schema xmlns:xsd="http://www.w3.org/2001/XMLSchema">
   <xsd:element name="topiclist">
      <xsd:complexType>
         <xsd:sequence>
            <xsd:element ref="category" minOccurs="0" maxOccurs="unbounded"/>
         </xsd:sequence>
      </xsd:complexType>
   </xsd:element>
   <xsd:element name="topics">
      <xsd:complexType>
         <xsd:sequence>
            <xsd:element ref="topic" minOccurs="0" maxOccurs="unbounded"/>
         </xsd:sequence>
      </xsd:complexType>
   </xsd:element>
   <xsd:element name="topic">
      <xsd:complexType>
         <xsd:simpleContent>
            <xsd:extension base="xsd:string">
```

```
                    <xsd:attribute ref="id"/>
                </xsd:extension>
            </xsd:simpleContent>
        </xsd:complexType>
    </xsd:element>
    <xsd:element name="category">
        <xsd:complexType>
            <xsd:all>
                <xsd:element ref="topics" minOccurs="0"/>
            </xsd:all>
            <xsd:attribute ref="Type"/>
        </xsd:complexType>
    </xsd:element>
    <xsd:attribute name="Type" type="xsd:string"/>
    <xsd:attribute name="id" type="xsd:string"/>
</xsd:schema>
```

Unless you are adding a completely new data source for some reason, you'll need to check the existing references in the `documentSchemas` section and make any necessary changes to the data model in the relevant files. Again, you may want to think of using version numbers to keep the schema references clear. If necessary, rename the files in `documentSchemas` and `files` sections of the XSF, and move on to modifying the appropriate `xmlToEdit` elements.

Document Upgrade

To update XML documents created from a template that predates a new specification, InfoPath uses upgrade parameters that are declared in the form definition file. Figure 9-3 shows the content model for this section of the XSF file.

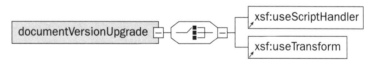

Figure 9-3: The `documentVersionUpgrade` content model.

documentVersionUpgrade

The `documentVersionUpgrade` element specifies how forms created with a previous version of a template will be upgraded to conform to the latest version. There are two ways you can perform upgrades: by using the XSLT defined in the `useTransform` subelement or by using scripting code.

```
<xsf:xDocumentClass>
    <xsf:documentVersionUpgrade>
    .

    .
    </xsf:documentVersionUpgrade>
</xsf:xDocumentClass>
```

useTransform

useTransform specifies that the upgrade will be handled by an XSLT file supplied by the newer version of the form template. When a user opens an older version form, InfoPath checks the inclusive minimum (oldest) and maximum (latest) version numbers. If the version is greater than or equal to the required minVersionToUpgrade attribute and the version is less than or equal to the optional maxVersionToUpgrade attribute, InfoPath runs the XSLT transform defined in the required transform attribute. The output of the transform becomes the data to be edited. minVersionToUpgrade is required to prevent data loss from existing forms that differ from the current structure.

```
<xsf:documentVersionUpgrade>
    <xsf:useTransform
        transform="upgrade.xsl"
        minVersionToUpgrade="0.0.0.0"
        maxVersionToUpgrade="1.0.0.5"/>
</xsf:documentVersionUpgrade>
```

useScriptHandler

When used with the documentVersionUpgrade element, useScriptHandler specifies that the upgrade will be processed by scripting code in the OnVersionUpgrade event handler in the form's primary script file.

useScripthandler has no attributes or child elements.

```
<xsf:documentVersionUpgrade>
    <xsf:useScriptHandler/>
<xsf:documentVersionUpgrade>
```

XSLT Example

Here's a partial XSLT upgrade example for adding a format element to a meta data schema. The default filename given by InfoPath is upgrade.xsl.

```
<?xml version="1.0" encoding="UTF-8" standalone="no"?>
<xsl:stylesheet xmlns:xsl="http://www.w3.org/1999/XSL/Transform"
xmlns:msxsl="urn:schemas-microsoft-com:xslt"
xmlns:xsi="http://www.w3.org/2001/XMLSchema-instance"
xmlns:my="http://schemas.microsoft.com/office/infopath/2003/myXSD/
2003-09-22T10:12:57" version="1.0">
    <xsl:output encoding="UTF-8" method="xml"/>
    <xsl:template match="/">
        <xsl:copy-of select="processing-instruction() | comment()"/>
        <xsl:choose>
            <xsl:when test="meta">
                <xsl:apply-templates select="meta" mode="_0"/>
            </xsl:when>
            <xsl:otherwise>
                <xsl:variable name="var">
                    <xsl:element name="meta"/>
                </xsl:variable>
                <xsl:apply-templates select="msxsl:node-set($var)/*" mode="_0"/>
            </xsl:otherwise>
```

```
          </xsl:choose>
      </xsl:template>
      <xsl:template match="meta" mode="_0">
          <xsl:copy>

<!--copy existing elements-->

              <xsl:element name="title">
                  <xsl:choose>
                      <xsl:when test="title/text()[1]">
                          <xsl:copy-of select="title/text()[1]"/>
                      </xsl:when>
                      <xsl:otherwise>
                          <xsl:attribute name="xsi:nil">true</xsl:attribute>
                      </xsl:otherwise>
                  </xsl:choose>
              </xsl:element>
                .
                .
<!--add new format element-->

              <xsl:element name="format">
              <xsl:copy-of select="format/text()[1]"/>
                </xsl:element>

 <!--continue existing elements-->

                .
                .

          </xsl:copy>
      </xsl:template>
</xsl:stylesheet>
```

Upgrading with Script

You've just seen how to use the `useScriptHandler` element to specify that the upgrade will be processed by scripting using the event handler. The `OnVersionUpgrade` event occurs when the version number of a form being opened is older than the version number of the template it is based on. During this event, InfoPath sets the XML document to read-only, and it is not validated against the schema.

In the following example, the event handler performs the same function as the preceeding XSLT style sheet:

```
Function XDocument: OnVersionUpgrade (eventObj)
{
    if (!XDocument.DOM.selectSingleNode("/meta/format"))
    {
        try
        {
            // Create a new format element
            var objItemNode = XDocument.DOM.selectSingleNode("/meta ")
                .ownerDocument.createElement("format");
```

```
            // Add the format element to the XML instance
        XDocument.DOM.selectSingleNode("meta")
            .appendChild(objItemNode);
        eventObj.ReturnStatus=true;
    }
    catch(ex)
    {
        XDocument.UI.Alert("There was an error inserting the " +
            "<format> node.\nDescription: " + ex.description);
        eventObj.ReturnStatus=false;
    }
    }
}
```

InfoPath Version Numbers

InfoPath uses version numbers, expressed as element attributes, in a number of form definition sections. Here we've drawn them together as a reminder of their purpose.

With the exception of the `productVersion` attribute, which omits a value for revision, the numbers are represented in the format nnnn.nnnn.nnnn.nnnn (major.minor.revision.build). The XSF schema type declaration shows the number pattern.

```
<xsd:simpleType name="xdSolutionVersion">
    <xsd:restriction base="xsd:string">
        <xsd:pattern value="(([0-9]{1,4}.){3}[0-9]{1,4})"/>
    </xsd:restriction>
</xsd:simpleType>
```

Element	Attribute	Purpose
xDocumentClass	solutionVersion	The version number of the form.
	solutionFormatVersion	The version number of the XSF file. It allows InfoPath to check if the form is compatible with the product version of InfoPath.
	productVersion	The version of the InfoPath application used to create a form. You can also use this number to target a specific version if you are editing the XSF outside of design mode.
useTransform	minVersionToUpgrade	Inclusive value for the oldest form that can be upgraded. Prevents running transforms on forms so different from the current one that there is a risk of losing data.

Element	Attribute	Purpose
	maxVersionToUpgrade	Inclusive value for the latest form that needs to be upgraded.
soultionProperties	lastVersionNeeding Transform	If a script is currently being used for the upgrade, this attribute contains the value of maxVersionToUpgrade to be used in an XSLT transform.

InfoPath Extensions

Before you leave this section on upgrading forms, we need to briefly mention a mechanism intended by Microsoft to detail minor upgrades to the XSF schema that can be used by specific future releases of InfoPath or by specific forms.

extensions

The extensions element is a wrapper for a set of extension declarations. Containing such extensions in this way means that any given version of InfoPath can ignore them unless required. Figure 9-4 shows the content model.

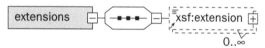

Figure 9-4: The extensions **content model.**

extension

Use of the extension element is reserved. It can contain elements of an open-content model. The required name attribute contains a unique name identifier for the extension.

```
<xsf:xDocumentClass>
    <xsf:extensions>
        <xsf:extension name="xdSpecialDate"
         .

         .

         open content model here

         .

         .

        </xsf:extension>
    <xsf:extensions>
<xsf:xDocumentClass>
```

Summary

Developing, testing, and upgrading in InfoPath have some common approaches. In this chapter you looked at the implications of various types of change to a form template, and the changes required in the documents that make up a form template.

If you are working with a preexisting schema and there are changes to it, you can find that InfoPath seems a bit intractable. We hope that some of the approaches suggested in this chapter will help get you around most upgrade problems. You'll see more gritty stuff next in Chapter 10, about form security issues and methods.

10

Security

The InfoPath security model is based on the Internet Explorer model, which attempts to protect your computer from unsafe operations by using security zones and levels.

In this chapter you explore the model in more detail and see how InfoPath also allows for other form security measures, including protecting form design, managing operations such as form merging and submission, and installing trusted forms.

You also review the way digital signatures are implemented in InfoPath and take a brief tour of the more important features of XML Digital Signature.

The Security Model

Internet Explorer implements security zones that allow you to control the level of access given to your computer by the Web sites that you visit. InfoPath uses some of these zones to determine the level of access that forms can have to system resources.

InfoPath users can set security levels, which also will apply to Internet Explorer, by choosing Tools⇨Options and clicking the Internet Options button.

The levels and the result of these settings for InfoPath are summarized in the table.

Zone	Result	Default Level
Restricted	InfoPath cannot open forms or access resources in this zone.	High
Internet	Forms may not access resources located on other domains.	Medium
Local Intranet	Forms can access resources on a different domain. Users are prompted to approve access.	Medium
Trusted Sites or Local Machine	Forms may access resources located on other domains. Users are not prompted to approve access.	Low

Cached Forms

In general, InfoPath forms run in a cached location that is denied access to critical system resources. Cached forms are identified by a URL or a URN. This identification determines the Internet Explorer security zone permissions they inherit.

URL-based forms are the default method of deployment when publishing a form. URL-based forms are said to be *sandboxed*, because they have restricted access to system resources, and other potential areas of risk. These forms inherit their security permissions, as well as their specific access rights such as cross-domain access, from the Internet Explorer security settings applicable to the original location of the form template.

InfoPath templates stored on a Web or SharePoint server run in the Internet or Local Intranet zones. Forms identified by a URL are cached to the user's computer, allowing for offline use of the form.

The URL is specified in the `publishUrl` attribute of the `xDocumentClass` element in the XSF file. `publishUrl` is set automatically when a form is published or deployed using InfoPath's design mode. When you open a form, InfoPath checks if the form has been moved from its original location. If the form template is moved from its original location, no new forms can be created based on that form template, unless this attribute is changed to the current location.

```
<xDocumentClass
    publishURL="http://someplace.net/forms/"
    .
    .
</xDocumentClass>
```

Cached forms that are identified by a URN using the `name` attribute inherit their permissions from the Local Machine zone, which is equivalent to the Trusted Sites zone. This type of form will have access to system and cross-domain resources, but users will be prompted to allow it every time that access is attempted.

Enabling Trusted Forms

If you need to give your users fuller access to system resources in a secure manner, you should consider using trusted forms. *Trusted forms* are those that are allowed full access to system resources and have a higher set of permissions than sandboxed forms. Form code can use external objects to access resources, ActiveX controls that are not marked as safe for scripting, and business logic provided by COM components.

You may also need to use a trusted form if you intend to make more than limited use of scripting. The InfoPath OM implements three levels of security that define how and where a member may be used, and each topic in the Object Model Reference specifies the level applying to the member. The levels and access permissions are as follows:

- ❑ *0.* No access restrictions
- ❑ *1.* Reserved
- ❑ *2.* Access by forms running in the same domain as the currently open form, or trusted forms
- ❑ *3.* Access by fully trusted forms only

Several OM members are set to security level 3, including key methods such as `Open`, `PrintOut`, and `SaveAs`.

You can enable or disable trusted forms in design mode by going to the General tab of the Options dialog box and checking the rather long-winded option starting with `Allow . . .` in the security options section. See Figure 10-1.

Before you can enable trusted forms, you must first enable submission, which we describe later in this chapter.

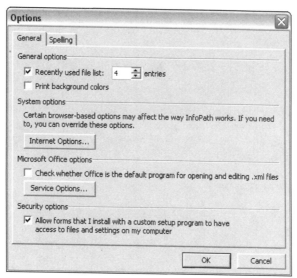

Figure 10-1: Setting the trusted form option.

Trusted forms also use URNs as identifiers. Perhaps you'll recall from Chapter 3 that in the form definition file, the `xDocumentClass` element has a `requireFullTrust` attribute. If this attribute is set to `"yes"`, the form is a fully trusted form. Again, the `name` attribute must contain the URN.

```
<xDocumentClass
    name="urn:metadata:newsline"
    requireFullTrust="yes"
    .
    .
    .
</xDocumentClass>
```

In the XML template file, you must also change the `href` attribute in the `mso-infoPathSolution` processing instruction to match the URN name.

```
<?mso-infoPathSolution
    solutionVersion="1.0.0.156"
    href="urn:metadata:newsline"
    productVersion="11.0.5531"
    PIVersion="1.0.0.0"?>
```

Registering Trusted Forms

Trusted forms must be registered on the client computer by an installation program or script so that they can be granted a higher level of permissions. In this case, the form gets the same permissions as an application running on the local machine.

Script

You can create a custom installation program by using the `RegisterSolution` method of the InfoPath `ExternalApplication` object to install the fully trusted form.

```
expression.RegisterSolution(ByVal bstrSolutionURL As String, [ByVal bstrBehavior As
String="overwrite"])
```

`bstrSolutionURL` is a required string value that specifies the URL of the template (XSN) or the form definition (XSF).

`bstrBehavior` is an optional string that specifies how the template is to be installed. If the form has already been registered, and default value of `"overwrite"` is used, the registration record will be overwritten. The other valid value, "new-only", will return an error in the same circumstances, so you can provide for inadvertent replacement.

One approach is to create a script:

```
oFInstall = new ActiveXObject("InfoPath.ExternalApplication");
oFInstall.RegisterSolution("D:\\Newsline\\metadata.xsn");
oFInstall.Quit();
oFInstall = null;
```

Another is to use the more robust Microsoft Windows Installer. You should use the `RegisterSolution` method in any case.

If you need to remove a fully trusted form, you should use the related `UnregisterSolution` method.

```
expression.UnregisterSolution(ByVal bstrSolutionURI As String)
```

`bstrSolutionURI` is a required string value that specifies the URI of the template. If the template can't be unregistered, the method returns an error.

Form Registration Tool

InfoPath SDK form registration tool is a command-line utility that simplifies the production of a trusted form and installation program. The file in the SDK Tools folder is RegForm.exe.

To use the tool, start a command prompt and enter the path to the tool, then type **RegForm** followed by the command-line switches you need. By default, the tool creates a JS file and a BAK file in the same folder that contains the form template that you are converting. The script file can be used to install the fully trusted form. The BAK file is a copy of the original form template.

The example uses the U, V, T, and MSI switches to output a file named metadata.msi.

```
RegForm /U urn:metadata:newsline /V 1.5.5.3 /T Yes /MSI M:\newsline\metadata.xsn
```

Switch	Description
/U	URN for the form template. If the URN is not specified, it is built using the specified FTand C parameters. If these are not specified, a globally unique identifier (GUID) value is generated.
/FT	Form template name.
/C	Company name.
/V	Version number of the form template if different from the number in the template. If no version number is present, the value 1.0.0.1 is used.
/T	Sets the requireFullTrust attribute to "Yes" (default is "No").
/O	Path and name of the output installation file if different from formtemplatefile.
/MSI	If you have Visual Studio .NET installed, you can output an MSI file. The tool also creates a Visual Studio .NET setup project that you can use to modify the installation code.
/? | /h | /help	Displays help for the tool.
formtemplatefile	The full path to the InfoPath form template to process.

Installing and Removing Trusted Forms

If you use a script for installation, you need to send all your users both the script and the template files. The script will register the form based on its location on the users' machines, so you must be sure that it uses the correct folder name.

If you use the RegForm tool to create a JS file for installing a fully trusted form, it will generate a dialog box that asks the user to confirm that they want to register the form, and final dialog box that confirms that the registration was successful.

To use an MSI installation, you need only distribute the MSI file. The MSI installer contains the form template file and automatically registers the form from the folder in which it is installed. A wizard guides the user through the process.

When trusted forms have been installed, they appear on the Custom Installed Forms tab in the Forms dialog box.

Security Best Practice

In the Security Guidelines section of the InfoPath Developer SDK, you will find best-practice advice from Microsoft. We recommend that you read these guidelines carefully and keep them in mind when you design your forms. Also bear in mind that InfoPath is closely related to the model of Internet Explorer, and be sure to keep abreast of any developments in this area that might impact InfoPath.

Controlling User Options

InfoPath provides several additional ways for you to control various aspects of form security, by controlling the options available to users.

Protecting a Form Design

You can protect the design of a form by enabling form protection. When protection is enabled, users will be unable to modify the form template when filling out a form.

Using this setting does not lock the form completely; rather, it disables the customization commands on the Tools menu, and the toolbar icon. Users can still open the form in design mode, but they will receive a warning that it is protected.

To enable form protection, choose the `Enable protection` check box on the General tab of the Form Options dialog box.

Merging Forms

You can configure a form template so that users can merge the data from multiple forms into one form. Usually, the data that is merged must be saved in a repeating field or in a field that is part of a repeating group, and the standard way of merging works reliably with forms that have identical schemas.

You'll learn more about merging forms in Chapter 14. At this time you'll just deal with enabling merging. To enable merging choose `Tools`⇨`Form Options`, and check `Enable form merging`. Figure 10-2 shows both protection and merging enabled.

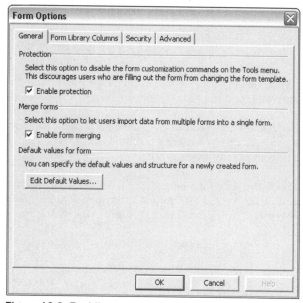

Figure 10-2: Enabling protection and merging.

Enabling Views

When you set view properties, you can decide whether users should be able to choose the view from the View menu and therefore edit the visible data. This option is only available if the current form has two or more views. If the default view is the only available view, no choices will appear.

To enable a view, first select it. Then choose View⇨Manage Views. Now check the Show on the View menu . . . check box in the View settings section of the General tab. See Figure 10-3.

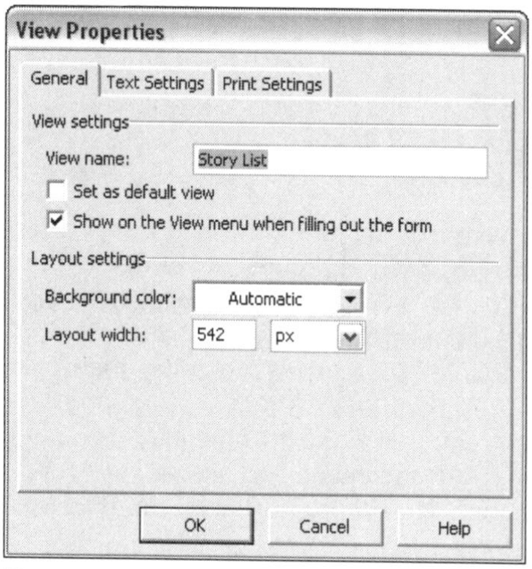

Figure 10-3: Enabling a view.

Enabling and Customizing Submission

You can design a form so that users can submit to a Web service, through HTTP, or by launching a script. Submitting forms is covered in more detail in Chapter 7.

To enable form submission, choose Tools⇨Submitting Forms and choose Enable submit. This enables other controls in the dialog box and lets you set other options

When you have enabled submission, you can customize the Submit command and the behavior of the form after submission. You can choose to enable a submit command on the file menu, modify the default command text Su&bmit, and include an access key.

You may also specify the form behavior after the user has submitted the form. There are options to close the form, create a new form, or leave the submitted form open. You can also customize the success and failure messages that you want to appear. Figure 10-4 shows the dialog box.

Figure 10-4: The Submit Options dialog box.

Digital Signatures

InfoPath allows users to sign entire forms using the method specified in the W3C XML Digital Signature recommendation. More generally, XML Signatures can be applied to any digital content, including XML, and may be applied to all or part of an object. Signatures may be the parent of the signed object or a child, or they may stand outside to object entirely. A signature provides an integrity check on a document. If any signed part is modified subsequent to signing, the signature will fail to verify.

In InfoPath, the signatures are children of the document. A form can be signed using one or more XML signatures at the level of the entire document. Because the signature is over the entire form, and any change by the user will invalidate the original signature, InfoPath makes signed forms read-only.

Users can sign and verify forms by choosing Tools⇨Digital Signatures or by using the Standard toolbar.

If a user opens a form with a signature, InfoPath checks for the existence of a signature. If the form is not signed, it is opened immediately. If a signature is present, InfoPath validates the signature. If the signature is valid, the form opens. If the signature is invalid, a warning dialog box is displayed.

Digital Certificates

Users must have a digital certificate installed on their computer before they can add a digital signature to a form. XML Signature depends on the use of pairs of public and private keys to transform the encrypted data. A signature encrypted with the private key can be decrypted with the public key. So the person verifying a signature with the public key must be sure that it belongs to the sender. A digital certificate validates the relationship between the subject of a certificate and their public key.

InfoPath will use only certificates that have a private key and that have a key usage value of "Digital Signature," and a purpose of "Client Authentication." Certificates that are valid in other Office applications, such as self-signed certificates used to sign VBA macros, may not be valid for digital signing in InfoPath.

XML Signature

The W3C recommendation specifies XML syntax and processing rules for creating and representing digital signatures. Unlike other digital signature standards, XML Signature has been designed specifically for the XML environment. XML Signature is quite flexible in that it can sign more than one kind of object, for example, some character-encoded XML in a form, or an embedded, binary encoded object like an image.

The entire process of applying signatures is complex, and we won't attempt to explain it here in any detail. But it is well worth understanding the process in outline and gaining a sense of the signature syntax.

Signatures are applied by reference to the URI of a signed object with a Reference element. In the example, the reference is to a complete document on the Web, but it could just as well be to an XML fragment in a containing document, such as #publicationTime. However, as you've seen, InfoPath allows signatures on entire forms only.

```
<Reference URI="http://newsline.net/20031010_ln1234_xml">
   .
   .
</Reference>
```

The Algorithm attribute of the DigestMethod element references the hash algorithm applied to extract a digest from the form. In this case, the reference is to SHA1, the Secure Hash Algorithm. The DigestValue element, which is base 64 encoded, contains the digest itself.

```
<Reference URI="http://newsline.net.ny7453_20031122.xml">
    <DigestMethod Algorithm="http://www.w3.org/2000/09/xmldsig#sha1" />
    <DigestValue>zM14ixa61vpUccMup4Ngai85nsdA=</DigestValue>
</Reference>
```

The references are wrapped in the `SignedInfo` element with two other elements. A canonization algorithm is defined in the `CanonicalizationMethod` element. Canonization tightens up the relatively lax approach of XML to such things as white space and the order of attributes, and ensures that signature validation doesn't fail owing to nonessential differences that can arise in XML processing. It chooses one path from all the possible XML output options, so that both sender and receiver can generate identical byte values.

The RSA public key algorithm is defined in the `Signature Method` element.

```
<SignedInfo>
    <CanonicalizationMethod Algorithm="http://www.w3.org/TR/2001/
REC-xml-c14n-20010315"/>
    <SignatureMethod Algorithm="http://www.w3.org/2000/09/xmldsig#rsa-sha1"/>
    <Reference URI="http://newsline.net.ny7453_20031122.xml">
        <DigestMethod Algorithm="http://www.w3.org/2000/09/xmldsig#sha1" />
        <DigestValue>zM14ixa61vpUccMup4Ngai85nsdA=</DigestValue>
    </Reference>
</SignedInfo>
```

The entire signature is contained in the `Signature` element. The `Id` attribute enables the identification of multiple signatures in business contexts, for example, where two signatures are needed on an expense claim.

The `SignatureValue` element contains the signed digest of the `SignedInfo` element, and the optional `KeyInfo` element can contain a number of key types and structures that identify the signer or their certificate. For example, the `KeyName` element might give the signer's e-mail address.

```
<Signature Id="j_fox">
    <SignedInfo>
        <CanonicalizationMethod Algorithm="http://www.w3.org/TR/2001/
REC-xml-c14n-20010315"/>
        <SignatureMethod Algorithm="http://www.w3.org/2000/09/xmldsig#rsa-sha1"/>
        <Reference URI="http://newsline.net.ny7453_20031122.xml">
            <DigestMethod Algorithm="http://www.w3.org/2000/09/xmldsig#sha1" />
            <DigestValue>zM14ixa61vpUccMup4Ngai85nsdA=</DigestValue>
        </Reference>
    </SignedInfo>
    <SignatureValue>a22tmXdsOzi90jkbdfMOP==</SignatureValue>
    <KeyInfo>
        <KeyName>j_fox@ln.newsline.com</KeyName>
</Signature>
```

As XML forms generated by InfoPath become commonplace, XML Signature will help create secure data as the basis of business transactions.

You can read more about the XML Signature recommendation at `www.w3.org/TR/xmldsig-core/`.

Signatures in Form Schema Design

Because the digital signature is located in a node in an XML form instance, you'll need to specify which node the signature is stored in when you design the form template. You do this by adding a group control bound to an element and incorporating the namespace.

```
<xs:element name="my:signatures1">
   <xs:complexType>
      <xs:sequence>
         <xs:any namespace="http://www.w3.org/2000/09/xmldsig#"
processContents="lax" minOccurs="0" maxOccurs="unbounded"/>
      </xs:sequence>
   </xs:complexType>
</xs:element>
```

Enabling Signatures

In design mode, you enable digital signatures by choosing Tools⇨Form Options, and selecting the Allow users to digitally sign this form check box on the Security tab. You can also select the group you have defined to contain the signatures. If you want users to sign the form before they submit it, select the If users submit this form . . . check box. See Figure 10-5.

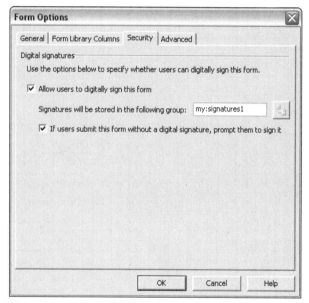

Figure 10-5: Enabling digital signatures.

You can't enable signatures if a form is created from a schema, database, or Web service without the digital signature namespace declaration, xmlns:ds="http://www.w3.org/2000/09/xmldsig#".

In Chapter 4 you learned about the XSF structure for signatures. If you enable signatures, InfoPath inserts the optional top-level documentSignatures element. The required signatureLocation attribute is an XPath expression pointing to the node containing the signature data.

```
<documentSignatures signatureLocation="/my:signatures1"/>
```

Summary

In this chapter you learned that the InfoPath security model is based on that of Internet Explorer. You learned about the distinctions between URL-based forms and URN-based trusted forms, and how to create trusted forms, using both scripting and the Form Registration tool, and also how to install them.

You also saw how InfoPath provides other types of security measures, including protecting form design, along with managing operations such as form merging and submission.

XML Signature is an important standard for developing validated business communication. You should now have a grasp of its purpose and functions and how it is implemented in InfoPath.

11

Customizing Forms

In this chapter, as a preliminary to the case study, you'll review the different approaches you can take with interface customization in InfoPath forms. The goal is to help you give your users a better experience when they work with your form application. Partly it's a question of good design practice, but you'll also find that InfoPath has some useful features that you can exploit. Namely:

❑ Controlling input

❑ Supporting better input

❑ Menus and toolbars

❑ Conditional formatting

❑ Look and feel

❑ Custom task pane

❑ Previewing forms

Let's look at each of these.

Controlling Input

In Chapter 6 you looked in some detail at ways of applying business logic through the use of XML schemas, rule-based validation, and scripting. Here you'll study some simple interface design methods that you can use with forms that are built from scratch.

Most of the time you'll be working with the Data tab on the control's Properties dialog box. We assume that by now you are quite familiar with the design mode interface, and our tips will therefore be summaries of actions rather than step-by-step instructions.

When a user saves a form containing data type errors or missing data, an error is displayed in a dialog box alert. Users can save invalid forms, but they can't submit these forms to a database, Web service, or other location.

InfoPath Data Types

If you develop a form from scratch with a blank form, building a schema as you go, you can assign an InfoPath data type to the control, or more exactly to the data source for the control. The following table gives the data types that you can use for text boxes and lists. The second column shows the equivalent XML schema data type.

InfoPath Type	Schema Type	Use
Text	string	Data such as names, addresses, phone numbers, social security numbers, and so on
Whole Number	integer	Positive or negative whole numbers, such as 1234, -1234, or $1,234
Decimal	double	Numbers with decimal places, such as 1234.12, -1234.12, or $1234.12
True/False	boolean	Data that should be either 1 (true) or 0 (false)
Hyperlink	anyURI	Hyperlinks, such as http://w3c.org
Date	date	Dates, such as 3/14/2007 or March 14, 2007
Time	time	Time, such as 9:46:55 or 09:46 A.M.
Date and Time	dateTime	Both date and time, such as 3/14/2007 11:30 A.M.

For example, if you want users to enter a value in euros into a text box for an amount, you can choose the decimal type and formatting options so that values typed in the text box are displayed with the € currency symbol.

If a user then types the wrong type of data, an inline alert appears. This takes the form of a dotted red line around the control. If the user right-clicks or moves the mouse pointer over the text box, additional information about the nature of the problem appears, in this case the error message "Only number allowed," as shown in Figure 11-1.

Figure 11-1: An inline alert.

Required Input

You can also specify that form data is required. When users open the form, a solid red underline appears under any controls that require data. As soon it is entered, the red underline disappears. This underline may not be prominent enough for all users, so you might consider using some additional formatting, for example, shading the background of the control if it is blank.

To set a control to required, select the `Cannot be blank` check box on the display tab of the Properties dialog box. When it is set, a screen hint appears when the cursor is over the control.

Setting Defaults

You can specify default values for controls. An example from our case study is that most stories are of the "Article" type. When a contributor adds a story of another type, or an editor decides to change it, they can type over the default value.

Defaults can be set in two ways. If the form schema contains a fixed element or attribute value, InfoPath will make that a default. Alternatively, you can enter or select a default on the Data tab of the Properties dialog box. The value is saved in the form template.

Read Only

If the contents of a control is fixed by default or set by script rather than users, you can choose to make it read-only to prevent users from making unwanted changes. You can do so by choosing the `Read-only` check box on the Display tab of the Properties dialog box.

Supporting Better Input

InfoPath can help you help your users in several ways. As always, the idea is to increase accuracy and consistency, and improve your users' experience.

Hints and Tips

On the Display tab you can also provide guidance to form users by specifying a placeholder or instructional text. So, to limit entry to a range of ages on a personnel form, you might add the text **Enter an age between 18 & 65**, as we have in Figure 11-2. This option is only available for text box, rich text box, and date picker controls.

Figure 11-2: A range of ages.

Sometimes the message you want to give is too long to fit in the available space, in which case a ScreenTip is more appropriate. You can enter one on the Advance tab, as shown in Figure 11-3. Tips are a great way to provide supplementary information about a control to anyone who uses the form. They can also provide alternate text for form images when the form is saved as a Web page.

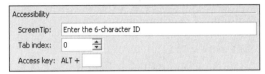

Figure 11-3: The Advance tab.

Naming Controls

When you add a control to a form, the default names and the labels that appear next to controls aren't guaranteed to be user-friendly. There are two likely reasons for this.

First, you may have been willed a schema with some obscure element and attribute names. How about `biblioentry.label` and `othercredit` from the widely used DocBook schema? They certainly mean something to a schema expert, but users will probably need assistance. You may even have used fairly user-unfriendly names yourself—we certainly have! In this case you can only make cosmetic changes to the labels, since the name box on the Data tab is disabled.

Second, InfoPath automatically assigns names like "field1" and "group2" to data sources that you add to a blank form. You can alter the default names to distinguish one control from another in the task pane and make them user-friendly too. When you drag a field onto the form, the new name will form the label text. When you change a name, remember that it must conform to the rules for XML element or attribute names. Names can't contain spaces. They must begin with an alphabetic character or under-score (_), and they can only contain alphanumeric characters, underscores, hyphens (-), and periods (.).

Controlling Input Options

Drop-down lists or list boxes, check boxes, and option buttons are all ways that you can set limits on user input.

Lists

If you have a large number of optional values, a drop-down list is a good choice, as it takes up very little screen space, in comparison to option buttons, for example. List boxes are also useful for shorter lists. You can set up the choice of values in a number of ways.

In the `List box entries` section of the tab, there are two alternatives. The most straightforward is to type in the values using the Add button on the Data tab (see Figure 11-4), but it may also be useful to use a secondary data source, such as an XML file or a database.

Figure 11-4: Adding values to a list box.

A third alternative is open to you if you have defined your own schema. In this event, you can use constraints in the schema to specify the list. When you bind the relevant schema element to the list control, InfoPath will populate the list from the schema.

Option Buttons

A single group of option buttons must be bound to a single data source field. On the Data tab, you can rename the field if allowed, set the value of the field when the button is selected, and choose the default (see Figure 11-5).

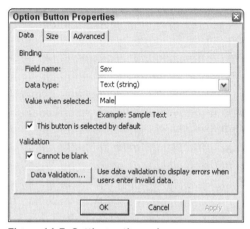

Figure 11-5: Setting option values.

Check Boxes

Check boxes may only be used with boolean data types. In the `Data type` dropdown you can rename the field if allowed, set the default value and choose between pairs TRUE/FALSE or 0/1.

Keyboard Actions

It's more than likely that your users will be fast keyboard operators, so you'll want to bear their needs in mind. If you assign a keyboard shortcut to a control, users can immediately navigate to it by pressing a combination of keystrokes. To add a shortcut, go to the `Advanced` tab and type a character in the `Access key` box.

If you decide to use keyboard shortcuts in your form, try to do so throughout, avoiding conflicts with menu commands. You also need to indicate to users that the shortcuts exist. In the example in Figure 11-6, we've underscored the "m" in the text box label to let users know that there's a shortcut.

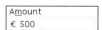

Figure 11-6: Underscored shortcut in the text box label.

As an additional help to keyboard users, you can set up a sequence of tab indexing, using the Advanced tab. The usual pattern is left to right and top to bottom on the form, following the workflow and skipping any read-only fields. Working this out often helps you spot potential problems and refine the layout.

Menus and Toolbars

In design mode, you can customize the commands used in menus and toolbars to insert, remove, or replace sections in a form. The same issues arise here as they do with field names. If you started with a blank form, you can quickly update all the menu commands associated with a section by changing the section name. Note that this modifies only those commands that currently contain the section name.

With a form based on a schema, when you can't change a section name, or if you want more control over specific commands, you'll need to customize each command name separately.

To make changes to commands, click `Customize Commands` on the Data tab, and choose an option from the `Action` drop-down list. The actions available will depend on the type of section you are working with. Now check the menu and toolbar locations you want to change, and type the command text in the `Command name` box. Figure 11-7 shows a repeating table.

Figure 11-7: Customizing a command for a repeating table.

New Menus and Toolbars

The Customize dialog box allows you to create a custom menu item or toolbar. Although you can add only built-in InfoPath commands to it, you can add new menus and toolbars that contain custom commands to a form. To do so, you have to define additional elements in the form definition file. It's been a while since you looked at these view structures, so here's a quick reminder of how menus and toolbars work.

Menus

To create a new menu, you place a `menu` element directly under the `view` element. InfoPath places these menus between the built-in `Table` and `Help` menus in the order you enter them in the form definition. You can use nested `menu` elements to create a cascading menu. Figure 11-8 shows an example.

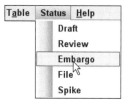

Figure 11-8: A new menu.

The `button` element is used to define menu items. The `caption` attribute labels the item, and the `name` attribute associates the button's `OnClick` event with a script. This is the XSF section for the same menu. You'll have to write an event handler for any menus you create.

```
<xsf:menu caption="Status">
    <xsf:button name="setDraft" caption="Draft"/>
    <xsf:button name="setReview" caption="Review"/>
    <xsf:button name="setEmbargo" caption="Embargo"/>
    <xsf:button name="setFile" caption="File"/>
    <xsf:button name="setSpike" caption="Spike"/>
</xsf:menu>
```

Toolbars

Adding a new toolbar works in a similar way. `button` elements provide the actions, and menus can nest sets of buttons. The only difference is that the toolbar element requires a `name` attribute as well as a caption.

Conditional Formatting

Conditional formatting is a feature in InfoPath that allows you to specify different formatting for controls in design mode. If the specified conditions occur when a user works on the form, the formatting is displayed. The formatting can apply to font styling and background color in controls, and you can also specify conditional visibility.

Conditional formatting is useful for calling attention to form values. However, people with impaired vision may not be able to see or distinguish colors, so you shouldn't rely on color alone to convey important or critical information.

The examples demonstrate how conditional formatting works. In Chapters 13 and 14 you'll see how to apply them in the case study.

Status Values

This example in Figure 11-9 uses different status values to switch icons in a repeating table.

Figure 11-9: Conditional formatting with status values.

Highlight Errors

Conditional formatting can be used to highlight a case where a user has entered invalid data. Suppose, using our earlier example, that a user has entered an amount over the authorized limit of € 1,500. Although InfoPath will highlight the text box with a red underline, changing the background color and making the text bold, as shown in Figure 11-10, immediately emphasizes the problem.

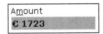

Figure 11-10: Emphasizing invalid data.

Hiding Information

Conditional visibility is a formatting option that allows you to show or hide a control on a form. It is a powerful tool for building dynamic forms. In Figure 11-11 we hide a section containing next of kin information, unless the address is different from the employee's.

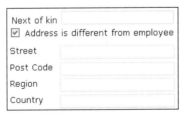

Figure 11-11: Conditional visibility.

It is important to remember that hiding a section is different from removing it. If you save while a section is hidden by conditional formatting, the contents of that hidden section are still saved as part of the form data.

Look and Feel

So far, you've done a lot to support your users by applying customization in a helpful way, reducing the likelihood that they'll make errors. As a final touch, you can give the form a consistent look and feel by setting up some view properties

Formatting Options

A quick way to get a consistent appearance in fonts and style is to set up text formatting options for the controls in the view. These options will also apply to new controls you insert.

In the Text Settings tab of the View Properties dialog box, select the type of control you want to format. Then choose the options you want to apply to the controls. Repeat for each type of control you want to format. To change the formatting of an individual control, select the control, and then use the commands on the Format menu.

Rich Text

Enabling character formatting for a control lets users format the information they enter when filling out a form. For instance, enabling character formatting lets users apply a color to text or make it bold.

This option is only available for rich text box, bulleted list, numbered list, and plain list controls. To enable character formatting for list controls, the data type these controls are bound to must be rich text XHTML.

Print Settings

On the Print Settings tab you can set the default print view, the page orientation, and values for header and footer text. You can print headers and footers using the following variables, which can be combined with text (for example, `Page &p of &P`).

Variable	Output
&u	Form address (URL)
&d	Date in short format
&D	Date in long format
&t	Time
&T	Time in 24-hour format
&p	Current page number
&P	Total number of pages
&b	Right-aligned text (following &b)
&b&b	Centered text (between &b&b)
&&	A single ampersand (&)

The InfoPath XSF schema provides for values for margin units and all four margins of the form page, but there is no design mode interface for setting them. You must set them by editing the form definition file like this, under the `view` element:

```
<xsf:printSettings
    .
    .
    .
    marginUnitsType="cm"
    topMargin="2"
    leftMargin="5"
    rightMargin="4"
    bottomMargin="2"
</xsf:printSettings>
```

Custom Task Pane

You can create a custom task pane to provide users with form-specific commands and Help content. Before enabling a custom task pane, you need to create additional resources, typically an HTML file. However, there's no real limit to what you can provide. It could be an XML source with XSL transform, with supporting CSS and JScript files. You may already have noted the example in Chapter 5 showing the use of a data source in a custom task pane, and in Chapter 14 you'll read about using one in more detail.

You can add the task pane file directly to your form template, so users can work with the form and task pane when they are not connected to a network, or you can link the HTML file to the form. Linking creates an absolute path to the custom task pane, so you should make sure that the location of the HTML file is accessible by users at all times.

To add a custom pane to a form, first choose Tools⇨Resource Manager, and add the HTML file that you plan to use. Then choose Tools⇨Form Options, and go to the Advanced tab. Check Enable custom task pane, and select the HTML file from the drop-down list in the Task pane location text box. Remember to add any additional files (HTML, CSS, etc.) to the Resource Manager if required. See Figure 11-12.

To link to an HTML, type the absolute file path in the Task pane location text box. If you don't provide an absolute path, you'll get a warning message.

Figure 11-12: Enabling a custom task pane.

Previewing Forms

You can use InfoPath's preview feature to test the functionality and appearance of your form before you make it available for users to fill out. However simple your form, you should make it a habit to preview your forms before you deploy them.

Preview is interactive and provides a simple way for you to test your form without leaving design mode. When you choose Preview Form, the form opens in a new window, where you can test it by entering data into controls.

Check on the features you have added, including:

- ❑ Formatting
- ❑ Validation
- ❑ Conditional formatting
- ❑ Look and feel
- ❑ Tab sequence
- ❑ Scripts

The Preview Window

When you are working in design mode, you can open the preview window by clicking the `Preview Form` button on the Standard toolbar or by choosing `File⇨Preview Form`.

When you preview a form, a preview window opens on top of the design mode window. This window contains a simulation of your form, so that you can see not only how it looks but also how it acts when you fill it out.

"Preview" appears in window title bar to let you know that you are in the preview window, and if you open a series of preview windows, they are numbered sequentially. Some menu commands are disabled because you are simulating user interaction rather than working on a regular form.

Using Sample Data

In addition to previewing a form, you can also use sample data to quickly test the appearance of your form. Sample data is placeholder text generated by InfoPath that appears in controls on your form. It shows an example of how text will appear in the control when a user fills it out. In design mode, choose `View⇨Sample Data` to toggle the view.

Another way to use sample data is when you make changes to a published template. In this event you need to confirm that the update doesn't cause errors to existing XML data. To preview one of these existing forms with the modified form template, choose `File⇨Preview Form⇨With data file` and open an XML data file to continue your tests.

Summary

This chapter completes our introductory review of InfoPath design features. In it you learned how to make good use of the design mode user interface controls, and we hope you'll be inspired to explore different ways of fine-tuning the form interface for your applications.

But there's more . . . Turn a page or two to read the background material on our case study.

12

Introducing the Case Study

In this chapter you learn about the background to the case study that you'll work through in the remainder of the book. It details the business requirements of a news and features service, and provides information about workflows and data structures.

We also introduce the three standards specified in the requirements: Publishing Requirements for Industry Standard Metadata (PRISM), the Resource Definition Format (RDF), and RDF Site Summary (RSS).

To round off this section, you'll also look at our first thoughts on a design solution.

Background

NewsLine, an English-language news and features service, requires a simple production support system for capturing meta data about stories, in XML format. This data is distributed to customers over the Internet. The service has news desks in New York, London, and Tokyo, each of which is responsible for processing material originating from contributors in their region. Customers who subscribe to the service need to get regular updates on current information from a news feed.

Information Capture

The Capture tool needs to be available to both contributors (who are freelance) and to news desk editors. Contributors are not connected to any in-house data sources. They submit content to editors at their news desks by e-mail.

The content of stories can consist of text only, or include or consist entirely of nontext media, such as photos or video/sound. Note that this requirement is not concerned with the processing of this multimedia content, but rather with describing these resources.

Contributors to the service get paid at individual contract rates. Each item therefore has to contain an identifier for the contributor.

Categorizing Stories

Contributors and editors require access to a subject vocabulary, from which they can select values to categorize stories. The vocabulary is relatively static. Broad, "flat" categories cover events, people, places, companies, industries, and organizations. This information needs to be available in a simple portable format that freelance users can easily download and update for use on their own machines.

It must be possible to choose a broad category and make one or more selections from a list of subjects. Examples include the following:

- *Events.* 2004 Olympics, Bali Bombing, September 11
- *People.* Kofi Annan, Tony Blair, George Bush
- *Places.* Boston, Milan, San Francisco, Sao Paulo
- *Companies.* AOL, Financial Times, Shell, Toyota
- *Industries.* Automotive, Electronics, Gas and Oil, Media
- *Organizations.* European Central Bank, NATO, Red Cross, United Nations

Monitoring Costs

A shared database of freelance writers and their contract rates is available to editors. The following information is maintained in a central database by the legal department:

- Contract number
- Name
- Item
    - Item type (text, photo, video/sound)
    - Units (100 words, 1 photo, 1 minute)
    - Contract rate per unit (in USD)
    - Examples: text,500,80; photo,1,125; video,8,100
- Address
- Telephone number
- Byline
- Home page
- E-mail address

When a story is approved by an editor and filed, the cost of the story to the relevant news desk must be calculated. Managers currently use Excel to monitor editorial budgets and require story costs to be aggregated in Excel under news desk headings.

Filing

The meta data from each news desk and the related stories are posted to a central back-end server ready for distribution and syndication. The service requires that selected meta data for each story is published cumulatively for a 24-hour cycle in RSS 1.0 format and updated at regular intervals. This enables subscribers to monitor news output and select stories for use.

Workflow

News desk managers need to be able to monitor the current status of stories in the workflow. Possible values for status are as follows:

- ❑ *Draft.* Not submitted by writer
- ❑ *In Review.* In news desk
- ❑ *Embargoed.* Approved but not used until a specified date/time
- ❑ *Filed.* Approved and available to service subscribers

The following dates and times on which changes of status took place must be updated automatically and persisted in the record.

- ❑ *Created.* First draft
- ❑ *Submitted.* Sent to news desk
- ❑ *Modified.* Draft/review/filed
- ❑ *Filed.* Filed
- ❑ *Spiked.* Put on hold
- ❑ *Embargoed.* Embargoed

PRISM

Like all media organizations, NewsLine wants to repurpose content in order to get a greater return on the investment made in creating it. Apart from first-use sales, the same material might be used in special packages for use by customers in later publication issues, such as in a topic retrospective or a photo series on a prominent individual. The company needs an approach that supports discovery by customers, rights tracking, and end-to-end meta data in the business process. Most published content already has meta data created for it. However, once content moves between systems in the information flow, the meta data is frequently discarded, only to be re-created later. The service has therefore decided to base their system on the PRISM standard for describing their stories.

PRISM is a specification developed by the publishing industry representatives. It defines a meta data vocabulary for syndicating, aggregating, and multipurposing content over a wide range of publication types. PRISM provides XML elements for the topics, formats, genre, origin, and contexts of a resource. It also provides for categorizing resources, using multiple subject description taxonomies. An important feature of the specification is its use of other standards: XML, RDF, Dublin Core, as well as various ISO formats and vocabularies. You can see details of PRISM 1.2 at www.prismstandard.org/.

Dublin Core Elements

In Chapter 3 we introduced the Dublin Core Metadata Initiative (DCMI) vocabulary for the form definition examples, so you'll be familiar with several elements by now. The core elements provide us with "pidgin" meta data terms that can be extended for requirements that are more specialized. As well as the core elements listed in the table that follows, DCMI also specifies a range of qualifiers that either refine the meaning of a core element or extend the vocabulary. For example, dc:date may be qualified to dc:created, dc:modified, or dc:issued.

The recommendation also covers encoding schemes that specify formats for values such as date, language, and country, or that define controlled vocabularies for place names or categories.

The table lists the 15 core elements in the dc namespace.

Element	Definition
dc:identifier	Identifier(s) for the resource.
dc:title	The name by which the resource is known.
dc:date	The date of publication or availability of the resource. The recommended format of the date is yyyy-mm-dd, where dates are encoded with the W3C Encoding rules—a profile based on ISO 8601. See *Date and Time Formats*, W3C Note, www.w3.org/TR/NOTE-datetime.
dc:creator	The primary creator(s) of the intellectual content of the resource, so it covers roles like composer, photographer and artist as well as author.
dc:contributor	Additional contributors to the creation or publication of the resource, such as editor or translator.
dc:description	A description of the resource.
dc:language	The principal language of the resource.
dc:format	The file format. DCMI recommends using the Internet Media Type (IMT) of the file. You can read about IMT values at www.isi.edu/in-notes/iana/assignments/media-types/media-types.
dc:type	Defines either the genre, or intellectual type, of the resource or its presentation.
dc:publisher	An identifier for the supplier of the resource.
dc:source	An identifier for source material for the resource, assuming it is derived from another format.
dc:coverage	Indicates geographic locations or periods of time that are subjects of the resource.
dc:subject	The subject of the resource.
dc:rights	Container element for specific rights data.
dc:relation	A reference to a related resource.

PRISM Elements

PRISM uses the Dublin Core element set as the foundation for its meta data. PRISM recommends practices for using the vocabulary and also augments it to allow more detailed descriptions. The augmentations are defined in three new namespaces.

`prism` is the main namespace. Most of its elements are more specific versions of elements from the Dublin Core. For example, `dc:date` is extended by elements like `prism:creationTime` and `prism:publicationTime`. Here is a selected list of elements.

Element	Definition
`prism:category`	The genre of the resource, such as election results vs. biographies.
`prism:distributor`	An identifier for the distributor of the resource.
`prism:edition`	An identifier for geographic or demographic versions of an issue.
`prism:issn`	ISSN for the publication.
`prism:number`	Part of volume and number identification for resource's publication.
`prism:startingPage`	Initial page number for the resource in its publication.
`prism:volume`	Part of volume and number identification of the resource's publication.
`prism:issueName`	An identifier for named issues.
`prism:creationTime`	Date and time the identified resource was first created.
`prism:modificationTime`	Date and time the resource was last modified.
`prism:publicationTime`	Date and time when the resource is released to the public.
`prism:receptionTime`	Date and time when the resource was received on current system.
`prism:event`	An event referred to in or described by the resource.
`prism:industry`	An industry referred to in or described by the resource.
`prism:location`	A location referred to in or described by the resource.
`prism:person`	A person referred to in or described by the resource.
`prism:organization`	An organization referred to in or described by the resource.
`prism:section`	The section, such as "news," "politics," and so on in which the resource might be placed.

Using keywords for describing the subjects of a resource rarely works well, because different people will use different keywords for the same subject. The recommended practice is to code the meta data from a well-defined set of subject terms that provide a common ground for both searcher and indexer. The PRISM Controlled Vocabulary, or `pcv` namespace, provides elements for specifying terms in a vocabulary, the relations between terms, and alternate names for the terms.

`pcv:broaderTerm`	Links to a broader (more general) concept in a vocabulary—for example, from "Dog" to "Mammal." Multiple broader term links are allowed.
`pcv:code`	Provides the unique identifier for the term.
`pcv:definition`	Provides a human-readable definition for the item in the vocabulary. Multiple definitions can be provided with different language attributes.
`pcv:Descriptor`	Grouping element for the information describing or defining a term. The definition must include a unique URI reference so that the term can be unambiguously identified.
`pcv:label`	Provides a human-readable label for the preferred name(s) of the term. Multiple labels can be provided, usually with different language attributes.
`pcv:narrowerTerm`	Links to a narrower (more specific) concept in the vocabulary. For example, from "Dog" to "Dalmatian." Multiple narrower term links are allowed.
`pcv:relatedTerm`	Links to a related term in the vocabulary, where the nature of the relation is not specified.
`pcv:synonym`	Provides alternate labels (synonyms) for the same property.
`pcv:vocabulary`	Provides a human-readable name identifying the vocabulary from which the term comes.

Knowing the rights status of material can be a problem for everyone in the supply chain. There is a number of proposals for rights management languages, but there is as yet no industry agreement on which proposal to accept. Some are very complex, supporting a wide range of rights transactions.

PRISM provides elements for basic tracking of rights. PRISM Rights Language (PRL), using the `prl` namespace, was defined to provide simple elements that let people say if an item can or can't be used, depending on conditions of time, geography, and industry. Several `prism` namespace elements are also relevant to rights issues.

`prism:copyright`	A copyright statement for this resource.
`prism:expirationTime`	Time at which the right to reuse expires.
`prism:releaseTime`	Time as which the right to reuse a resource begins, and the resource may be published.
`prism:rightsAgent`	Name and contact information of a rights agent.
`prl:geography`	Specifies geographic restrictions.
`prl:industry`	Specifies restrictions on the industry in which the resource may be reused.
`prl:usage`	Specifies ways that the resource may be reused.

The PRL Processing Model

Sets of declarations in PRL can be treated as RDF statements (see next section) and evaluated to determine if a resource can be used in a particular way. Conditions such as `prl:industry` and `prl:greography` and also `prism:expirationTime` and `prism:releaseTime` elements can evaluate to boolean values. Usage may be one of a set of controlled vocabulary terms that evaluate to the URI references `#none`, `#use`, `#not applicable`, and `#permissionsUnkown`. In PRL, expressions must appear only within the scope of a `dc:rights` element, or an `rdf:Bag` element if there are multiple statements. See PRISM 1.2 for further details of the processing logic.

RDF/XML

The *Resource Description Framework* (RDF) is a general-purpose language for representing information on the Web, intended for describing and exchanging meta data about online resources. RDF can also be used to represent information about anything that can be identified on the Web.

You can read the full W3C's RDF Specification at `http://www.w3.org/RDF/`, but a gentler introduction comes in the form of the RDF Primer at `http://www.w3.org/TR/2004/REC-rdf-primer-20040210/`.

RDF/XML is a vocabulary for expressing RDF statements about resources in XML. Suppose you want to make a statement about a contributor to the online version of the InfoPath XSF Reference in Appendix B of this book. In English you might say something like this:

`http://www.wrox.com/books/0764557130_xsfref.html` has a contributor whose name is Ian Williams.

This combination of object (URL), predicate (contributor), and subject (Ian Williams) is known as a *triple*. By processing a set of triples, an application may be able to infer relationships between the objects. The hope of RDF proponents is that such applications will contribute to the semantic Web of the future. For now, we'll focus on the more practical aspects of RDF/XML use.

The RDF/XML for this statement could be

```
<rdf:Description rdf:about="http://www.wrox.com/books/0764557130_xsfref.html"
    <dc:contributor>Ian Williams</contributor>
</rdf:Description>
```

Further properties of the resource, such as publisher, date, and subject, can be added inside the description.

RDF Syntax

The following table contains a brief explanation of the meaning of the elements and attributes you'll see in this chapter.

Name	Type	Meaning
rdf:RDF	element	Root element for a resource description. Indicates that the XML expresses RDF.
rdf:Description	element	Starts the resource description and contains the list of its properties.
rdf:about	attribute	Contains the URI for the resource.
rfd:ID	attribute	An alternative to rdf:about that points to another resource rather than a URI.
rdf:type		Indicates that the resource belongs to a defined class.
rdf:Bag	element	Container for elements in any order.
rdf:Seq	element	Container for elements in an ordered sequence.
rdf:Alt	element	Container for property values that are equivalent, for example, alternative titles.
rdf:li	element	A list item that is a child element of Bag, Seq, and Alt.

A PRISM description in RDF may be as simple as a few elements from the Dublin Core with literal values. The following example describes a photograph, giving basic information on its title, photographer, format, and so on:

```
<?xml version="1.0" encoding="UTF-8"?>
<rdf:RDF xmlns:rdf="http://www.w3.org/1999/02/22-rdf-syntax-ns#"
        xmlns:dc="http://purl.org/dc/elements/1.1/"
        xml:lang="en-US">
    <rdf:Description rdf:about="http://newsline.net/ln/043_20030924.jpg">
        <dc:title>Tony Blair at the 2003 Labour Party Conference</dc:title>
        <dc:description>Prime Minister Blair addresses the annual conference
in Brighton England, still defiant about Britain's role in the Iraq conflict.
        </dc:description>
        <dc:creator>Alf White</dc:creator>
        <dc:format>image/jpeg</dc:format>
        <prism:person>Blair, Tony</prism:person>
    </rdf:Description>
</rdf:RDF>
```

PRISM uses RDF because of its abilities for dealing with descriptions of varying complexity. Currently, a great deal of meta data uses simple string values, such as:

```
<dc:coverage>United Kingdom</dc:coverage>
```

Over time we expect uses of the PRISM specification to become more sophisticated, moving from simple literal values to more structured values. Some publishers already use sophisticated controlled vocabularies; others are barely using manually supplied keywords. Some examples of the different kinds of values that can be given are

```
<dc:coverage rdf:resource="rdf:about="http://prismstandard.org/vocabs/ISO-3166/GB">
```

and

```
<dc:coverage>
  <pcv:Descriptor rdf:about="http://prismstandard.org/vocabs/ISO-3166/GB">
    <pcv:label xml:lang="en">United Kingdom</pcv:label>
    <pcv:label xml:lang="fr">Royaume Uni</pcv:label>
  </pcv:Descriptor>
</dc:coverage>
```

Note also that there are elements whose meanings are similar and are subsets of other elements. For example, the geographic subject of a resource could be given with

```
<prism:subject>United Kingdom</prism:subject>
<dc:coverage>United Kingdom</dc:coverage>
```

or

```
<prism:location>United Kingdom</prism:location>
```

Any of those elements might use the simple literal value or a more complex structured value.

RSS

RDF Site Summary 1.0 (RSS) is a format for syndication and descriptive meta data. The primary application of RSS is as a lightweight syndication protocol for distributing headlines and links. An RSS summary describes a "channel" consisting of items and their URLs. Each item consists of a title, link, and brief description. You can find details of RSS 1.0 at http://web.resource.org/rss/1.0/spec. Like PRISM, RSS is an XML application. It conforms to the W3C's RDF Specification and may be extended using XML-namespace and/or RDF-based modules.

The following is a basic sample RSS 1.0 document, making use of only the core RSS 1.0 element set:

```
<?xml version="1.0"?>

<rdf:RDF
   xmlns:rdf="http://www.w3.org/1999/02/22-rdf-syntax-ns#"
   xmlns="http://purl.org/rss/1.0/">
   <channel rdf:about="http://www.xml.com/xml/news.rss">
      <title>XML.com</title>
      <link>http://xml.com/pub</link>
      <description>XML.com features a rich mix of information and services
      for the XML community.
      </description>
      <image rdf:resource="http://xml.com/universal/images/xml_tiny.gif" />
      <items>
         <rdf:Seq>
```

```
            <rdf:li resource="http://xml.com/pub/2000/08/09/xslt/xslt.html" />
            <rdf:li resource="http://xml.com/pub/2000/08/09/rdfdb/index.html" />
         </rdf:Seq>
      </items>
   </channel>

   <image rdf:about="http://xml.com/universal/images/xml_tiny.gif">
      <title>XML.com</title>
      <link>http://www.xml.com</link>
      <url>http://xml.com/universal/images/xml_tiny.gif</url>
   </image>
   <item rdf:about="http://xml.com/pub/2000/08/09/xslt/xslt.html">
    <title>Processing Inclusions with XSLT</title>
    <link>http://xml.com/pub/2000/08/09/xslt/xslt.html</link>
    <description>
     Processing document inclusions with general XML tools can be
     problematic. This article proposes a way of preserving inclusion
     information through SAX-based processing.
    </description>
   </item>
   <item rdf:about="http://xml.com/pub/2000/08/09/rdfdb/index.html">
      <title>Putting RDF to Work</title>
      <link>http://xml.com/pub/2000/08/09/rdfdb/index.html</link>
      <description>Tool and API support for the Resource Description Framework
      is slowly coming of age. Edd Dumbill takes a look at RDFDB,
      one of the most exciting new RDF toolkits.
      </description>
   </item>
</rdf:RDF>
```

RSS Elements

The outermost level in every RSS 1.0-compliant document is the RDF element. The opening RDF tag associates the rdf namespace prefix with the RDF syntax schema and establishes the RSS 1.0 schema as the default namespace for the document.

The channel element contains meta data describing the channel itself, including a descriptive title for the channel and a brief description of the channel's content. The link element provides a URL to the described resource. The URL of the channel element's rdf:about attribute must be unique with respect to any other rdf:about attributes in the RSS document, and is a URI that identifies the channel. Most commonly, this is either the home page being described or a URL where the RSS file can be found. The contained image element associates the optional top-level image element and this channel. The value of the rdf:resource attribute must be identical to that of the image element's rdf:about attribute.

The top-level image element gives the URL of the associated image.

The items element provides an optional RDF table of contents, associating the document's items with this site summary. Each item's rdf:resource must be the same as the associated item element's rdf:about attribute.

An rdf:Seq (sequence) element is used to contain all the items to denote item order for rendering and reconstruction.

While commonly a news headline, the `item` element can be just about anything: discussion posting, job listing, software patch—any object with a URI. There may be a minimum of one item per RSS document. While RSS 1.0 does not enforce an upper limit, for backward compatibility with RSS 0.9 and 0.91, a maximum of 15 items is recommended. The `rdf:about` attribute must be unique in the RSS document. The URI should be identical to the value of the `link` subelement if possible.

RSS Modules

A key difference between RSS 1.0 and earlier versions is that the specification is extended by putting specific functions into modules. Adding and removing functions is then just a matter of the inclusion of a module set that best matches a requirement.

Modules are available for Dublin Core, Content, and Syndication, and there is a recent proposal for a PRISM module, parts of which you can see in this example based on an issue of *Nature* magazine:

```xml
<?xml version="1.0" encoding="utf-8"?>
<rdf:RDF
    xmlns:rdf="http://www.w3.org/1999/02/22-rdf-syntax-ns#"
    xmlns="http://purl.org/rss/1.0/"
    xmlns:dc="http://purl.org/dc/elements/1.1/"
    xmlns:prism="http://prismstandard.org/namespaces/1.2/basic/"
>
<channel rdf:about="http://www.nature.com/cgi-
taf/dynapage.taf?file=/nature/journal/v424/n6950/index.html">
    <title>Nature</title>
    <description>International weekly journal of science</description>
    <link>http://www.nature.com/cgi-
taf/dynapage.taf?file=/nature/journal/v424/n6950/index.html</link>
    <dc:publisher>Nature Publishing Group</dc:publisher>
    <dc:language>en-GB</dc:language>
    <dc:rights>Copyright (C) 2003 Nature Publishing Group</dc:rights>
    <prism:publicationName>Nature</prism:publicationName>
    <prism:issn>0028-0836</prism:issn>
    <prism:publisher>Nature Publishing Group</prism:publisher>
    <prism:copyright>Copyright (C) 2003 Nature Publishing Group</prism:copyright>
    <prism:rightsAgent>permissions@nature.com</prism:rightsAgent>
    <items>
        <rdf:Seq>
            <rdf:li rdf:resource="http://dx.doi.org/10.1038/424709a"/>
            <rdf:li rdf:resource="http://dx.doi.org/10.1038/424709b"/>
                .
                .
        </rdf:Seq>
    </items>
</channel>
  <item rdf:about="http://dx.doi.org/10.1038/424709a">
    <title>If it ain't broke, don't fix it (much)</title>
    <link>http://dx.doi.org/10.1038/424709a</link>
    <description>Modest structural reforms could help the US National Institute
of Health to maintain its independence - and the public's confidence.</description>
    <dc:title>If it ain't broke, don't fix it (much)</dc:title>
    <dc:identifier>doi:10.1038/424709a</dc:identifier>
```

```
    <dc:source>Nature 424, 709 (2003)</dc:source>
    <dc:date>2003-08-14</dc:date>
    <prism:publicationName>Nature</prism:publicationName>
    <prism:publicationDate>2003-08-14</prism:publicationDate>
    <prism:volume>424</prism:volume>
    <prism:number>6950</prism:number>
    <prism:category
rdf:resource="http://prismstandard.org/vocabularies/1.2/category.xml#column"/>
    <prism:section>Editorials</prism:section>
    <prism:startingPage>709</prism:startingPage>
</item>
    .
    .
    .
</rdf:RDF>
```

The "Other" RSS

Somewhat confusingly, there is another standard using the RSS acronym, now at version 2.0, designed for a similar purpose but using a different approach. You can read about it at `http://blogs.law.harvard.edu/tech/rss`.

RSS 0.9 was introduced in by Netscape as a channel description format and content-gathering mechanism. A by-product was the use of RSS as a syndication format. RSS 1.0 builds on version 0.9.

Renamed "Rich Site Summary," RSS 0.91 was included as one of the syndication formats in the Userland Manila product and related services, where it brought together the approaches of Weblog and syndication. Dave Winer at Userland has now put its derivative, RSS 2.0, in the public domain under a Creative Commons license.

A Preliminary Design

Before you move on to the case study, we thought it might be useful if we sketched out our first thoughts on a design for the NewsLine InfoPath application.

Workflow

Figure 12-1 is a skeletal diagram showing the form templates as individual contributor files, then merged into a single news desk file. There are components for processes and data sources, and some related XML input and outputs. We haven't attempted to show supplementary files like XSLT templates, XSDs, and so on.

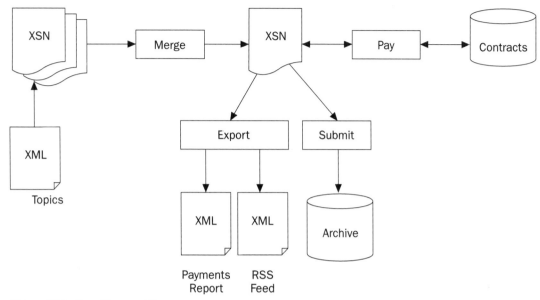

Figure 12-1: NewsLine workflow.

The table lists the components and their purpose.

Component	Purpose
XSN contributor template	View interface for data entry on local machines.
XML topics file	Secondary data source with subject categories.
Merge	Custom merge incorporating status change.
XSN desk template	Views with added content and functions.
Contacts	Secondary data source. Access database with contract details.
Pay	Calculates payment due to contributor.
Export	Transforms XML to Excel data source, and RSS for news feed.
Post	Posts stories to archive.
Archive	Story archive on SQL Server.

XML Schema

RDF/XML is certainly verbose and (some say) hard to understand. Whatever you think about it, the good news is that you don't need to use RDF/XML in the raw just yet. Provided you know what is needed in the outputs for the NewsLine application, you can develop any convenient vocabulary and use XSLT to transform it to the target schema. That's what we've done here.

Figure 12-2 shows a content model diagram containing the minimum of what we seem to need for a basic form. You'll find that this model needs refinement as we go along. At this point we haven't produced a schema listing. From the diagram you should be able to work out what we intend to map on to the DC and PRISM elements for output.

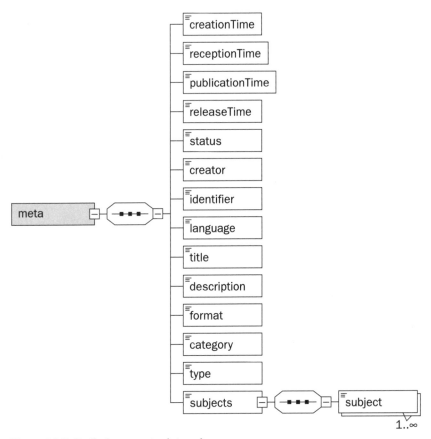

Figure 12-2: Preliminary meta data schema.

Summary

In this chapter you've seen the requirements of the NewsLine service, as background for the case study that you'll work through in the following chapters.

You also reviewed in outline the reasons for NewsLine's choice of three important meta data standards: PRISM 1.2, RDF, and RSS 1.0. Having seen our first thoughts on a design, perhaps you'll have begun to think of how you might apply them when it comes to building an XML vocabulary for the NewsLine InfoPath application.

That comes up next in Chapter 13, where you'll step through the form design process, with a look at data input structures and a main schema for InfoPath. In Chapter 14 you'll work through the template implementation in detail. Chapters 15 and 16 cover the ADO processing logic for payment calculations and for posting to the archive server. In Chapter 17 you'll look at schemas for the Excel and RSS outputs, and see examples of the XSLT transforms that might be applied to achieve them.

13

Input Data Structures

In this chapter you look at the XML schema for the meta data capture form. As you develop the form schema, you'll also need to consider the three data output requirements in conjunction with meeting the PRISM and RSS standards.

To help things along, we've created a form template showing one possible solution to the application problem. As we go along we'll suggest alternative approaches that you might want to explore.

The template files for this section are contained in the download from the Wrox Web site. In the ch13 folder, the form files are already extracted. If you haven't already done so, we suggest you download the file now. You can get it at www.wrox.com.

Your overall task in schema design is to create a robust set of data structures for capturing and processing the meta data. This means developing schemas that express the data content at each processing stage, and the constraints that will contribute to validating user input.

Altogether you'll need to consider the structure of three schemas.

Schema	Purpose	Filename
Infopath	Main InfoPath form	meta.xsd
Excel	Target data structure to load into Excel	payments_report.xsd
RSS	Regular news feed	rss.xsd

You'll cover the output data structure design in Chapter 17.

Top-Level Elements

Remember that your form schema is a structure that needs to meet a number of needs. It has to be friendly enough that a sequence of different users can get on with their jobs without being nagged for invalid input. The design should be informed by the required outputs, but at this point you don't have to conform to specific output syntaxes. You can use XSLT to transform to the target vocabulary when you output the data, provided that the right content and semantics have been captured.

Schema Declaration

Your form schema declaration will start with the WSX `schema` element and `namespace` attribute:

```
<xsd:schema xmlns:xs="http://www.w3.org/2001/XMLSchema">
  .
  .
  .
<xsd:schema>
```

Ideally, you would be able to use the schemas developed by DC or PRISM, but that won't work for two reasons. First of all, the published DC schema contains abstract elements that InfoPath can't handle, and second, PRISM hasn't published an XML schema.

It will, however, make sense to declare a NewsLine or `nl` namespace for this application.

```
<xsd:schema xmlns:xs="http://www.w3.org/2001/XMLSchema"
  xmlns:nl="http://newsline.net/schemas/meta_01_20031103">
  .
  .
  .
<xsd:schema>
```

Root Element

The root element for the form has the basic purpose of allowing multiple stories to be merged into a single XML file. Much of the time contributors and editors will work with individual meta data descriptions. There are two cases where multiple stories come into play. One is where a contributor or editor wants to keep a set of related material together—a text and a number of photos, for example. The second case is when a desk editor needs to aggregate stories for export to Excel. We use the name `resourceList` for the element.

Apart from requiring at least one meta data entry, what do you need to include? We think a form header carrying some fixed information about the relevant desk would help the labeling process when it comes to news feed and archiving processes. The header is pulled in with an `xsd:include`. This makes it possible to have separate header files for each of the news desks.

The attributes `deskID` and `deskName` are clear enough. The `email` attribute is there to provide a `mailto` address for a button action that launches the contributor's e-mail application.

```
<xsd:element name="formHeader">
    <xsd:complexType>
        <xsd:attribute name="deskID" type="xsd:string" use="required"
```

```
fixed="ln"/>
        <xsd:attribute name="deskName" type="xsd:string" use="required"
fixed="London"/>
        <xsd:attribute name="email" type="xsd:string" use="required"
fixed="ln.contrib@newsline.net"/>
        <xsd:attribute name="period" type="xsd:date" use="optional"/>
      </xsd:complexType>
    </xsd:element>
```

Then, as you'll see under *Conditional Formatting and Display*, we've introduced a `categoryFilter` element that will help manage long lists of stories. Note that this is distinct from the `category` element that belongs to the individual story meta data.

Our suggested structure looks like this:

```
<xsd:schema xmlns:xs="http://www.w3.org/2001/XMLSchema"
  xmlns:nl="http://newsline.net/schemas/meta_01_20031103">
    <xsd:include schemaLocation="header.xsd"/>
    <xsd:element name="resourceList">
      <xsd:complexType>
        <xsd:sequence>
          <xsd:element name="categoryFilter"/>
          <xsd:element ref="formHeader"/>
          <xsd:element ref="meta" maxOccurs="unbounded"/>
        </xsd:sequence>
      </xsd:complexType>
    </xsd:element>
      .
      .
<xsd:schema>
```

Meta Data Element

You can use any name you choose for the meta data element; in our example we've used `meta` as the container element for the individual resource descriptions.

At the end of the editorial process, you'll need to generate a unique identifier for each resource, so the `id` attribute in the `meta` element is declared inside a complex type. Here it is optional, since it won't be completed by contributors.

The `language` attribute defines the language of the meta data, not the content of the stories. In the example, we've used the encoding from *ISO 639-2 Codes for the representation of names of languages, Part 2: alpha-3 code*, which specifies the three-letter codes for languages. The three-letter structure allows more codes and finer granularity. The value is fixed as `"eng"` for English.

You'll fill in this content model with references to global element declarations. We've chosen to use an `xsd:sequence` element.

```
<xsd:element name="meta">
  <xsd:complexType>
    <xsd:sequence>
```

```
               .
               .
        </xsd:sequence>
        <xsd:attribute name="id" type="xsd:string" use="optional"/>
        <xsd:attribute name="language" type="xsd:string" fixed="eng"/>
    </xsd:complexType
</xsd:element>
```

Fixed Information

The requirement specifies the distribution of stories in English. You should nonetheless add a `language` element to the schema, though it needn't appear on the form in any view. It should, however, go in the RSS and the archive output, so that customers are in no doubt about the content.

```
<xsd:element name="language" default="eng">
    <xsd:simpleType>
        <xsd:restriction base="xsd:string">
            <xsd:length value="3"/>
        </xsd:restriction>
    </xsd:simpleType>
</xsd:element>
```

User Input

Recall that we have two types of form users: contributors and editors. Contributors to the NewsLine service will usually not be connected to the company network when they create stories. Entering meta data needs to be quick and simple.

Creator

Each contributor needs to enter a unique identifier that is stored in the `userID` attribute. When a story is approved, the identifier is used to look up details of the contributor's contract rates, to generate a byline for the story, and to create a link to a short biography and a list of stories by the contributor on the NewsLine Web site.

```
<xsd:element name="creator">
    <xsd:complexType>
        <xsd:simpleContent>
            <xsd:extension base="xsd:string">
                <xsd:attribute name="userID" type="xsd:string" use="required"/>
                <xsd:attribute name="byline" type="xsd:string" use="optional"/>
                <xsd:attribute name="url" type="xsd:string" use="optional"/>
            </xsd:extension>
        </xsd:simpleContent>
    </xsd:complexType>
</xsd:element>
```

A possible modification you might make here is a restriction of the string to conform to a business rule about user identifiers, thus providing a limited degree of local validation.

Title Description and Language

The `title` element provides a short title for the story. You may want to restrict the length of this element so that the title text will easily fit into news feed and other meta data listings. Our length of 150 characters in the example is somewhat arbitrary. If you think a longer title may be needed, consider adding an optional element.

```
<xsd:element name="title">
   <xsd:simpleType>
      <xsd:restriction base="xsd:string">
         <xsd:maxLength value="150"/>
      </xsd:restriction>
   </xsd:simpleType>
</xsd:element>
```

The `description` element is intended for a single paragraph, plain-text summary of the story's content:

```
<xsd:element name="description"/>
```

Story File

The `content` element records a temporary filename for the content that the meta data describes. The value is any convenient name that makes it easy for the news desk to correlate meta data and content when it arrives. In our example a persistent identifier is assigned later.

```
<xsd:element name="content">
   <xsd:complexType>
      <xsd:attribute name="file" type="xsd:string" use="required"/>
   </xsd:complexType>
</xsd:element>
```

The `format` element defines the Internet Media Type (IMT) of the story content. For this element we suggest using a drop-down list with user-friendly names and hiding the `type` attribute value.

```
<xsd:element name="format" type="formatType"/>
```

In our example we've defined a format type to constrain the options that users can choose for the `type` attribute.

```
<xsd:complexType name="formatType">
   <xsd:simpleContent>
      <xsd:extension base="xsd:string">
         <xsd:attribute name="type">
            <xsd:simpleType>
               <xsd:restriction base="xsd:string">
                  <xsd:enumeration value="text/xml"/>
                     <xsd:enumeration value="image/png"/>
                     <xsd:enumeration value="image/jpeg"/>
                  <xsd:enumeration value="audio/mpeg"/>
                  <xsd:enumeration value="video/mpeg"/>
               </xsd:restriction>
            </xsd:simpleType>
```

```
            </xsd:attribute>
        </xsd:extension>
    </xsd:simpleContent>
</xsd:complexType>
```

Editors

The main tasks of a news desk editor are to check the details of the meta data, add or modify any information, and approve the story for distribution. If a story needs to be withheld until a particular date and time (embargoed), the editor needs to indicate this in the meta data, so that both customers and NewsLine sales staff can be made aware of this special status.

In our solution we provide an optional Embargoed section in the Desk view. When an editor chooses this option, the `releaseTime` field is displayed, and the editor can enter a date and a time. Our schema specifies the `xsd:dateTime` data type, which takes the format 2003-09-30T10:10:10. Because the business operates over multiple time zones, a zone indicator is also needed.

```
<xsd:element name="releaseTime" type="xsd:dateTime"/>
```

Editors also need to select the `type` element from a drop-down list. `type` defines how a story is presented. For example, financial information could be presented in a text table or a graph, and a JPEG file could be a map, photo, or drawing.

```
<xsd:element name="type" type="resourceType"/>
```

We also propose a short list of resource types:

```
<xsd:simpleType name="resourceType">
    <xsd:union>
        <xsd:simpleType>
            <xsd:restriction base="xsd:string">
                <xsd:enumeration value="Article"/>
                <xsd:enumeration value="Illustration"/>
                <xsd:enumeration value="Photo"/>
                <xsd:enumeration value="Sound"/>
                <xsd:enumeration value="Video"/>
            </xsd:restriction>
        </xsd:simpleType>
    </xsd:union>
</xsd:simpleType>
```

For this application we'll assume that most contributions will be treated as "work for hire." In these cases, all rights belong to NewsLine. However, NewsLine might also use secondary materials in their output that belong to third parties or are controlled by their agents. The goal here is to inform NewsLine customers who to contact for permissions.

So, the required `rights` element allows a choice between `rightsAgent` and `copyright` elements. `copyright` is the default with the fixed value of `"NewsLine Inc"`.

```
<xsd:element name="rights" use="required">
    <xsd:complexType>
```

```
        <xsd:choice>
            <xsd:element ref="rightsAgent"/>
            <xsd:element ref="copyright"/>
        </xsd:choice>
    </xsd:complexType>
</xsd:element>
        .
        .
<xsd:element name="rightsAgent" type="xsd:string"/>
<xsd:element name="copyright" type="subjectType" fixed="NewsLine Inc"/>
```

Conditional Formatting and Display

If you want to include any controls that determine conditional formatting in a form, you'll have to include elements for them in your schema.

In our scenario, there isn't much scope for conditional formatting in the capture view. However, in one news desk view, we decided to emphasize the status of a form.

Status

The status element itself is set by default when a contributor fills out a form:

```
<xsd:element name="status" type="statusType"
```

Here's the type definition:

```
<xsd:simpleType name="statusType">
    <xsd:union>
        <xsd:simpleType>
            <xsd:restriction base="xsd:string">
                <xsd:enumeration value="Draft"/>
                <xsd:enumeration value="In Review"/>
                <xsd:enumeration value="Spiked"/>
                <xsd:enumeration value="Filed"/>
                <xsd:enumeration value="Embargoed"/>
            </xsd:restriction>
        </xsd:simpleType>
    </xsd:union>
</xsd:simpleType>
```

Then for the status field, we create five formatting elements, one for each status value. They'll contain icons that display next to the status field in the interface.

```
<xsd:element name="iconDraft" xsd:type="string"/>
<xsd:element name="iconReview" xsd:type="string"/>
<xsd:element name="iconSpiked" xsd:type="string"/>
<xsd:element name="iconEmbargoed" xsd:type="string"/>
<xsd:element name="iconApproved" xsd:type="string"/>
```

A section control bound to the `iconDraft` element contains the formatting rule, which hides the section if the content of the `status` element is not `"Draft"`. Formatting matches to text values are case-sensitive.

Here's an XSLT template fragment for the view, showing the conditional formatting for the `iconDraft` element:

```
<xsl:template match="iconDraft" mode="_13">
    <div class="xdSection xdRepeating" title="" style="PADDING-LEFT: 1px;
MARGIN: 0px; WIDTH: 24px; HEIGHT: 24px" align="left" xd:CtrlId="CTRL25"
xd:xctname="Section" tabIndex="-1">
        <xsl:attribute name="style">PADDING-LEFT: 1px; MARGIN: 0px;
WIDTH: 20px; HEIGHT: 20px;
            <xsl:choose>
                <xsl:when test="status != &quot;Draft&quot;">DISPLAY: none
                </xsl:when>
            </xsl:choose>
        </xsl:attribute>
        <div>
            <img style="WIDTH: 24px; HEIGHT: 24px" height="24" src="msoA607E.gif"
width="24"/>
        </div>
    </div>
</xsl:template>
```

Category Filter

When editors have merged data from a series of story forms, it is likely that the Desk view will become rather long. To make the list easier to handle, we decided to create a Story List view and add a filter for the different resource categories. Again, we've used a drop-down list of category names.

```
<xsd:element name="category" type="resourceCategory">
```

The `type` declaration contains a selection of PRISM resource categories. You may recall from Chapter 12 that these specify the genre of the story, as distinct from its presentation.

```
<xsd:simpleType name="resourceCategory">
    <xsd:union>
        <xsd:simpleType>
            <xsd:restriction base="xsd:string">
                <xsd:enumeration value="Analysis"/>
                <xsd:enumeration value="Bulletin"/>
                <xsd:enumeration value="Cartoon"/>
                <xsd:enumeration value="Column"/>
                <xsd:enumeration value="Biography"/>
                <xsd:enumeration value="Feature"/>
                <xsd:enumeration value="Financial Statement"/>
                <xsd:enumeration value="Interview"/>
                <xsd:enumeration value="Opinion"/>
                <xsd:enumeration value="Portrait"/>
                <xsd:enumeration value="Press Release"/>
                <xsd:enumeration value="Profile"/>
                <xsd:enumeration value="Review"/>
                <xsd:enumeration value="Transcript"/>
```

```
        </xsd:restriction>
      </xsd:simpleType>
    </xsd:union>
  </xsd:simpleType>
```

Here's part of the HTML `select` element in the XSLT for the view:

```
.
.
<select class="xdComboBox xdBehavior_Select" title="" size="1"
xd:binding="categoryFilter" xd:boundProp="value" tabIndex="0"
xd:xctname="DropDown" xd:CtrlId="CTRL1" style="WIDTH: 130px">
   <xsl:attribute name="value">
      <xsl:value-of select="filter_category"/>
   </xsl:attribute>
   <option value="Any">
      <xsl:if test="categoryFilter=&quot;Any&quot;">
         <xsl:attribute name="selected">selected</xsl:attribute>
      </xsl:if>Any category...
   </option>
   <option value="analysis">
      <xsl:if test="categoryFilter=&quot;analysis&quot;">
         <xsl:attribute name="selected">selected</xsl:attribute>
      </xsl:if>analysis
   </option>
   <option value="biography">
      <xsl:if test="categoryFilter=&quot;biography&quot;">
         <xsl:attribute name="selected">selected</xsl:attribute>
      </xsl:if>biography
   </option>
   <option value="column">
      <xsl:if test="categoryFilter=&quot;column&quot;">
         <xsl:attribute name="selected">selected</xsl:attribute>
      </xsl:if>column
   </option>
   .
   .
</select>
   .
   .
```

A repeating table contains the story elements in the listing. Two conditions set up the relationship between the filter and the table:

```
categoryFilter   category AND categoryFilter   "Any"
```

A match of the value in the drop-down list with any resource category element in the story hides everything but that category; choosing `Any` displays all the story data. Part of the repeating table XSLT shows the logic:

```
   .
   .
<tbody xd:xctname="RepeatingTable">
   <xsl:for-each select="resourceList/meta">
<tr>
```

```
      <xsl:attribute name="style">;
         <xsl:choose>
            <xsl:when test="category != resource_filter and resource_filter!=
            &quot;Any&quot;">DISPLAY: none</xsl:when>
         </xsl:choose>
      </xsl:attribute>
      <td>
         <span class="xdTextBox" hideFocus="1" title="Title" xd:binding="title"
          tabIndex="0" xd:xctname="PlainText" xd:CtrlId="CTRL3" style="WIDTH:100%">
            <xsl:value-of select="title"/>
         </span>
      </td>
         .
         .
      </tr>
   </xsl:for-each>
</tbody>
      .
      .
```

External Sources

One secondary data source applies to both the Contributor and the Desk views of the form. Both contributors and editors use a subject lookup feature when adding subject terms to the meta data. This provides a controlled vocabulary of terms and related encodings.

The form schema offers a choice of one or more of company, country, event, industry, organization, or person, using the type attribute:

```
<xsd:element name="subject">
   <xsd:complexType>
      <xsd:attribute name="id" type="xsd:string"/>
      <xsd:attribute name="type" type="xsd:string"/>
      <xsd:attribute name="name" type="xsd:string"/>
   </xsd:complexType>
</xsd:element>
```

The lookup source is an XML file containing topics derived from a topic map maintained by NewsLine. This is a convenient way to support unconnected contributors. In our scenario the data is fairly static, and the file can be updated regularly by the relevant news desk. There will be core topics of use to contributors in every region, but not all topics have to go to everyone. We think it will be easy to maintain and will perform well, and the company won't have to pay for the development and deployment of a more complex system. You'll read more about how to use XML sources and how we handle the form data in the next chapter.

The subject element is contained in a subjects element wrapper:

```
<xsd:element name="subjects">
   <xsd:complexType>
      <xsd:sequence>
         <xsd:element ref="subject" maxOccurs="unbounded"/>
      </xsd:sequence>
   </xsd:complexType>
</xsd:element>
```

Script Processing

In our example we make fairly extensive use of script-based code functions. Mostly the code is there to supplement schema validation, improve accuracy, and apply business rules. What follows here is an overview of the implications for the form schema. You'll read more about the details of scripting in Chapters 15 and 16.

Identifier

The meta data `identifier` element will contain the URL for the story content. This value will be added when a unique ID is generated for the meta data. The identifier is based on a concatenation of the date of approval, the desk ID, the `id` attribute of the `meta` element, and the file extension, for example, `20030922_NY1234_xml`.

```
<xsd:element ref="identifier"/>
```

Dates

In the sample design, all date information on the form, except for the `releaseTime` element, is script-driven, and we assume that all these fields in the form will be read-only.

`creationTime` is automatically generated when the user creates a new form. The other values are generated on subsequent changes of workflow status. `modificationTime` records any change of status to the meta data. `receptionTime` is added when an editor merges stories at a news desk. `publicationTime` is the time when a story is filed. `releaseTime` is only specified if a story is embargoed.

```
<xsd:element name="creationTime" type="xsd:dateTime" nillable="true"/>
<xsd:element name="receptionTime" type="xsd:dateTime" nillable="true"/>
<xsd:element name="modificationTime" type="xsd:dateTime" nillable="true"/>
<xsd:element name="publicationTime" type="xsd:dateTime" nillable="true"/>
<xsd:element name="releaseTime" type="xsd:dateTime" nillable="true"/>
```

Creator

When a story gets to the news desk, the only information about the contributor is his or her userID. When the payment lookup takes place, a script copies the `byline` and `url` attribute values from the data source.

Workflow

The `status` element defaults to a value of `"Draft"` when the contributor creates a new form, and is modified by script or XSLT code each time there is a change of status. It is therefore a read-only field in the UI. You've already seen how an icon is used to highlight the current status of the form.

Payments

A second external source is used to get contributor data from a table on a central database server. It is used in the Desk view. When an editor approves a story, the value in the `userID` is used in a script to query a table containing the user's full name and the contract rate for the contribution.

Script logic calculates the payment to contributors and stores the value in the payment element. At present, all contributors get paid in U.S. dollars. There are Web services that provide currency exchange, so it would be fairly simple to add a function to convert the contract dollar rate to a local currency value, such as the euro or yen.

```xsd
<xsd:element name="payment">
    <xsd:complexType>
        <xsd:attribute name="amount" type="xsd:decimal" use="required"/>
        <xsd:attribute name="currency" fixed="USD">
            <xsd:simpleType>
                <xsd:restriction base="xsd:string"/>
            </xsd:simpleType>
        </xsd:attribute>
    </xsd:complexType>
</xsd:element>
```

Filing the Story

Submitting a form involves posting the form data for a single story (not the entire form) to an archive server using ADO scripting.

Script Actions Review

Since quite a lot of script code is running under the hood, here's a summary of the user events and script actions you'll need to cover in your code.

User Event	Script Actions
New form	Sets creationTime and modificationTime
Embargo story	Updates modifiedTime
Authorize payment	Calculates payment amount using lookup values
Sets status to Filed (if not embargoed)	
Updates modifiedTime	
Sets publicationTime	
Validates releaseTime > publicationTime	
Completes creator element attributes	
File story	Transforms to archive format
Submits ADO or HTTP post to server	

The Form Schemas

To round things off for this section, we'll list the entire form schema. Figure 13-1 shows the content model.

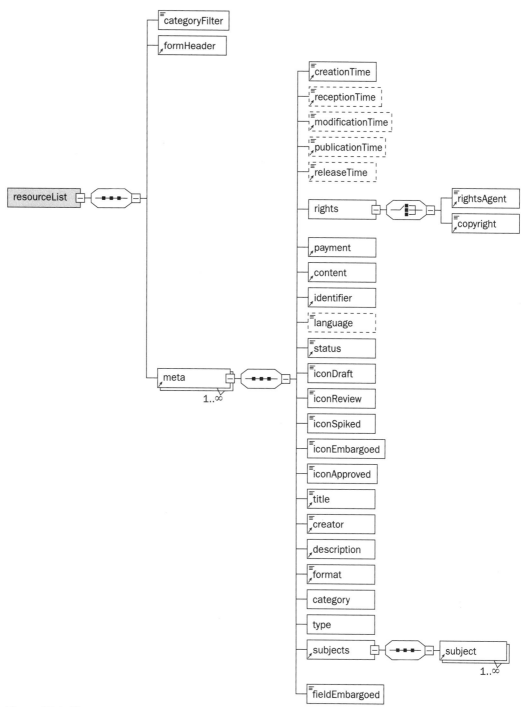

Figure 13-1: The meta data form content model.

The following lists the entire form schema:

```xml
<?xml version="1.0" encoding="UTF-8"?>
<xsd:schema xmlns:xs="http://www.w3.org/2001/XMLSchema"
elementFormDefault[I1]="qualified" attributeFormDefault="unqualified">
    <xsd:include schemaLocation="header.xsd"/>
    <xsd:element name="resourceList">
        <xsd:complexType>
            <xsd:sequence>
                <xsd:element name="categoryFilter"/>
                <xsd:element ref="formHeader"/>
                <xsd:element ref="meta" maxOccurs="unbounded"/>
            </xsd:sequence>
        </xsd:complexType>
    </xsd:element>
    <xsd:element name="meta">
        <xsd:complexType>
            <xsd:sequence>
                <xsd:element name="userID" type="xsd:string" use="required"/>
                <xsd:element ref="creationTime"/>
                <xsd:element ref="receptionTime" minOccurs="0"/>
                <xsd:element ref="modificationTime" minOccurs="0"/>
                <xsd:element ref="publicationTime" minOccurs="0"/>
                <xsd:element ref="releaseTime" minOccurs="0"/>
                <xsd:element ref="payment"/>
                <xsd:element ref="content"/>
                <xsd:element ref="identifier"/>
                <xsd:element name="language" default="eng" minOccurs="0">
                    <xsd:simpleType>
                        <xsd:restriction base="xsd:string">
                            <xsd:length value="3"/>
                        </xsd:restriction>
                    </xsd:simpleType>
                </xsd:element>
                <xsd:element ref="status"/>
                <xsd:element name="iconDraft" type="xsd:string"/>
                <xsd:element name="iconReview" type="xsd:string"/>
                <xsd:element name="iconSpiked" type="xsd:string"/>
                <xsd:element name="iconEmbargoed" type="xsd:string"/>
                <xsd:element name="iconApproved" type="xsd:string"/>
                <xsd:element ref="title"/>
                <xsd:element ref="creator"/>
                <xsd:element ref="description"/>
                <xsd:element ref="format"/>
                <xsd:element name="category" type="resourceCategory"/>
                <xsd:element name="type" type="resourceType"/>
                <xsd:element ref="subject"/>
            </xsd:sequence>
            <xsd:attribute name="id" type="xsd:string" use="optional"/>
            <xsd:attribute name="language" type="xsd:string" fixed="eng"/>
        </xsd:complexType>
    </xsd:element>
    <xsd:element name="creationTime" type="xsd:dateTime"/>
    <xsd:element name="receptionTime" type="xsd:dateTime"/>
    <xsd:element name="modificationTime" type="xsd:dateTime"/>
    <xsd:element name="publicationTime" type="xsd:dateTime"/>
```

```xsd
<xsd:element name="releaseTime" type="xsd:dateTime"/>
<xsd:element name="content">
   <xsd:complexType>
      <xsd:attribute name="file" type="xsd:string" use="required"/>
   </xsd:complexType>
</xsd:element>
<xsd:element name="title">
   <xsd:simpleType>
      <xsd:restriction base="xsd:string">
         <xsd:maxLength value="150"/>
      </xsd:restriction>
   </xsd:simpleType>
</xsd:element>
<xsd:element name="status" type="statusType"/>
<xsd:element name="format" type="formatType"/>

<xsd:simpleType name="resourceCategory">
   <xsd:union>
      <xsd:simpleType>
         <xsd:restriction base="xsd:string">
            <xsd:enumeration value="Analysis"/>
            <xsd:enumeration value="Bulletin"/>
            <xsd:enumeration value="Cartoon"/>
            <xsd:enumeration value="Column"/>
            <xsd:enumeration value="Biography"/>
            <xsd:enumeration value="Feature"/>
            <xsd:enumeration value="financialStatement"/>
            <xsd:enumeration value="Interview"/>
            <xsd:enumeration value="Opinion"/>
            <xsd:enumeration value="Portrait"/>
            <xsd:enumeration value="Press Release"/>
            <xsd:enumeration value="Profile"/>
            <xsd:enumeration value="Review"/>
            <xsd:enumeration value="Transcript"/>
         </xsd:restriction>
      </xsd:simpleType>
   </xsd:union>
</xsd:simpleType>

<xsd:simpleType name="resourceType">
   <xsd:union>
      <xsd:simpleType>
         <xsd:restriction base="xsd:string">
            <xsd:enumeration value="Article"/>
            <xsd:enumeration value="Graph"/>
            <xsd:enumeration value="Illustration"/>
            <xsd:enumeration value="Photo"/>
            <xsd:enumeration value="Video"/>
            <xsd:enumeration value="Web Page"/>
         </xsd:restriction>
      </xsd:simpleType>
   </xsd:union>
</xsd:simpleType>

<xsd:complexType name="formatType">
   <xsd:simpleContent>
```

```
            <xsd:extension base="xsd:string">
                <xsd:attribute name="type">
                    <xsd:simpleType>
                        <xsd:restriction base="xsd:string">
                            <xsd:enumeration value="xml"/>
                            <xsd:enumeration value="html"/>
                            <xsd:enumeration value="png"/>
                            <xsd:enumeration value="svg"/>
                            <xsd:enumeration value="mpg"/>
                        </xsd:restriction>
                    </xsd:simpleType>
                </xsd:attribute>
            </xsd:extension>
        </xsd:simpleContent>
    </xsd:complexType>

    <xsd:simpleType name="statusType">
        <xsd:union>
            <xsd:simpleType>
                <xsd:restriction base="xsd:string">
                    <xsd:enumeration value="Draft"/>
                    <xsd:enumeration value="In Review"/>
                    <xsd:enumeration value="Filed"/>
                    <xsd:enumeration value="Embargoed"/>
                    <xsd:enumeration value="Spiked"/>
                </xsd:restriction>
            </xsd:simpleType>
        </xsd:union>
    </xsd:simpleType>

    <xsd:complexType name="subjectType">
        <xsd:simpleContent>
            <xsd:extension base="xsd:string">
                <xsd:attribute name="id"/>
            </xsd:extension>
        </xsd:simpleContent>
    </xsd:complexType>

    <xsd:element name="creator">
        <xsd:complexType>
            <xsd:simpleContent>
                <xsd:extension base="xsd:string">
                    <xsd:attribute name="userID" type="xsd:string" use="required"/>
                    <xsd:attribute name="byline" type="xsd:string" use="optional"/>
                    <xsd:attribute name="url" type="xsd:string" use="optional"/>

                </xsd:extension>
            </xsd:simpleContent>
        </xsd:complexType>
    </xsd:element>

    <xsd:element name="subject">
        <xsd:complexType>
            <xsd:choice minOccurs="0" maxOccurs="unbounded">
                <xsd:element ref="company"/>
```

```
                <xsd:element ref="country"/>
                <xsd:element ref="event"/>
                <xsd:element ref="industry"/>
                <xsd:element ref="organization"/>
                <xsd:element ref="person"/>
            </xsd:choice>
        </xsd:complexType>
    </xsd:element>
    <xsd:element name="identifier"/>
    <xsd:element name="description"/>
    <xsd:element name="company" type="subjectType"/>
    <xsd:element name="country" type="subjectType"/>
    <xsd:element name="event" type="subjectType"/>
    <xsd:element name="industry" type="subjectType"/>
    <xsd:element name="organization" type="subjectType"/>
    <xsd:element name="person" type="subjectType"/>
    <xsd:element name="rightsAgent" type="xsd:string"/>
    <xsd:element name="copyright" type="subjectType" fixed="NewsLine Inc"/>

    <xsd:element name="payment">
        <xsd:complexType>
            <xsd:attribute name="amount" type="xsd:decimal" use="required"/>
            <xsd:attribute name="currency" fixed="USD">
                <xsd:simpleType>
                    <xsd:restriction base="xsd:string"/>
                </xsd:simpleType>
            </xsd:attribute>
        </xsd:complexType>
    </xsd:element>

    <xsd:element name="rights">
        <xsd:complexType>
            <xsd:choice>
                <xsd:element ref="rightsAgent"/>
                <xsd:element ref="copyright"/>
            </xsd:choice>
        </xsd:complexType>
    </xsd:element>
</xsd:schema>
```

Summary

In this chapter you looked in detail at the schema for the meta data capture form. You learned that there are several issues to consider in the schema design. In addition to defining elements or attributes to contain meta data describing the stories, you had to consider business-related administrative meta data. User interface requirements also made an impact, and you had to add elements to accommodate the requirements of conditional formatting.

In Chapter 17 you'll move on to consider the two closely related output data structures in conjunction with the requirement to meet the PRISM and RSS standards, and look at the XSLT transforms. But before that, you'll tackle ADO scripts for calculating payments and archive posting.

14

Implementing the Template

In this chapter you assemble your form components into three views and look at techniques for merging stories, using an XML file as a secondary data source and adding a task pane to help your users.

We'll illustrate how our proposed user interface looks and how you might go about dealing with some specific design issues. Essentially, you'll step through the three views in sequence, looking at the more interesting points and dealing with some simple scripts and some XSLT as you go.

Rounding things off, you'll examine ways to construct a basic help system, with a feature to switch views from the task pane.

Defining the Data Source

Your first task is to select the XML schema. When InfoPath looks at a schema, it may find some ambiguity about root elements, as in this case, where there are several possibilities. To load our example schema, choose the file meta1.2.xsd from the case_study folder, and select the `resourceList` element. Figure 14-1 illustrates the interface.

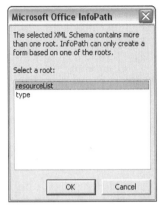

Figure 14-1: Choosing a root element.

When you have loaded the file, the data source task pane should look like Figure 14-2.

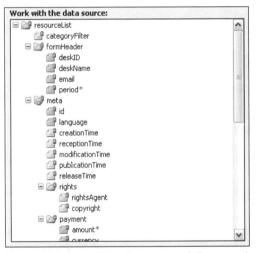

Figure 14-2: Part of the data source fully expanded.

Not all controls appear in all three views. The following table shows the mapping of schema elements (or their attributes) in the different views.

Element	Contributor	Desk	Story List
formHeader			
Status			
createdTime			
modifiedTime			
publishedTime			
receivedTime			
releaseTime			
fieldEmbargoed			
iconDraft			
iconReview			
iconPublished			
iconEmbargoed			
iconSpiked			
Creator			
Content			
Type			
Format			
Category			
Extent			
Payment			
Title			
Description			
Subjects			
Rights			

Contributor View

The Contributor view is pretty simple. We've set it as the default because that's how most users will want to see it. We've also allowed all users to see all the views. Of course, it would be possible to package the form into separate configurations for contributors and desk editors, with appropriate restrictions, and deploy two versions of the template.

The first thing to note here is that the form allows multiple meta elements. So contributors can batch up items if they wish. The labels for the controls differ from the unfriendly names of elements and attributes, even though that is sometimes just a matter of a shift to uppercase. We've used ScreenTips where possible and have a simple work-based tab sequence. Figure 14-3 shows the view.

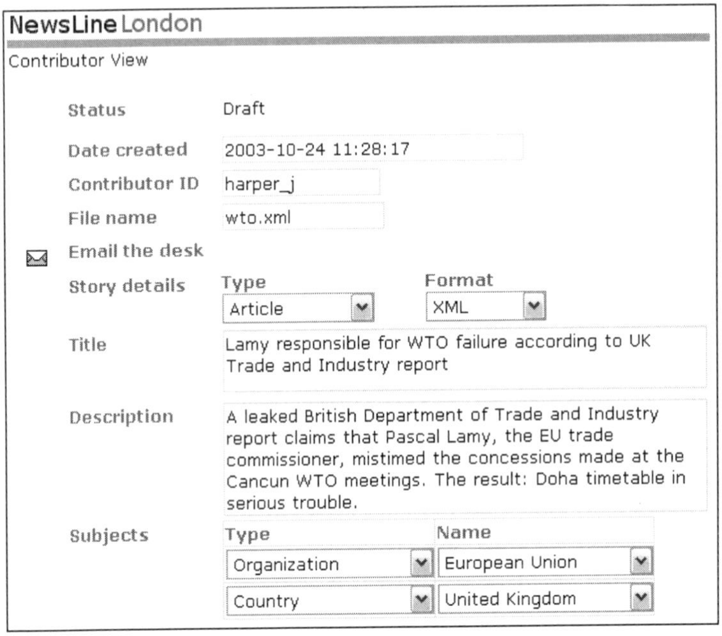

Figure 14-3: The Contributor view.

The `Status` control is set to Draft as a schema default and is read-only.

The `Date created` control is bound to the `creationTime` element. Here we set its value with a script. There are several date-setting calls to be made during a form life cycle, so first we include a couple of script functions for ISO 8601 date and time.

```
function getDateString(oDate)

    { // Use today as default value.
    if (oDate == null) oDate = new Date();

    var m = oDate.getMonth() + 1;
    var d = oDate.getDate();
```

```
    if (m < 10) m = "0" + m;
    if (d < 10) d = "0" + d; // (YYYY-MM-DD)

    return oDate.getFullYear() + "-" + m + "-" + d;
    }
function getTimeString(oTime)
    {
    if (oTime == null) oTime = new Date();

    var h = oTime.getHours();
    var m = oTime.getMinutes();
    var s = oTime.getSeconds();
    var ms = oTime.getMilliseconds();

    if (h < 10) h = "0" + h;
    if (m < 10) m = "0" + m;
    if (s < 10) s = "0" + s;
    if (ms < 100) ms = "0" + (ms < 10 ? "0" : "") + ms; // (HH:MM:SS.SSS)

    // ISO 8601 time (HH:MM:SS.SSS).
    return h + ":" + m + ":" + s + "." + ms;
    }
```

Then we use the OnLoad event to get current date and time values and build a string for the form. The control formatting takes care of the display, which is also read-only. One simple way to prevent an update of creationTime taking place on subsequent open actions is to compare it with a default value. Note that we also call a setModified function.

```
function XDocument::OnLoad(oEvent)
    {
    var formDate = new Date();
    var formTime = new Date();
    var createdNode = XDocument.DOM.selectSingleNode("//creationTime");

    //if default value is there set new date time
    if(createdNode.text=="2003-01-01T00:00:00")
        createdNode.text= getDateString(formDate) + "T" + getTimeString(formTime);
        setModified();
    }
function setModified()
    {
    var formDate = new Date();
    var formTime = new Date();
    var modifiedNode = XDocument.DOM.selectSingleNode("//modificationTime");

    modifiedNode.text= getDateString(formDate) + "T" + getTimeString(formTime);
    }
```

The default behavior when a user e-mails a form is for InfoPath to attach the XML schema and any form images to the message, and include the HTML for the form in the body. NewsLine wants a way to package up the story and its meta data.

Figure 14-4 shows how we set up the hyperlink icon next to `Email the desk`. In the dialog box, the value of the `Data source` option is set to `concat("mailto:", ../formHeader/@email, "?subject=", title)`. When the user clicks the icon, it opens Outlook with the correct e-mail address for the contributor's desk, along with the story title as the subject. We decide on a simple manual solution, but it would be quite easy to create a script to do the attachments and turn the hyperlink into a button to kick off the message process. You may recall seeing one way of managing that process in Chapter 7, under *Integrating with Applications and Services*.

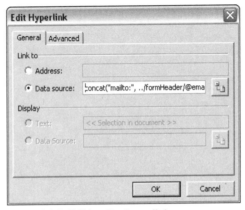

Figure 14-4: Editing the hyperlink.

In `Story details`, the `Type` and `Format` controls are bound to the related elements. Because the schema constrains the possible values for both elements, InfoPath populated the drop-down options automatically. The only change we had to make is for user-friendly display names in the Format properties.

`Subjects` contains two lists contained in a repeating table. The lists are populated from a secondary data source. You'll get to the details of how that is constructed in a short while.

Desk View

The Desk view is more complex. Several controls are copies of those in the Contributor view, though the layout is sometimes different.

The first time that story meta data appears in a Desk view is when it has been merged into an existing Desk view after arriving at the desk. Later in this chapter you'll learn more about how that merge process operates.

In the meantime we'd like to briefly cover additional controls that appear in the view, and which we discussed in Chapter 13.

Conditional Formatting

In Chapter 11 you saw how to add conditional formatting rules to objects on a form—how you can highlight a control by changing text style, color, or background, or hide an object entirely.

In our design, a table cell in the Desk and Story List views contains a group of status icons, each of which is inside a section control. The section controls are bound to their respective icon data source elements, for example, iconReview. Each section control contains a conditional formatting rule that hides the section when the content of the status element does not match the icon. Figure 14-5 shows the layout.

Figure 14-5: The conditional formatting section for status icons.

Figure 14-6 shows the rule for the iconReview element binding. The section control hides the section if the content of the status element is not "In Review."

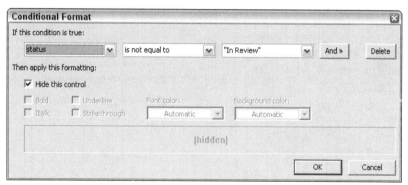

Figure 14-6: The Conditional Format dialog box with the rule for the "In Review" status.

Here's the XSLT template fragment for the view, showing the conditional formatting for the iconReview element:

```
<xsl:template match="iconReview" mode="_18">
   <div class="xdSection xdRepeating" title="" style="PADDING-RIGHT: 0px;
PADDING-LEFT: 0px; PADDING-BOTTOM: 0px; MARGIN: auto auto 0px; WIDTH: 27px;
PADDING-TOP: 0px; HEIGHT: 13px" align="left" xd:CtrlId="CTRL10"
xd:xctname="Section" tabIndex="-1">
      <xsl:attribute name="style">PADDING-RIGHT: 0px; PADDING-LEFT: 0px;
PADDING-BOTTOM: 0px; MARGIN: auto auto 0px; WIDTH: 27px; PADDING-TOP: 0px;
HEIGHT: 13px;
         <xsl:choose>
```

```
        <xsl:when test="../status != &quot;In Review&quot;">DISPLAY:
none</xsl:when>
        </xsl:choose>
    </xsl:attribute>
    <div>
        <img title="In Review" style="WIDTH: 24px; HEIGHT: 24px"
height="24" src="47826624.gif" width="24"/>
    </div>
  </div>
</xsl:template>
```

We use similar formatting to hide the embargo date and time until the status element is set to "Embargoed" by a button in the view. Here the fieldEmbargoed element is bound to a date picker control inside a section. Figure 14-7 shows the arrangement.

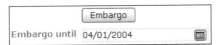

Figure 14-7: The conditional formatting section for the embargo date control.

Unbound Controls

Three further changes of status involve actions by an editor. Button controls for Embargo, File, and Spike set the respective status values.

The date controls Last modified and Received are set by script code or XSLT. Received is set when a form is merged, and Last modified gets an update with every status change.

```
function CTRLembargo_story::OnClick(eventObj)
    {
    var statusNode = XDocument.DOM.selectSingleNode("//status");
    statusNode.text = "Embargoed";
    }
```

Because of the conditional formatting, the Embargo until control is made visible as soon as the value for status is changed by the script.

Before a story is filed, an editor needs to complete the Extent control. When the editor clicks the File button, Identifier is automatically completed, and Filed gets filled in too. Both changes are scripted, along with the other fields completed at this time: Byline and Payment. Figure 14-8 shows the date controls and buttons. The scripting is described in Chapters 15 and 16.

Created	24/10/2003 00:00:00	Last modified	04/01/2004 19:09:05
Received	04/01/2004 19:09:05	Filed	
	Embargo		File Spike

Figure 14-8: Date controls and buttons in the Desk view.

Replacement Elements

In the Desk view you need to handle the choice between the `copyright` and `rightsAgent` elements. When you drag the rights element onto the form, InfoPath forms a section containing two nested sections within it. The second of these is an optional section. In design mode the interface looks like Figure 14-9.

Figure 14-9: The design mode interface for the Rights controls.

In the XSF file, InfoPath has included an `xReplace` component.

```
<xmlToEdit name="rightsAgent_13" item="/resourceList/meta/rights/copyright"
container="/resourceList/meta/rights">
    <editWith caption="Rights Agent" xd:autogeneration="template"
component="xReplace">
        <fragmentToInsert>
            <chooseFragment>
                <rightsAgent/>
            </chooseFragment>
        </fragmentToInsert>
    </editWith>
</xmlToEdit>
<xmlToEdit name="copyright_14" item="/resourceList/meta/rights/rightsAgent"
container="/resourceList/meta/rights">
    <editWith caption="Copyright" xd:autogeneration="template" component="xReplace">
        <fragmentToInsert>
            <chooseFragment>
                <copyright>NewsLine Inc</copyright>
            </chooseFragment>
        </fragmentToInsert>
    </editWith>
</xmlToEdit>
```

You'll need to modify the interface by setting user-friendly values for the `Replace` commands in each of the two sections. Right-click and choose `Properties` and click `Customize Commands` to show the Section Commands dialog box. The values for the Copyright section should look like Figure 14-10.

213

Figure 14-10: Customizing the Copyright replacement section.

Story List View

The Story List view is intended to simplify long listings of stories and to give editors an overview of story status. It uses a repeating table for all the stories, with a filter to simplify the view if necessary.

Using additional views like this one is one of the more attractive features of InfoPath. They are easy to create, providing different perspectives on form data for separate user groups. Creating a new view is easy; just clone the one you are working with using copy and paste, and add or subtract elements and attributes using the Data Source task pane. You can change the layout and modify other UI features.

Print View Settings

We think that the Story List is the most likely print view, so we've made it the default and used a landscape layout. Figure 14-11 shows the Properties dialog box with the settings, including values for the header and footer text.

Figure 14-11: The Print Setting tab values for the Story List view.

Story List Filter

In the Story List view we want to filter the stories by category using a drop-down control placed above the repeating table containing the stories. Figure 14-12 shows an unfiltered list.

Figure 14-12: The Category filter.

The filter control, which is bound to the `categoryFilter` element, contains a list matching the allowed `category` element `name` attribute values. Here's part of the HTML `select` element in the XSLT for the view:

```
.
.
.
<select class="xdComboBox xdBehavior_Select" title="" size="1"
xd:binding="categoryFilter" xd:boundProp="value" tabIndex="0"
xd:xctname="DropDown" xd:CtrlId="CTRL1" style="WIDTH: 130px">
   <xsl:attribute name="value">
```

```
         <xsl:value-of select="filter_category"/>
    </xsl:attribute>
    <option value="Any">
       <xsl:if test="categoryFilter=&quot;Any...&quot;">
          <xsl:attribute name="selected">selected</xsl:attribute>
       </xsl:if>Any category...
    </option>
    <option value="analysis">
       <xsl:if test="categoryFilter=&quot;analysis&quot;">
          <xsl:attribute name="selected">selected</xsl:attribute>
       </xsl:if>analysis
    </option>
    <option value="biography">
       <xsl:if test="categoryFilter=&quot;biography&quot;">
          <xsl:attribute name="selected">selected</xsl:attribute>
       </xsl:if>biography
    </option>
    <option value="column">
       <xsl:if test="categoryFilter=&quot;column&quot;">
          <xsl:attribute name="selected">selected</xsl:attribute>
       </xsl:if>column
    </option>
      .
      .
      .
</select>
      .
      .
      .
```

Two conditions in the properties of the repeating table set up the relationship between the filter (which is outside the table in the layout) and the table control:

```
categoryFilter   category AND categoryFilter   "Any"
```

A match of the value in the drop-down list with any resource category element in the story hides everything but that category; choosing Any displays all the story data. Part of the repeating table XSLT shows the logic:

```
      .
      .
      .
<tbody style="mso-spreadsheet-section: dynamic" xd:xctname="repeatingtable">
   <xsl:for-each select="meta">
      <tr>
         <xsl:attribute
            name="style">;
            <xsl:choose>
               <xsl:when test="../categoryFilter != category/@name
and ../categoryFilter != &quot;Any&quot;">DISPLAY: none
               </xsl:when>
            </xsl:choose>
         </xsl:attribute>
         <td>
```

```
            <div>
                <xsl:apply-templates select="iconDraft" mode="_1"/>
            </div>
                .
                .
            </td>
        </tr>
    </xsl:for-each>
</tbody>
    .
    .
    .
```

Merging New Stories

The form-merging feature in InfoPath is designed to combine the data from multiple forms into a single form. Microsoft also calls this process "data aggregation'" If merging forms is enabled, users can choose File⇨Merge Forms and select one or more forms (the source) to add to the one that is already open (the target).

When new story meta data arrives from NewsLine contributors, editors will merge or import the new material into their existing forms. Of course, it would be possible for them to use the standard interface provided in InfoPath. However, to meet the NewsLine requirement, you'll also need to update the status value and two dates on all the imported stories.

One way to do this is to use XSLT in a custom merge. Merging can include some or all of the data in the source and target forms. In this case you'll do a simple copy of existing data in the source. Then you'll change the status value to "In Review" and set the receptionTime and the modificationTime.

Making a Custom Transform

The default merging operation works well for forms that are based on the same XML schema. But it is also possible to override the default merge operation, or even merge forms based on different schemas.

To do this, you can create an XSLT script that contains aggregation instructions for the merge. The transform is applied at merge time to create an XML DOM document containing the information to be imported, together with annotations specifying how to incorporate this information into the target document. These annotations are XML attributes with values that serve as aggregation instructions specifying how each node should be merged with the target form.

Because we are merging forms from a single schema, we don't need to follow this approach in much detail. So we'll just briefly note the purpose of these attributes in the agg namespace http://schemas.microsoft.com/office/InfoPath/2003/aggregation.

A full explanation of the use of the attributes and their values with examples are available in the *InfoPath Developer SDK*.

Attribute	Value	Purpose
select		An absolute XPath expression that identifies the target form element.
action	Insert	Inserts the source element as a child of the target element in select.
	Replace	Replaces each of the target elements referred to by the select attribute with the source element.
	mergeAttributes	The attributes of the source element in select are merged with the attributes of each of the target elements.
	Delete	Each of the target elements in select are deleted from the target form.
select child		Provides a way to select a specific location for the insert operation.
order	Before | after (default)	Specifies whether a source element is inserted before or after an existing target element.

Creating the XSLT

From Chapter 4 you'll recall the XSF declarations for importing in the importParameters element. You'll need to make appropriate entries here. The name attribute of the xsf:importSource element contains the form template's name. Usually, you can leave this empty. The schema attribute contains the name of a schema file. The transform attribute contains the name of the transform that you'll use for merging.

```
<xsf:importParameters enabled="yes">
   <xsf:importSource name="" schema="meta1.2.xsd" transform="merge.xsl"/>
</xsf:importParameters>
```

There must also be references in the files section of the form definition file to any custom transform files. Here we show the references to merge.xsl and the included file, date.msxsl.xsl, that handles the date/time value production:

```
<xsf:file name="merge.xsl">
   <xsf:fileProperties>
      <xsf:property name="fileType" type="string" value="resource"/>
   </xsf:fileProperties>
</xsf:file>
<xsf:file name="date.msxsl.xsl">
   <xsf:fileProperties>
      <xsf:property name="fileType" type="string" value="resource"/>
   </xsf:fileProperties>
</xsf:file>
```

When designing your transform, decide whether you want to use merging from XML location paths or merging from InfoPath aggregation instructions. You can start with a simple identity transform that copies all the source data across.

```xml
<?xml version="1.0"?>
<xsl:stylesheet version="1.0" xmlns:xsl="http://www.w3.org/1999/XSL/Transform"
xmlns:agg="http://schemas.microsoft.com/office/infopath/2003/aggregation"
xmlns:target="http://schemas.microsoft.com/office/infopath/2003/aggregation-target"
xmlns:my="http://schemas.microsoft.com/office/infopath/2003/myXSD/2003-05-29T20:30:
47">

  <xsl:template match="/">
      <xsl:copy>
      <xsl:apply-templates select="@* | node()" />
      </xsl:copy>
  </xsl:template>

  <xsl:template match="@* | node()">
      <xsl:copy>
      <xsl:apply-templates select="@* | node()" />
      </xsl:copy>
  </xsl:template>

</xsl:stylesheet>
```

Now you can override the basic transform with templates for the elements that need updating. The status element is straightforward:

```xml
<xsl:template match="status">
    <status>In Review</status>
</xsl:template>
```

Date/time values are a little more complex. Because there are no date-related functions in XSLT 1.0, you'll need to use one of the useful EXSLT recommended extensions to obtain a system value.

We've used the EXSLT dateTime extension developed by Chris Bayes. It employs a function to be used with the Microsoft XSLT engine. To include it, you'll need to make the following additions to the namespace declarations and specify the func:script element. The function date:dateTime always returns a UTC date with the appropriate time zone value.

Then you can call the new function to return a value, and make the updates.

```xml
xmlns:date="http://exslt.org/dates-and-times"
xmlns:func="http://exslt.org/functions"
xmlns:msxsl="urn:schemas-microsoft-com:xslt"
extension-element-prefixes="date msxsl">
    <func:script
    language="exslt:msxsl"
    implements-prefix="date"
    src="date.msxsl.xsl"/>

    <xsl:include href="date.msxsl.xsl"/>
```

```
<xsl:variable name="datetime"
    select="concat(substring(date:dateTime(),1,19),'Z')"/>
    .
    .
    .
<xsl:template match="receptionTime">
    < receptionTime >
        <xsl:value-of select="$datetime"/>
    </ receptionTime >
</xsl:template>
<xsl:template match="modificationTime">
    <modificationTime>
        <xsl:value-of select="$datetime"/>
    </modificationTime>
</xsl:template>
    .
```

Using an XML Data Source

In the last chapter we outlined the structure of the `subject` element and mentioned that it could be populated from an external XML data source. Now you'll see how to go about doing this using a repeating table containing bindings to the `subject` element attributes `type` and `name`.

XSF Structure

Back in Chapters 4 and 5 you looked at the structure of the data adapter entries in the XSF file and some of the ways you can incorporate them in InfoPath forms. The `xmlFileAdapter` element defines a data adapter for retrieving information from an XML data source.

```
<xsf:dataObjects>
    <xsf:dataObject name="topics" schema="topics.xsd" initOnLoad="yes">
        <xsf:query>
            <xsf:xmlFileAdapter fileUrl="topics.xml"/>
        </xsf:query>
    </xsf:dataObject>
</xsf:dataObjects>
```

The Topic Schema

When you select a secondary data source, InfoPath creates a schema file for it and adds appropriate values to the `files` and the `documentSchema` sections of the XSF file. Because we're dealing with a controlled data source, we shouldn't have to be concerned here about whether the data selected is valid. However, it will be important that the values the user selects are validated in the XML application used to create the topics.

Using company and country are a little more specific than `prism:organization` and `prism:location`. NewsLine uses organization for major public bodies and nongovernmental organizations.

Here's the listing for the topic schema. Figure 14-13 shows the content model.

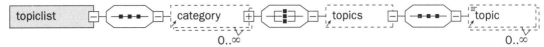

Figure 14-13: The topic schema content model.

```xml
<?xml version="1.0"?>
<xsd:schema xmlns:xsd="http://www.w3.org/2001/XMLSchema">
    <xsd:element name="topiclist">
        <xsd:complexType>
            <xsd:sequence>
                <xsd:element ref="category" minOccurs="0"
maxOccurs="unbounded"></xsd:element>
            </xsd:sequence>
        </xsd:complexType>
    </xsd:element>
    <xsd:element name="topics">
        <xsd:complexType>
            <xsd:sequence>
                <xsd:element ref="topic" minOccurs="0"
maxOccurs="unbounded"></xsd:element>
            </xsd:sequence>
        </xsd:complexType>
    </xsd:element>
    <xsd:element name="topic">
        <xsd:complexType>
            <xsd:simpleContent>
                <xsd:extension base="xsd:string">
                    <xsd:attribute ref="id"></xsd:attribute>
                </xsd:extension>
            </xsd:simpleContent>
        </xsd:complexType>
    </xsd:element>
    <xsd:element name="category">
        <xsd:complexType>
            <xsd:all>
                <xsd:element ref="topics" minOccurs="0" maxOccurs="1"></xsd:element>
            </xsd:all>
            <xsd:attribute ref="Type"></xsd:attribute>
        </xsd:complexType>
    </xsd:element>
    <xsd:attribute name="Type" type="xsd:string"></xsd:attribute>
    <xsd:attribute name="id" type="xsd:string"></xsd:attribute>
</xsd:schema>
```

In the next listing we've shown a partial list of countries from the data maintained by the London desk. You'll recall from the Chapter 12 that PRISM specifies the broad prism:location element for subjects.

We've added ISO 3166 three-letter codes for countries in the id attribute. Possibly the three-figure numeric encoding provided by ISO would be a better choice, as it is apparently more stable—just think of all the relatively recent name changes in former Soviet Union, Eastern Europe, and the Balkans, for example.

```
<topiclist>
    .
    .
    <category Type="Country">
        <topics>
            <topic id="AND">Andorra</topic>
            <topic id="AUT">Austria</topic>
            <topic id="BLR">Belarus</topic>
            <topic id="BEL">Begium</topic>
            <topic id="BIH">Bosnia Herzegowina</topic>
            <topic id="BGR">Bulgaria</topic>
            <topic id="HRV">Croatia</topic>
            <topic id="CYP">Cyprus</topic>
            <topic id="CZE">Czech Republic</topic>
            <topic id="DNK">Denmark</topic>
                .
                .
                .
            <topic id="SWE">Sweden</topic>
            <topic id="CHE">Switzerland</topic>
            <topic id="UKR">Ukraine</topic>
            <topic id="GBR">United Kingdom</topic>
            <topic id="VAT">Vatican</topic>
            <topic id="YUG">Yugoslavia</topic>
        </topics>
    </category>
    .
    .
</topiclist>
```

For industry, we've slightly adapted the top level of the European *Statistical Classification of Economic Activities* (NACE Rev. 1) encoding. It's very similar to the U.S. Census NIACS classification, which you might prefer to use.

```
<category Type="Industry">
    <topics>
        <topic id="A">Agriculture</topic>
        <topic id="F">Construction</topic>
        <topic id="M">Education</topic>
        <topic id="J">Finance</topic>
        <topic id="B">Fishing</topic>
        <topic id="N">Health &amp; Social Work</topic>
        <topic id="H">Hotels &amp; Restaurants</topic>
        <topic id="D">Manufacturing</topic>
        <topic id="C">Mining</topic>
        <topic id="L">Public Administration</topic>
        <topic id="K">Real Estate &amp; Business</topic>
        <topic id="O">Recreation &amp; Membership</topic>
        <topic id="G">Retail &amp; Wholesale</topic>
        <topic id="I">Transportation &amp; Communication</topic>
        <topic id="E">Electricity, Water &amp; Gas</topic>
    </topics>
</category>
```

After this, listing becomes pretty arbitrary. We've simply used some names and events that have appeared in recent news and features (in Europe, as we both live there).

Populating the Subject List

In the Contributor and Desk views the subjects are grouped together in a repeating table. In each table row there are two drop-down lists bound to the subject element type and name attributes. Both lists use the topic list, topics.xml, as a data source. Choosing a subject Type filters the available choices under Name. Figure 14-14 shows the form interface.

Figure 14-14: The subject lists.

When you select a drop-down menu and choose Properties, you'll note that the Data tab contains options for entering the list manually or using a data source. When you click Secondary Data Source, you can browse to locate the XML file. We decided to include topics.xml in the template rather than having to be concerned with deploying multiple files.

Once the file is selected, you can set up values for Entries, Value, and Display name in the Properties dialog box. Entries is an XPath expression to the element you wish to use. In Figure 14-15 we show the values for the Type drop-down list.

Figure 14-15: Data source entries in the Properties dialog box.

You do the same for the name attribute binding, except this time you use /topiclist/topics/topic as the path and choose the topic element.

Now it's time to modify the XSLT in the two views so that the list in the Name drop-down list is filtered by the type attribute value. This is how the control looks initially:

```
<div>
   <select class="xdComboBox xdBehavior_Select" title="" style="WIDTH: 100%"
size="1" xd:binding="@name" xd:CtrlId="CTRL45" xd:xctname="DropDown" value=""
xd:boundProp="value" tabIndex="0">
      <xsl:attribute name="value">
         <xsl:value-of select="@name"/>
      </xsl:attribute>
      <xsl:choose>
         <xsl:when test="function-available('xdXDocument:GetDOM')">
            <option/>
            <xsl:variable name="val" select="@name"/>
```

223

```
                <xsl:for-eachselect="xdXDocument:GetDOM(&quot;topics&quot;)
    /topiclist/category/topics/topic">
                <option>
                    <xsl:attribute name="value">
                        <xsl:value-of select="."/>
                    </xsl:attribute>
                    <xsl:if test="$val=.">
                        <xsl:attribute name="selected">selected</xsl:attribute>
                    </xsl:if>
                    <xsl:value-of select="."/>
                </option>
            </xsl:for-each>
        </xsl:when>
        <xsl:otherwise>
            <option>
                <xsl:value-of select="@name"/>
            </option>
        </xsl:otherwise>
    </xsl:choose>
  </select>
</div>
```

In the example, you need to add the predicate `[@Type=current()/@type]` to the `select` attribute of the `xsl:for each` statement, to act as the filter on the list of topic names.

The `select` attribute now reads as follows:

```
select="xdXDocument:GetDOM(&quot;topics&quot;)/topiclist/category[@Type=current()/@
type]/topics/topic">
```

Preserving XSLT Customization

When you have made a change to an existing XSLT view transform that was generated by InfoPath, and you want to ensure that it can't be subsequently altered by design mode editing of the form, you can protect a form area. As it happens, we haven't protected the formatting in our form, but if you want to you can do it with one of your own projects. Here's how it works.

The key to preserving customization is to use the `mode` attribute on a few XSL elements—`xsl:apply-templates`, and `xsl:template`. The `mode` attribute allows you to switch the processing of an element based on its value. For instance, you might want to output a `url` element as plain text in one case and in another make it the `href` attribute of a link. To do this in the first case, you would use

```
<xsl:apply-templates select="url" mode="plain"/>
```

For the hyperlink you would use

```
<xsl:apply templates select="url" mode="link"/>
```

You would also create two `xsl:template` elements, each with the relevant `mode` attribute setting.

In InfoPath you use the special xd:preserve value for the mode attribute, like this:

```
<xsl:apply-templates select="subjects" mode="xd:preserve"/>
   .
   .
<xsl:template match ="subjects" mode="xd:preserve">
   .
   . some processing in here
   .
</xsl:template>
```

In design mode only, the control or controls in your form are surrounded with a red box with the text Preserve Code Block, as shown in Figure 14-16. The form retains the original appearance and operation when you fill it out.

Preserve Code Block

Figure 14-16: Design mode preserved code.

Adding a Custom Task Pane

In Chapter 11 you covered the basic requirements for creating a custom task pane. Here you work through the process of building a simple help file, a related CSS style sheet, and JScript to add a function to switch views between Desk and Story List.

You'll need to create at least one HTML file for your custom pane. We've opted for a short section for each view with basic guidelines on the use of controls in the view. You might choose XHTML for the help file, as we have. XHTML allows you to extend the vocabulary with other XML elements in a modular way.

Help Text

The structure of the help text is simple:

❑ A heading for each view, followed by a table

❑ The table itemizes the controls on the form and tells the user how to complete them, or how they are completed automatically

❑ Links to other pages

Figure 14-17 shows the help text for the Contributor view task pane.

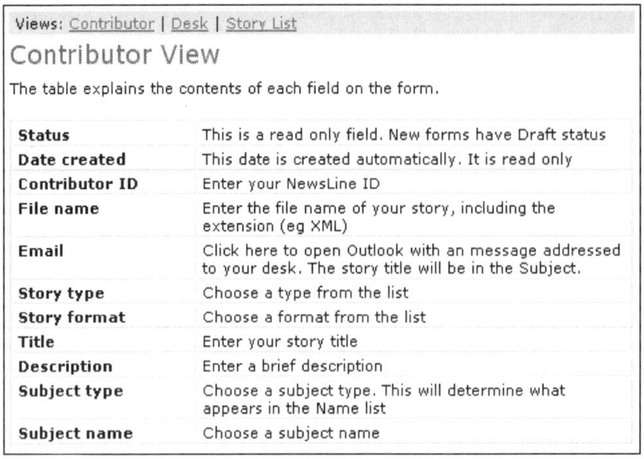

Figure 14-17: Help for the Contributor view.

Here's part of the HTML text for the task pane, taskpane.html. The file contains a small area at the top with links to the script function SwitchView(). There's a <div> element for each help text, only the first of which is initially visible. We've shown the help text for the Contributor view.

```html
<html>
    <head>
        <link href="newsline.css" rel="stylesheet" type="text/css" />
    </head>
    <body onLoad="InitializeTaskPane()">
        <table>
            <tr class="context">
                <td>Views:
                <a href="" onClick="SwitchView(0);return false;">Contributor</a>|
                <a href="" onClick="SwitchView(1);return false;">Desk</a> |
                <a href="" onClick="SwitchView(2);return false;">Story List</a>
                </td>
            </tr>
        </table>
        <div id="Contributor" style="display:block" viewRef="Contributor">
            <h1>Contributor View</h1>
            <p>The table explains the contents of each field on the form.</p>
            <br />
            <table>
                <tr>
                    <th width="30%" valign="top" align="left">Status</th>
                    <td valign="top">This is a read only field. New forms have
Draft status</td>
                </tr>
                <tr>
                    <th valign="top" align="left">Date created</th>
                    <td valign="top">This date is created automatically.
It is read only</td>
                </tr>
                <tr>
                    <th valign="top" align="left">Contributor ID</th>
                    <td valign="top">Enter your NewsLine ID</td>
```

```
            </tr>
            <tr>
                <th valign="top" align="left">File name</th>
                <td valign="top">Enter the file name of your story, including
the extension (eg XML)</td>
            </tr>
            <tr>
                <th valign="top" align="left">Email</th>
                <td valign="top">Click here to open Outlook with a message
addressed to your desk. The story title will be in the Subject.</td>
            </tr>
            <tr>
                <th valign="top" align="left">Story type</th>
                <td valign="top">Choose a type from the list</td>
            </tr>
            <tr>
                <th valign="top" align="left">Story format</th>
                <td valign="top">Choose a format from the list</td>
</tr>
            <tr>
                <th valign="top" align="left">Title</th>
                <td valign="top">Enter your story title</td>
            </tr>
            <tr>
                <th valign="top" align="left">Description</th>
                <td valign="top">Enter a brief description</td>
            </tr>
            <tr>
                <th valign="top" align="left">Subject type</th>
                <td valign="top">Choose a subject type. This will determine
what appears in the Name list</td>
            </tr>
            <tr>
                <th valign="top" align="left">Subject name</th>
                <td valign="top">Choose a subject name</td>
            </tr>
        </table>
    </div>
    <div id="Desk" style="display:none" viewRef="Desk">
     .
     .
     .
    </div>
    <div id="StoryList" style="display:none" viewRef="Story List">
     .
     .
     .
    </div>
   </body>
</html>
```

Switching Views

To switch views, we've adapted an example from the InfoPath SDK. The following script initializes an array of view names. SwitchView hides/shows a view based on the iViewId parameter passed by the onClick event on the help page. It does so by using the external property of the task pane, which returns a reference to the xDocument object associated with the pane, and the object's SwitchView method.

```
<script>
   var gaViewList = new Array()
   var gintCurrentView = 0
   var gstrOriginalURL = window.external.Window.XDocument.Solution.URI.replace
(/.*\/\/\/(.*)\\.*$/, "$1").replace(/%20/g, " ")

   function InitializeTaskPane()
        {
            gaViewList = [Contributor, Desk, StoryList]
            //ContextHeader.innerText = gaViewList[gintCurrentView].headerText
        }

   function SwitchView(iViewId)
        {
            // wrap around to array start
            if (iViewId >= gaViewList.length)
               iViewId = 0

            // hide the old view help
            gaViewList[gintCurrentView].style.display = "none"

            try
            {
            //switch the view
window.external.Window.XDocument.View.SwitchView(gaViewList[iViewId].viewRef)
            }
            catch(ex)
            {
            // in case the view isn't switched yet
               return
            }

            // Show the view help
            gaViewList[iViewId].style.display = "block"

            // Set the new current Id
            gintCurrentView = iViewId
        }
</script>
```

Summary

In this chapter you've seen how we went about implementing the form interface for the case study. It's not the only possible solution, of course, and there are many improvements and changes you could make to enhance the design.

You also looked at how to merge forms with a custom XSLT transform and how to protect your transforms against possible overwriting by InfoPath. Then you learned about making a simple implementation of a custom task pane.

Now you move on to two chapters covering the use of ADO scripting in the meta data application.

15

ADO Scripts for Rates

In this chapter, you see how to use ADO scripts to calculate the payment for each contribution approved by the editor. The computation is based on some input data present in meta document and other information from a local Access database. We also introduce the database structure for rates and other relevant information, the XML source element, and computation scripts needed to calculate the payment amount to the contributor. For completeness, you will see also how to update and complete some information about the contributor and the story when the editor approves the content.

Rating Process

In Chapter 13, you saw how script actions were applied during the publishing process. In this chapter, you investigate payment authorization.

When the editor receives the stories from the contributor and approves them, he or she must calculate the amount due to the contributor based on the extent of content received. As you have seen previously (Chapter 12), the payment approval is started by the editor clicking the Filed button in the Desk view, which invokes a script action, AuthorizePayment.

Filed and spiked are mutually exclusive states, since "spike" effectively stops publication or at least puts it on hold.

The script sets the following data values in the XML document:

❑ Sets the status to Filed

❑ Updates the modificationTime

❑ Completes the creator element: url and byline attributes

❑ Sets the meta/@id and identifier

❑ Completes the payment element

Some data is set and updated directly by the script without requiring additional information, whereas in other cases, such as `payment` element, the computation depends on lookup tables present in the contracts database.

You could invoke the `AuthorizePayment` function in several ways. For example, you could explicitly use a task pane link command or a view button control. You could also intercept the `OnAfterChange` event for the `status` element, so that when it is set to `Filed`, it starts updating and setting the payment values. We've chosen this last approach in this chapter.

Status Update

When the editor finishes the review phase, he or she must decide whether to publish each story or not. We use `OnAfterChange` event, as explained previously, making sure that the script operates differently if the `status` is set to `Spiked` or `Filed`.

Then, the function skeleton is as follows:

```
function msoxd__status::OnAfterChange(eventObj)
{
  if(eventObj.Operation == "Insert" && eventObj.Site.text == "Filed")
  {
   // code here
  }

  if(eventObj.Operation == "Insert" && eventObj.Site.text == "Spiked")
  {
   // code here
  }
}
```

Depending on the status of the story, some action is applied. If the `status` is `Spiked`, you have to update the `modificationTime` element with the current time. This can be done by simply changing the element content for all `meta` elements with `status` equal to `Spiked`:

```
if(eventObj.Operation == "Insert" && eventObj.Site.text == "Embargoed")
{
  var objMetaNodes = XDocument.DOM.selectNodes("//meta");

  for (var i = 0; i < objMetaNodes.length; i++)
  {
   UpdateModificationTime(objMetaNodes.item(i));
  }
}
```

`UpdateModificationTime` is a custom function that selects the `modificationTime` node and sets the current date and time:

```
function UpdateModificationTime(metaNode)
{
 var modTime = metaNode.selectSingleNode("modificationTime");
 modTime.nodeTypedValue = GetCurrentDateTime();
}

function GetCurrentDateTime()
{
 var now = new Date();
 return now.getFullYear() + "-" + (now.getMonth() + 1) + "-" +
   now.getDate() + "T" + now.getHours() + ":" + now.getMinutes() + ":" +
now.getSeconds();
}
```

If the story is accepted (status = Filed), you have to compute more information. Some of these, as you will see later, depend on database content.

Database Meta Data

Most of the changes to the XML data during the approval process depend on database lookup. We decided to use Microsoft Access in this sample.

In Chapter 12 you may have noted the information required to rate the stories sent by contributors. Figure 15-1 shows the meta data model of the database needed for rate calculation and meta model update.

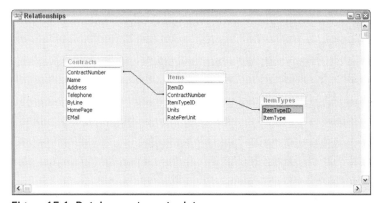

Figure 15-1: Database rate meta data.

The Contracts table contains all the values we need about contributors. Depending on item type, each contract defines the amount per unit. In this way, you have a rate per unit for each item type, and in this case study you have five items for each contract.

Completing the Creator and Identifiers Data

When the editor approves the story, InfoPath must update and complete the following `meta` elements and attributes:

❑ Complete the `creator` element: `url` and `byline` attributes

❑ Set the `meta/@id` and `meta/identifier`

`meta/@id` is calculated as `deskID` concatenated with an auto increment integer saved in a database table. The `meta/identifier` is given by the concatenation of the date, `deskID`, and story file extension (see `meta/content/@file` to get the filename).

Defining Identifiers

The identifiers, `meta/identifier` and `meta/@id`, are subject to a little elaboration. The former is just a concatenation of several elements contained in the `meta` element:

```
function CalculateIdentifier(meta)
{
 var identifier = metaNode.selectSingleNode("identifier");
 var deskID     = metaNode.selectSingleNode("//formHeader/@deskID");
 var file       = metaNode.selectSingleNode("content/@file");
 var date       = metaNode.selectSingleNode("modificationTime");

 // get the file extension
 var ext = file.text.substr(file.text.length - 3);

 // set identifier
 identifier.noteTypedValue = date.text + deskID.text + ext;
}
```

The `meta/@id` content is the result of the concatenation of `deskID` and a unique identifier. A script that uses a database table that stores the last identifier used produces that unique identifier:

```
function GetUniqueID()
{
 // Constants
 adOpenForwardOnly = 0;
 adLockReadOnly = 1;
 adCmdText = 1;

 // db values
 var id;

 try
 {
  // Connection string
  var strConn = "Provider=Microsoft.Jet.OLEDB.4.0;" +
      "Data Source=D:\Documents\Books\InfoPath\Samples\case\DataBase.mdb;" ;
  var objRs = new ActiveXObject("ADODB.Recordset");
```

```
// Command text
var strComm = "SELECT ID FROM IDs";

// Open the connection to database and execute the SQL statement
objRs.Open(strComm, stroConn,adOpenForwardOnly, adLockReadOnly, adCmdText);

// Move to the first (and unique) record
objRs.MoveFirst();

// Load the id
id = objRs("ID");

// Close the recordset
objRs.Close();

// Increment by one
id += 1;

// Command text
var strComm = "UPDATE IDs SET ID = " + id;

// Open the connection to database and execute the SQL statement
objRs.Open(strComm, stroConn,adOpenForwardOnly, adLockReadOnly, adCmdText);
// Close the recordset
objRs.Close();

objRs = null;

return id;
}
catch(e)
{
XDocument.UI.Alert("An error occurred during the rating calculation.");
return 0;
}
}
```

As you can see from the preceding code, you connect to the database table IDs and load the last ID value used, and then you increment by one and update the value's table. The new ID is returned by the function. To complete meta/@id attribute, you need to concatenate the ID created and deskID as follows:

```
function SetId(metaNode)
{
var deskID = metaNode.selectSingleNode("//formHeader/@deskID");
var id     = metaNode.selectSingleNode("@id");
id.nodeTypedValue = deskID + GetUniqueID();
}
```

The code must be applied for each story of the source XML document as shown before:

```
function msoxd__status::OnAfterChange(eventObj)
{
```

233

```
if(eventObj.Operation == "Insert" && eventObj.Site.text == "Filed")
{
 var objMetaNodes = XDocument.DOM.selectNodes("//meta");

 for (var i = 0; i < objMetaNodes.length; i++)
 {
  UpdateModificationTime(objMetaNodes.item(i));
  CalculateIdentifier(objMetaNodes.item(i));
  SetId(objMetaNodes.item(i));
 }
}

if(eventObj.Operation == "Insert" && eventObj.Site.text == "Embargoed")
{
 var objMetaNodes = XDocument.DOM.selectNodes("//meta");

 for (var i = 0; i < objMetaNodes.length; i++)
 {
  UpdateModificationTime(objMetaNodes.item(i));
 }
}
}
```

Completing Creator Data

When the contributor mails his or stories, the contributor provides a user identifier. The editor, during the approval process, needs to convert that information to a url and byline, as specified in Chapter 13. This information is part of the table Contracts and can be recovered through a query:

```
function UpdateCreator(meta)
{
 var creatorID = metaNode.selectSingleNode("creator/@userID");

 // Constants
 adOpenForwardOnly = 0;
 adLockReadOnly = 1;
 adCmdText = 1;

 // db values
 var byline;
 var url;

 try
 {
  // Connection string
  var strConn = "Provider=Microsoft.Jet.OLEDB.4.0;" +
    +Data Source=D:\Documents\Books\InfoPath\Samples\case\DataBase.mdb; ";
  var objRs = new ActiveXObject("ADODB.Recordset");

  // Command text
  var strComm = "SELECT byline, url FROM Contracts WHERE ContractNumber = " +
creatorID;
```

```
    // Open the connection to database and execute the SQL statement
    objRs.Open(strComm, stroConn,adOpenForwardOnly, adLockReadOnly, adCmdText);

    // Move to the first (and unique) record
    objRs.MoveFirst();

    // Load the data
    byline = objRs("byline");
    url = objRs("url");

    // Close the connection
    objRs.Close();
    objRs = null;

    // Update the fields
    metaNode.selectSingleNode("creator/@byline").nodeTypedValue = byline;
    metaNode.selectSingleNode("creator/@url").nodeTypedValue = url;
    }
    catch(e)
    {
    XDocument.UI.Alert("An error occurred during the rating calculation.");
    return 0;
    }
}
```

Since the preceding function must be computed for each story, you have to update the `msoxd__status::OnAfterChange` function as well:

```
function msoxd__status::OnAfterChange(eventObj)
{
 if(eventObj.Operation == "Insert" && eventObj.Site.text == "Filed")
 {
  var objMetaNodes = XDocument.DOM.selectNodes("//meta");

  for (var i = 0; i < objMetaNodes.length; i++)
  {
   UpdateModificationTime(objMetaNodes.item(i));
   UpdateCreator(objMetaNodes.item(i));
  }
 }

 if(eventObj.Operation == "Insert" && eventObj.Site.text == "Embargoed")
 {
  var objMetaNodes = XDocument.DOM.selectNodes("//meta");

  for (var i = 0; i < objMetaNodes.length; i++)
  {
   UpdateModificationTime(objMetaNodes.item(i));
  }
 }
}
```

This way, anytime you modify the status, you get all contributor information correctly set.

Calculating the Payment

Script logic calculates the payment to contributors, using the `extent` and `type` attribute values from the `type` element, together with a database rate. The script then sets the value in the `payment` element. At present, all contributors are paid in U.S. dollars.

The `type` attribute of the `type` element is used to identify the rate per unit from the Item table, and with `type/@extent` you can define how many units to pay. These values in conjunction with the rate per unit (RatePerUnit in Item table) are used for the calculation. For example, if the contributor sends a story containing 1,000 words (then `type` equal to article), the article will be paid 100 U.S. dollars because for each 100 words (Units in Item table) the writer is paid 10 U.S. dollars.

In the script code, you then have to query the database rate by creator ID (`ContractNumber`) and `type` (`ItemType`) and get back `Units` and `RatePerUnit` in order to calculate the payment value. To do so, you can create a JScript function that connects to the Access database, gets the data required depending on the input values, and then closes the connection:

```
function CalculatePaymentAmount(creatorID, type, extent)
{
// Constants
adOpenForwardOnly = 0;
adLockReadOnly = 1;
adCmdText = 1;

// db rate values
var units = 0;
var ratePerUnit = 1;

try
{
// Connection string
var strConn = "Provider=Microsoft.Jet.OLEDB.4.0;" +
   "Data Source=D:\Documents\Books\InfoPath\Samples\case\DataBase.mdb; ";
var objRs = new ActiveXObject("ADODB.Recordset");

// Command text
var strComm = "SELECT Items.Units, Items.RatePerUnit ";
strComm += "FROM (Contracts INNER JOIN Items ON ContractNumber =
Items.ContractNumber) ";
strComm += "INNER JOIN ItemTypes ON Items.ItemTypeID = ItemTypes.ItemTypeID ";
strComm += "WHERE (((Contracts.ContractNumber)=" + creatorID +
") AND ((ItemTypes.ItemType)=" + type + "));";

// Open the connection to database and execute the SQL statement
objRs.Open(strComm, stroConn, adOpenForwardOnly, adLockReadOnly, adCmdText);

// Move to the first (and unique) record
objRs.MoveFirst();

// Load the data
units = objRs("Units");
ratePerUnit = objRs("RatePerUnit");
```

```
 // Close the connection
 objRs.Close();
 objRs = null;
}
catch(e)
{
 XDocument.UI.Alert("An error occurred during the rating calculation.");
 return 0;
}

// Calculate the payment
 return extent / units * ratePerUnit;
}
```

CalculatePaymentAmount requires three parameters as input: creatorID is the author identification number, type is the content category, and extent is the number of units of the preceding type. These elements (and attributes) are selected from the meta node, as you will see later. The payment node gets its value from the CalculatePaymentAmount function as shown previously.

```
function CalculatePayments(metaNode)
{
 var payment   = metaNode.selectSingleNode("payment/@amount");
 var creatorID = metaNode.selectSingleNode("creator/@userID");
 var type      = metaNode.selectSingleNode("type/@type");
 var extent    = metaNode.selectSingleNode("type/@extent");

 payment.nodeTypedValue = CalculatePaymentAmount(creatorID, type, extent);
}
```

CalculatePaymentAmount accepts the meta node currently processed. To process it, you have complete msoxd__status::OnAfterChange function:

```
function msoxd__status::OnAfterChange(eventObj)
{
 if(eventObj.Operation == "Insert" && eventObj.Site.text == "Filed")
 {
  var objMetaNodes = XDocument.DOM.selectNodes("//meta");

  for (var i = 0; i < objMetaNodes.length; i++)
  {
   UpdateModificationTime(objMetaNodes.item(i));
   CalculatePayments(objMetaNodes.item(i));
  }
 }

 if(eventObj.Operation == "Insert" && eventObj.Site.text == "Embargoed")
 {
  var objMetaNodes = XDocument.DOM.selectNodes("//meta");

  for (var i = 0; i < objMetaNodes.length; i++)
  {
   UpdateModificationTime(objMetaNodes.item(i));
  }
 }
}
```

The current payment rating process works only for U.S. dollars. You might want to look ahead to a variant that adopts a multicurrency approach, where you can calculate the payments depending on a currency property in the contracts table.

Summary

In this chapter, you saw how to calculate payments for user contributions. Our approach includes integration with a lookup database, which can be decentralized for small user groups (Microsoft Access), or in other scenario, centralized (Microsoft SQL Server). In either case, the integration is done with scripts implemented in InfoPath and invoked by the editor.

In the next chapter you will see how to post all news stories to the central database to archive them.

16

ADO Scripts for Posting

All news stories are processed by the editor when they come from authors. After the complete processing phase, the editor must persist on a data storage. In previous chapters, you saw how to save and load data into a local database like Microsoft Access. In an enterprise, you normally have a database server such as Microsoft SQL Server. In this chapter, you see how to save all stories to a database like SQL Server.

Persistency Strategy

Software engineering provides several ways to store data in a database. You can, for example, map each XML element to a data table and each leaf node and attribute to a field of the data table. This is obviously not a general solution, since the two data structures, XML and database, are not always comparable on a one-to-one basis. In fact, the XML structure is hierarchical, whereas the database is relational. In our case, we have an exception, since the XML structure adapts very well to the relational one. The only problem is that we have to write a lot of code to save the news.

Another solution consists of saving the whole XML document in a single data table BLOB (Binary Large Object) field. This approach simplifies the programming code to write but involves several complications for searching algorithms used by customers. How do you retrieve all stories of a given category or status? You should open all documents and load inside in order to retrieve the information required.

A possible alternative to the preceding approaches is to have a hybrid solution, then save only sensitive data and the remaining as a BLOB field. In this way, the indexed values are then saved as single field values and the remainder as a single file containing the whole XML story. This is the approach we will pursue in this case study.

Archive Meta Data

One of the most important answers the analyst must provide when talking about data storage is what values must be indexed for further searches. Well, we identified a set of indexed values useful for a complete search engine:

- ❑ meta/@id
- ❑ creator/@userID
- ❑ status
- ❑ category
- ❑ publicationTime
- ❑ subject/@type
- ❑ subject/@name
- ❑ type/@type

With this information required for each story (meta), we can design the database diagram as shown in Figure 16-1.

Figure 16-1 shows a normalized form of database model. The main table is a meta table and contains the following fields definition:

```
CREATE TABLE [dbo].[Meta] (
  [MetaID] [varchar] (10) NOT NULL,
  [ContributorID] [int] NOT NULL ,
  [StatusID] [int] NOT NULL ,
  [CategoryID] [int] NOT NULL ,
  [SubjectTypeID] [int] NOT NULL ,
  [SubjectNameID] [int] NOT NULL ,
  [PublicationTime] [datetime] NOT NULL ,
  [ResourceTypeID] [int] NOT NULL ,
  [WholeStory] [text] NOT NULL
)
```

The MetaID field is taken from the XML document and includes the desk ID. The contributor ID refers to a lookup table that contains all information about the contributors:

```
CREATE TABLE [dbo].[Contributors] (
  [ContributorID] [int] NOT NULL ,
  [FirstName] [varchar] (50)  NOT NULL ,
  [LastName] [varchar] (50)  NOT NULL ,
  [email] [varchar] (100)  NOT NULL,
   // all other contributor fields here
)
```

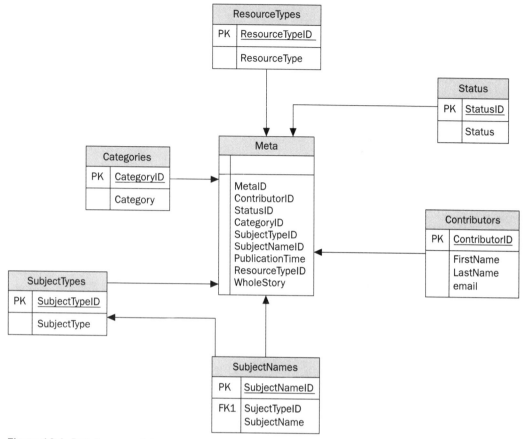

Figure 16-1: Database model.

When the user searches for news about a given contributor, they will search it from the `Contributors` table. The second lookup table is the `Status` one:

```
CREATE TABLE [dbo].[Status] (
  [StatusID] [int] NOT NULL ,
  [Status] [varchar] (10)  NOT NULL
)
```

This second table contains all available statuses of the story: Draft, In Review, Filed, Embargoed, and Spiked. The third table is the resource categories:

```
CREATE TABLE [dbo].[Categories] (
  [CategoryID] [int] NOT NULL ,
  [Category] [varchar] (20)  NULL
)
```

This table contains all possible categories of the resource, such as Analysis, Bulletin, Cartoon, Column, Biography, and so on. `SubjectTypes` and `SubjectNames` are two related lookup tables because for each subject type there is a list of subject names available, as stated in the file `topic.xml` shown in Chapter 13.

Then the table structures are defined as follows:

```
CREATE TABLE [dbo].[SubjectTypes] (
  [SubjectTypeID] [int] NOT NULL ,
  [SubjectType] [varchar] (50)  NOT NULL
)

CREATE TABLE [dbo].[SubjectNames] (
  [SubjectNameID] [int] NOT NULL ,
  [SubjectTypeID] [int] NOT NULL ,
  [SubjectName] [varchar] (50)  NULL
)
```

The last lookup table is the resource type that contains the story types such as Article, Illustration, Photo, Sound, and Video. Its structure is defined as follows:

```
CREATE TABLE [dbo].[ResourceTypes] (
  [ResourceTypeID] [int] NOT NULL ,
  [ResourceType] [varchar] (50)  NOT NULL
)
```

Saving the Stories

Once the meta data of the database is defined, you can write the code to save all stories inside it. As for the database choices, you have several strategies to save XML data into the database. You can use a SQL Server stored procedure that gets the XML document to do everything using OPENXML rowset provider, or you can write all code using ADO.

For portability reasons, we would adopt a saving strategy that is independent of the database server. Then, all code will be written in InfoPath using ADO components. Before you proceed writing code, you have to consider two factors:

❑   Atomicity

❑   Double insert

Suppose that the editor is reviewing five stories and decides to save them on his company database storage. For some reason the third story raises an exception, and the editor tries saving again. If you don't manage that kind of issue, you could find in your database seven stories instead of five, since in the first try, two stories were saved successfully and in the second try all five stories were saved again. To solve this kind of issue, you have to save in a transactional (atomic) connection that guarantees that if one error is raised for any reason, no records are saved to the database. To inhibit a double insert of the same story, before you save, you have to verify that the story isn't already present in the database. If it is, you have to update it.

The saving process is then organized in the manner shown in Figure 16-2.

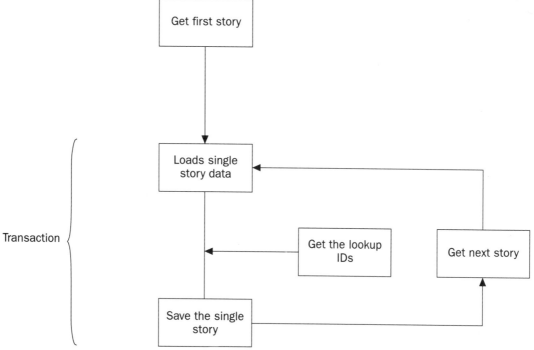

Figure 16-2: Saving process.

Loading and Saving the Stories

The first step of the saving process is to load all stories entered and save them one by one:

```
function Save()
{
 var metaNodes = XDocument.DOM.selectNodes("//meta");
 for(var i = 0; i < metaNodes.length; i++)
  SaveSingleStory(metaNodes.item(i));
}
```

SaveSingleStory is the function that saves a single meta element into the database. Since we must work on a single atomic transaction, we have to open the connection before the cycle starts and close it after all stories are saved:

```
function Save()
{
 var adoCn = null;
 var metaNodes = XDocument.DOM.selectNodes("//meta");

 // Check the node precence
```

```
 if(metaNodes.length > 1)
  return;

 try
 {
  // Connection string
  var strConn = "Provider=SQLOLEDB.1;Integrated Security=SSPI;" +
     "Persist Security Info=False;Initial Catalog=NewsLine;Data Source=.";
  adoCn = new ActiveXObject("ADODB.Connection");

  adoCn.Open(strConn);
  adoCn.BeginTrans();

  for(var i = 0; i < metaNodes.length; i++)
   SaveSingleStory(metaNodes.item(i), adoCn);

  adoCn.CommitTrans();
 }
 catch(e)
 {
  XDocument.UI.Alert("An error occurred during the saving.");
  if(adoCn != null && adoCn.State == 1)
  {
   adoCn.RollbackTrans();
   adoCn.Close();
  }
 }
}
```

When the connection is opened, a new transaction starts. Then, all database operations done with that connection object are under the same transaction. If one of the operations fails, the rollback is invoked and no operations are persisted. If all saving proceeds correctly, the transaction is then committed.

Saving a Story

SaveSingleStory is the function that saves a single story into the database. Before that, you must collect all indexed values with the correct identifier:

```
function SaveSingleStory(meta, cn)
{
 var metaID = meta.selectSingleNode("@id").text;
 var creatorID = meta.selectSingleNode("creator/@userID").text;
 var status = meta.selectSingleNode("status").text;
 var category = meta.selectSingleNode("category/@name").text;
 var pubTime = meta.selectSingleNode("publicationTime");
 var type = meta.selectSingleNode("type/@type").text;

 // code continue...
}
```

If all values are valid, you can proceed in getting the correct lookup IDs. To do so, you have to implement some functions that get the id from the database. For example, to get the id of the status, you can query the Status table as follows:

```
function getStatusID(status)
{
 var adoCn = null;
 var id = 0;
 try
 {
  // Connection string
  var strConn = "Provider=SQLOLEDB.1;Integrated Security=SSPI;" +
     "Persist Security Info=False;Initial Catalog=NewsLine;Data Source=.";
  adoCn = new ActiveXObject("ADODB.Connection");
  var adoCmd = new ActiveXObject("ADODB.Command");

  adoCmd.CommandText = "SELECT StatusID FROM Status WHERE Status = '" + status +
"'";
  adoCmd.CommandType = 1; //adCmdText

  adoCn.Open(strConn);
  adoCmd.ActiveConnection = adoCn;

  var rs = adoCmd.Execute();
  rs.MoveFirst();
  id = rs("StatusID");
 }
 catch(e)
 {
  if(adoCn != null && adoCn.State == 1)
   adoCn.Close();
  throw e;
 }

 return id;
}
```

By the way, you can ensure that all lookup IDs query the lookup data tables the same way. Once you have collected all IDs, you can check to see whether or not the meta data has been saved already:

```
function IsMetaPresent(metaID, cn)
{
 var present = false;

 try
 {
  var adoCmd = new ActiveXObject("ADODB.Command");

  adoCmd.CommandText = "SELECT COUNT(MetaID) AS NR FROM Meta WHERE MetaID = '" +
     metaID + "'";
  adoCmd.CommandType = 1; //adCmdText
  adoCmd.ActiveConnection = cn;

  var rs = adoCmd.Execute();
  rs.MoveFirst();
  if(rs("NR") > 0)
   present = true;
 }
```

```
catch(e)
{
 throw e;
}

return present;
}
```

If the preceding function returns `false`, that `meta` ID isn't present in the data table and you can save it. Otherwise, you can only update the record with new information. The new story is inserted into the `meta` table with an `insert` SQL statement:

```
function NewMeta(metaID, contributorID, statusID, categoryID, subjectTypeID,
    subjectNameID, publicationTime, resourceTypeID, meta, cn)
{
 try
 {
  var adoCmd = new ActiveXObject("ADODB.Command");

  adoCmd.CommandText = "INSERT INTO Meta VALUES( '" + metaID + "', " +
    contributorID + "," + statusID + "," + categoryID + "," + subjectTypeID + "," +
    subjectNameID + ",'" + publicationTime + "'," + resourceTypeID + ",'" + meta   +
"')";
  adoCmd.CommandType = 1; //adCmdText
  adoCmd.ActiveConnection = cn;

  adoCmd.Execute();
 }
 catch(e)
 {
  throw e;
 }
}
```

If the story is already present, you have to update the record content:

```
function UpdateMeta(metaID, contributorID, statusID, categoryID, subjectTypeID,
    subjectNameID, publicationTime, resourceTypeID, meta, cn)
{
 try
 {
  var adoCmd = new ActiveXObject("ADODB.Command");

  adoCmd.CommandText = "UPDATE Meta SET ContributorID = " +
    contributorID + ", StatusID = " + statusID + ", CategoryID = " + categoryID +
    ", SubjectTypeID = " + subjectTypeID + ", SubjectNameID = " +
    subjectNameID + ", PublicationTime = '" + publicationTime + "', ResourceTypeID =
" +
    resourceTypeID + ", WholeStory = '" + meta   + "'" +
    " WHERE MetaID = '" + metaID + "'";
  adoCmd.CommandType = 1; //adCmdText
  adoCmd.ActiveConnection = cn;
```

```
    adoCmd.Execute();
    }
    catch(e)
    {
      throw e;
    }
  }
```

As a final step, you can complete the `SaveSingleStory` function:

```
function SaveSingleStory(meta, cn)
{
 var metaID = meta.selectSingleNode("@id").text;
 var creatorID = meta.selectSingleNode("creator/@userID").text;
 var status = meta.selectSingleNode("status").text;
 var category = meta.selectSingleNode("category/@name").text;
 var pubTime = meta.selectSingleNode("publicationTime");
 var type = meta.selectSingleNode("type/@type").text;

 var statusID = getStatusID(status);
 var contributorID = getContributorID(creatorID);
 var categoryID = getStatusID(category);
 var subjectTypeID = getStatusID(subjectType);
 var subjectNameID = getStatusID(subjectName);
 var resourceTypeID = getResourceType(resourceType);

 if(IsMetaPresent(metaID, cn))
  UpdateMeta(metaID, contributorID, statusID, categoryID, subjectTypeID,
     subjectNameID, pubTime, resourceTypeID, meta.xml, cn);
 else
  NewMeta(metaID, contributorID, statusID, categoryID, subjectTypeID,
     subjectNameID, pubTime, resourceTypeID, meta.xml, cn);
}
```

Summary

In this chapter you saw how to save all stories into a database using ADO objects from InfoPath scripts. The database model (meta data) has been designed considering the breakpoint between the flexibility of the search engine and writing as few lines of code as possible. This is the choice of the authors, and you can make any variations you choose.

In the next chapter you see how to merge the NewsLine data to Excel.

17

Output Data Structures

In Chapter 13 you analyzed the input data structures for the NewsLine application. Now its time to look into the output data structures and transforms needed to push your InfoPath meta data to Excel, to RSS news feeds, and to the NewsLine customer Web site.

First we've included a brief digression into the new XML features in Excel 2003. If you are already completely familiar with XML lists, the mapping interface and procedures, and importing and exporting XML, you can skip this section.

Next you'll look into the Excel export data schema and how to map the output on to the payment analysis spreadsheet. To wind up the case study, you'll consider a modular structure that will support both the RSS output for the news feed and the XML/RDF archived and delivered as HTML in the customer interface.

XML in Excel

If you have used Office XP, you'll be aware that you can open and save Excel spreadsheets in an XML vocabulary designed specifically for Excel, now called SpreadsheetML. This format opened up access to other programs and made it easier to create Excel spreadsheets.

Excel 2003 allows you to work with other XML vocabularies. You can use XML schemas of your own design with a workbook and map the schema elements to Excel objects. The mappings can then be used to import data files conforming to the schema and to write XML data using save or export functions.

Excel now uses three separate namespaces for spreadsheet elements. We're mainly interested in the x2 namespace, which covers mapping in Excel 2003.

- ❑   ss   XML Spreadsheet 2002 namespace `urn:schemas-microsoft-com:office:spreadsheet`

- ❑   x   XML Spreadsheet 2000 namespace `urn:schemas-microsoft-com:office:excel`

- ❑   x2   XML Spreadsheet 2003 namespace `urn:schemas-microsoft-com:office:excel2`

Excel 2003 does not support the following XML schema constructs:

- ❑   `xsd:any`

- ❑   `xsd:anyAttribute`

- ❑   `abstract` and `substitutionGroup` attributes on elements and types

Recursive elements are supported, but only to *one* level.

XML Maps

XML maps are objects created by Excel each time you add an external XML schema to a workbook. A map describes the relationship between schema objects and spreadsheet locations.

Mapping allows a spreadsheet to exist independently of the underlying data and separates the data in a workbook from its presentation. The data remains ready to be consumed by any number of other systems that understand XML.

A workbook can support multiple maps, all of which have distinct names. One reason you might want to use two maps is when the data to import belongs to one schema and the calculated results (for export) need to be in a different vocabulary. Another is that you might wish to import separate series of data at different times on to separate sheets in the same workbook, using a single schema.

The XML Maps dialog box allows you to define new mappings by adding, removing, and renaming schemas. See Figure 17-1.

You create this mapping in a similar way to InfoPath. The XML Source task pane displays the data source, and you can drag schema objects onto the spreadsheet. See Figure 17-2.

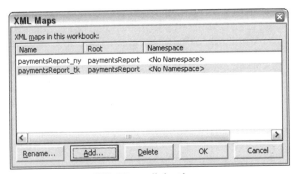

Figure 17-1: The XML Maps dialog box.

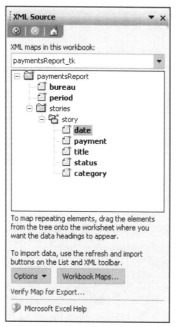

Figure 17-2: The XML Source
task pane.

Lists

Lists are a new feature in Excel that bring more structure to a range in a worksheet. Lists have distinct columns, column headings, and an insert row for adding more data. XML lists are those where a column is related to an element in an XML map. These lists are created automatically when you drag a repeating element onto a worksheet. The List toolbar, shown in Figure 17-3, includes buttons for import, export, charting, and map properties commands.

Figure 17-3: The List and XML toolbar.

Mapped Cells

As well as mapping repeating elements to a column, you can map a nonrepeating element to an individual XML mapped cell. This is the preferred way to handle single occurring items in an XML data source. You might want to do this to place an author, title, and date at the top of a report, for example.

In Figure 17-4, the values at C4 and C5 are mapped cells, while the range B13-F19 contains XML lists. Cell B20 shows an asterisk, indicating the insert row. Note that the total row (C21-F21) is contained within the lists range. It automatically moves down to accommodate added rows. Optional properties for totals cells include total (D21) and count (F21). Each cell in the header row (B13-F13) contains a drop-down list with sort options.

	A	B	C	D	E	F	G
1							
2		**Contributor Payments**					
3							
4		Bureau	New York				
5		Period	2003-11-05				
6							
7		Budget	$5,000.00				
8			$3,055.00				
9		Difference	$1,945.00				
10							
11		Average	$509.17				
12							
13		Identifier ▾	Date ▾	Payment ▾	Status ▾	Category ▾	
14		ny1234	10/10/2003	800	Filed	Feature	
15		ny1235	10/10/2003	420	Embargoed	Review	
16		ny1236	10/10/2003	300	Draft	Bulletin	
17		ny1237	11/10/2003	625	Filed	Opinion	
18		ny1238	11/10/2003	420	Embargoed	Review	
19		ny1239	11/10/2003	490	Draft	Column	
20		*					
21		Total ▾		3055		6	
22							

Figure 17-4: XML list and mapped cell.

Denormalized Data

The XML features in Excel 2003 are, naturally enough, optimized for tabular data. The team at Microsoft aimed to make it possible for users to import data from as wide a range of sources as possible, even if they could not always export it again.

The looser the XML structure, and the more inconsistent the data, the less likely it is a candidate for viewing or processing in a spreadsheet. You could end up with very sparse tables in extreme cases.

If you map a repeating element onto a column, and these elements are associated with single instances of other data, Excel will by default "denormalize" the data set by repeating the single-instance data for each row in the XML list. Excel can import the XML, and "fill down" the date and desk across all titles, but it can't round-trip the information by exporting it through the same schema.

If the data looks like this:

```
<paymentsReport>
    <bureau>New York</bureau>
    <period>2003-11-05</period>
    <stories>
        <story>
            <identifier>ny1234</identifier>
            <date>2003-10-10</date>
            <payment>800.00</payment>
            <status>Filed</status>
```

```
            <category>Feature</category>
        </story>
        <story>
            <identifier>ny1235</identifier>
            <date>2003-10-10</date>
            <payment>420.00</payment>
            <status>Embargoed</status>
            <category>Review</category>
        </story>
        <story>
            <identifier>ny1236</identifier>
            <date>2003-10-10</date>
            <payment>300.00</payment>
            <status>Draft</status>
            <category>Bulletin</category>
        </story>
    </stories>
</paymentsReport>
```

Excel will render a denormalized listing like the one in Figure 17-5 if the file is imported with default settings.

	A	B	C	D	E	F	G
1	bureau	period	identifier	date	payment	status	category
2	New York	05/11/2003	ny1234	10/10/2003	800	Filed	Feature
3	New York	05/11/2003	ny1235	10/10/2003	420	Embargoed	Review
4	New York	05/11/2003	ny1236	10/10/2003	300	Draft	Bulletin

Figure 17-5: A denormalized listing.

The same issue arises if there is a hierarchy of lists within lists in the mapping—for example, multiple title elements each containing multiple subjects.

So if you want to be able to import and export identical data structures, you have two options. You either need to do some denormalizing before you import the data or (better) avoid the default behavior by creating mapped cells for all the single-instance data, as we illustrated in Figure 17-4.

XML Map Schema

The structure for the mapping of XML elements is defined in the XML Spreadsheet Schema (XMLSS). In this section we present an outline of this structure and focus on the Field element mapping. For a more detailed explanation you should read the documentation in both the *Excel XML Toolkit* and *Microsoft Office 2003 XML Schema References*. You can obtain the schema references at the following URL:

www.microsoft.com/downloads/details.aspx?FamilyId=FE118952-3547-420A-A412-00A2662442D9&displaylang=en

Each singly mapped cell or table is represented by an Entry element. One or more Entry elements are grouped together to form a Map. One or more Map elements may appear within the MapInfo element, which in turn occurs within the top-level Workbook element of the XMLSS file after all other child elements within the Workbook. The Schema element contains the related schema. The content model is in Figure 17-6.

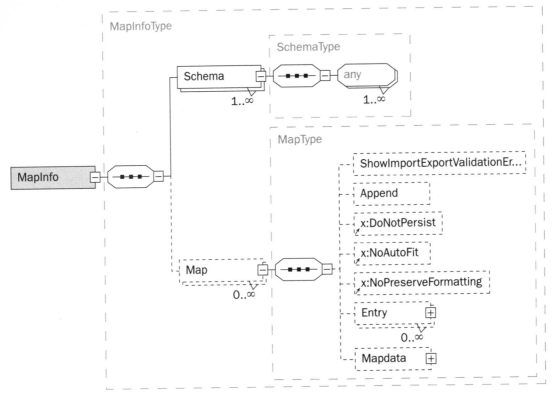

Figure 17-6: The `MapInfo` **content model.**

Within the `Entry` element, much of the content is concerned with positioning or the view of data on the spreadsheet. The `Field` element is the one holding the mapping to your imported schema, and we'll concentrate on that.

There must be at least one `Field` element containing the mapping for a single value, or a repeating element.

`Aggregate` specifies the aggregate type for a column, such as Average, Sum, or Count, if there is a totals row for the field.

The optional `AutoFilterColumn` element persists sort and filter information related to a column.

`Cell` defines the style, formula, or default value for the mapped cell. In formulas, Excel uses the R1C1 rather than the A1 notation for cell references.

`DataValidation` specifies the validation that should be performed whenever data is entered in the cell by a user.

`Range` contains a relative reference to the first value (table) or only absolute reference (single cell) for a field. Again, RC notation is used.

XPath is an expression relative to Entry/XPath used to retrieve data from nodes in the underlying XML document. If an XPath is specified, the XSDType of the value pointed to should also be present.

See Figure 17-7 for the content model.

Object Model

You can use the Excel VBA object model to add schemas to a workbook, map a schema to a sheet, import and export data, and find data and ranges with XPath expressions. There isn't space here to go into the XML OM in any detail, but since we're focused here on importing data, we'll review the import methods of the Workbook class.

You can use the OpenXML method when loading data from a file into a workbook. This is the programmatic equivalent of using Open from the File menu to open an XML file in Excel. The following table lists the different options for opening XML files in Excel and their purpose.

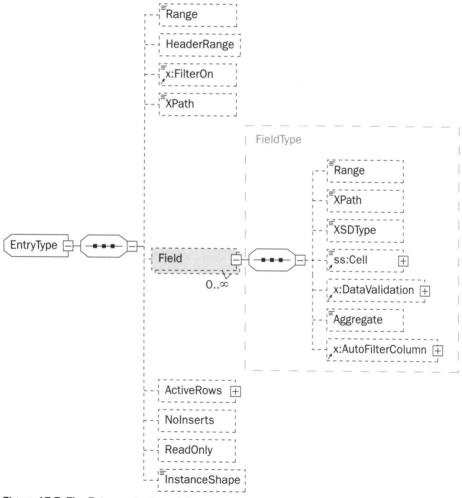

Figure 17-7: The Entry content model.

Option	Purpose
xlXmlLoadImportToList	Load the data from the source file into an XML list.
xlXmlLoadMapXml	Create an XML map based on the data in the source file.
xlXmlLoadOpenXml	Load the data from the source file as a new workbook.
xlXmlLoadPromptUser	Prompt the user with a dialog box for choosing one of the other three options.

Importing XML is different in that, rather than opening an XML file as a separate workbook, Excel places the data in an existing workbook, either creating a worksheet or creating an XML list in an existing one.

The XMLImport method specifies a URL as the source for the XML This method accepts four parameters, detailed in the following table.

Parameter	Description
URL	A string that refers to the URL target that hosts the XML data (required).
XMLMap	An instance of the XMLMap class. In other words, if the workbook already has an XML map in place, you can use that map. If you want Excel to create a map automatically when the import occurs, then pass Nothing as the parameter (required).
Overwrite	A boolean value that indicates whether or not the newly imported data should overwrite existing data (optional).
Destination	A reference to the cell range where the imported is placed in a worksheet (optional).

The last method, XMLImportXML, is similar to XMLImport, except that instead of importing data based on a URL, the method accepts the actual data string as its first parameter. All other parameters are the same.

Payments Analysis

InfoPath provides a standard UI method for exporting forms to Excel. This will meet many basic requirements.

Excel's default behavior is to load the XML file into a new workbook, in a single table with the top left at A1. This is definitely not what we want for the NewsLine data. We need a well-designed template, and we want to map our values rather than getting the denormalization Excel would otherwise impose.

Export Schema

For the Excel export schema, you'll want to select a subset of the information contained in a resource listing. NewsLine managers are probably not going to be interested in the details of contributors, titles, and most of the other meta data. However, they might want to do some simple analysis of bureau performance against budget and be able to pin down the contribution that different story categories make to costs.

Our proposed solution allows the editor-in-chief at each bureau to export daily payments listings that can be cumulated by management to view against a weekly budget. This arrangement also has potential for interbureau comparisons at a company-wide level.

Here's the schema. Figure 17-8 shows the content model.

```xml
<?xml version="1.0" encoding="UTF-8"?>
<xsd:schema xmlns:xs="http://www.w3.org/2001/XMLSchema"
elementFormDefault="qualified" attributeFormDefault="unqualified">
    <xsd:element name="paymentsReport">
        <xsd:complexType>
            <xsd:sequence>
                <xsd:element ref="bureau"/>
                <xsd:element ref="period"/>
                <xsd:element ref="stories"/>
            </xsd:sequence>
        </xsd:complexType>
    </xsd:element>
    <xsd:element name="bureau" type="xsd:string"/>
    <xsd:element name="period" type="xsd:date"/>
    <xsd:element name="stories">
        <xsd:complexType>
            <xsd:sequence maxOccurs="unbounded">
                <xsd:element ref="story"/>
            </xsd:sequence>
        </xsd:complexType>
    </xsd:element>
    <xsd:element name="story">
        <xsd:complexType>
            <xsd:sequence>
                <xsd:element ref="identifier"/>
                <xsd:element ref="date"/>
                <xsd:element ref="payment"/>
                <xsd:element ref="status"/>
                <xsd:element ref="category"/>
            </xsd:sequence>
        </xsd:complexType>
    </xsd:element>
    <xsd:element name="identifier">
        <xsd:simpleType>
            <xsd:restriction base="xsd:string">
                <xsd:length value="6"/>
```

```
        </xsd:restriction>
      </xsd:simpleType>
    </xsd:element>
    <xsd:element name="date" type="xsd:date"/>
    <xsd:element name="payment">
      <xsd:simpleType>
        <xsd:restriction base="xsd:decimal">
          <xsd:fractionDigits value="2"/>
        </xsd:restriction>
      </xsd:simpleType>
    </xsd:element>
    <xsd:element name="status" type="xsd:string"/>
    <xsd:element name="category" type="xsd:string"/>
  </xsd:schema>
```

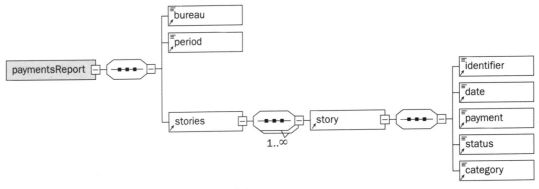

Figure 17-8: The paymentsReport content model.

Export Transform

The payments report export transform loops through the daily resource list, selecting the data subset needed to populate new XML files. Here we truncate the values for identifier and publicationTime elements to clarify the output. The status element is there so that payments on spiked and embargoed stories can be identified, and category allows managers to analyze costs by story type.

```
<?xml version="1.0" encoding="UTF-8"?>
<xsl:stylesheet version="1.0" xmlns:xsl="http://www.w3.org/1999/XSL/Transform" >
  <xsl:output method="xml"/>
  <xsl:template match="resourceList">
    <paymentsReport>
      <bureau>
        <xsl:value-of select="formHeader/@deskName"/>
      </bureau>
      <period>
        <xsl:value-of select="formHeader/@period"/>
      </period>
```

```
            <stories>
            <xsl:for-each select="meta">
                    <xsl:apply-templates select="."/>
                    <xsl:sort select="publicationTime"/>
            </xsl:for-each>
            </stories>
        </paymentsReport>
    </xsl:template>
    <xsl:template match="meta">
        <xsl:variable name="date" select="substring(publicationTime,1,10)"/>
        <xsl:variable name="id" select="substring(identifier,10,6)"/>
        <story>
            <date>
               <xsl:value-of select="$date"/>
            </date>
            <identifier><xsl:value-of select="$id"/></identifier>
            <payment><xsl:value-of select="payment/@amount"/></payment>
            <status><xsl:value-of select="status"/></status>
            <category><xsl:value-of select="category"/></category>
        </story>
    </xsl:template>
</xsl:stylesheet>
```

In this transform and in those for RSS and archive output, you'll probably note that there's something missing: a method of expressing the output result tree as a document URL. This is because there is no standard method of doing so in XSLT 1.0. Several XSLT processors have extension elements. For example, the Saxon processor uses the `saxon:output` element (or `xsl:document` if you specify XSLT1.1 in the namespace declaration).

XSLT 2.0 is now an advanced Working Draft, and we'll soon have the `xsl:result-document` element to use consistently on all processors supporting the standard. In the meantime you'll need to use the function provided by your favorite XSLT tool.

You saw an XML export instance earlier. Here's a fragment again:

```
<paymentsReport>
    <bureau>New York</bureau>
    <period>2003-11-05</period>
    <stories>
        <story>
            <identifier>ny1234</identifier>
            <date>2003-10-10</date>
            <payment>800.00</payment>
            <status>Filed</status>
            <category>Feature</category>
        </story>
          .
          .
    </stories>
</paymentsReport>
```

Importing the Data

Now it's time to map the schema onto a cell in a spreadsheet and import the data. First, you'll step through the process manually using the Excel interface. Then you'll consider the options for using VBA and the Excel object model to automate the import actions.

Manual Import

You'll need the following files from the folder for this chapter:

- ☐ Template   ny_unmapped.xls
- ☐ Examples   ny_mapped.xls and ny_imported.xls
- ☐ Schema   paymentsReport.xsd
- ☐ Two files to import   day1.xml and day2.xml

The first step in mapping is to import the schema.

1. Open the template ny_unmapped.xls.

2. Choose File⇨Save As ny_test.xls to preserve the template in its original state.

3. Choose Data⇨XML⇨XML Source to display the XML Source pane, and click the XML Maps button.

4. In the XML Maps dialog box, click Add and select paymentsReport.xsd. Excel opens the Multiple Roots dialog box. Select the paymentsReport element and click OK.

5. Back in the XML Maps dialog box, click Rename, and rename the map as paymentsReport_ny. Now close the dialog box. The schema is displayed in the Source pane, and the List and XML toolbar pops up.

6. Select the story element and drag it onto the cell marked Identifier. The nested elements are dragged with their parent and form a set of XML lists.

7. Now drag the bureau and period elements next to the labels at the top of the sheet. These are now mapped cells.

8. At the bottom of the XML Source pane, click Verify Map for Export. You should get an alert confirming that the map is exportable. Your sheet should look something like ny_mapped.xls.

Before you import any data, you'll need to set up some map properties to allow your user to append data to the sheet (as distinct from replacing it):

1. Choose Data⇨XML⇨Map Properties to show the Properties dialog box.

2. In the options section at the bottom of the dialog box, choose Append new data to existing XML lists.

3. Check all the other options and click OK.

Now you can import the two data files:

1. Choose Data⇨XML⇨Import, and import day1.xml. This is an example of one day's input for a bureau. The data appears in the XML lists and mapped cells.

2. Click anywhere in an XML list and click the Toggle Total Row button in the List toolbar. This adds a total row to the lists.

3. In the drop-down list in the totals cell at the bottom of the Payments column, choose Sum to show the total.

Now you can use any available Excel features to work with the figures. We've chosen to do a simple comparison between payments and budget, with a figure to show an average for any category.

To add power to the spreadsheet, you might choose to create additional maps for data from the other bureaus. Using similar layouts on separate tabs, you could map to additional XML lists and graph inter-bureau comparisons. As a final touch you might define a new schema to export the comparative information to the company intranet.

Using the Excel Object Model

The Excel OM provides three import methods from the Workbook class to get XML data into a spreadsheet:

❑   OpenXML loads data from a file into a workbook and is equivalent to using File⇨Open to open an XML file, with its attendant disadvantages.

❑   XMLImportXML accepts an XML data string value and imports it.

❑   XMLImport is closest to the approach we took with the manual process, and we've chosen it for our example.

XMLImport accepts four parameters, detailed in the following table, and returns XlXmlImportResult.

Parameter	Type	Use	Description
URL	String	Required	A reference to the URL source of the XML data.
ImportMap	XMLMap	Required	A reference to an existing map. If you want to create a map automatically when the import occurs, then pass "Nothing" as the parameter.
Overwrite	Boolean	Optional	If destination is not specified, Overwrite determines whether the imported data should overwrite existing data or be appended to it. This corresponds to the setting in the XML Map Properties dialog box. The default is True.
Destination	Range	Optional	Refers to the top left of the cell range where the XML lists are placed. For obvious reasons you should not pass this parameter in cases where a map already exists.

To start the import process, you might place a button associated with a VBA macro on a sheet.

This example imports a data file into a sheet that already contains a map and appends the data. Excel places it in the mapped XML list. Because you specified the existing XML map when calling ImportXML, you do not need to worry about where the data is dropped. The value xmlData is an absolute path, so you will need to modify it to suit your file location. The sample file is ny_import_om.xls.

```
Private Sub importPayments_Click()
    Dim xmlData As String
    Dim paymentMap As XmlMap
    Set paymentMap = ThisWorkbook.XmlMaps("paymentsReport_ny")
    On Error Resume Next
    xmlData = "D:\infopath\project2\code\excel\day1.xml"
    ThisWorkbook.XmlImport xmlData, paymentMap, False
    If Err.Number = 0 Then
        MsgBox "Data from " & xmlData & " was successfully imported"
    Else
        MsgBox "There was an error importing" & xmlData
    End If
End Sub
```

There is an interesting range of XML-related objects and methods in the OM, which we haven't space to explore here. We encourage you to use them to improve on this simple example and to learn about the structure of the Excel mapping interface.

RSS News Feed

NewsLine has decided to structure the customer view of RSS feeds by news desk, reckoning that most of their initial customer take-up will come from local time zones. The update frequency of the feeds is every eight hours, and the information in a feed cumulates for 24 hours, after which a daily archive is available.

XML Data to RSS

Here's an instance of an RSS 1.0 news feed of NewsLine stories, based on the proposed PRISM module you saw in Chapter 12. Because the meta data schema design has been informed by these standards, you haven't too much of a task to transform the data using XSLT. (If you skimmed the details of PRISM and RDF, you might want to revisit that chapter for an explanation of the RSS structure and vocabulary details.)

To keep the listing manageable, we've first shown the root rdf:RDF element and the channel element and its partial contents, with only a few items for the London desk feed. Most of the channel informa-tion is boilerplate, except for the rdf:about attribute of the channel element, where the URI of the channel is specific for each desk, and for the items listed in identifier sequence as rdf:li elements.

```
<?xml version="1.0" encoding="utf-8"?>
<rdf:RDF
    xmlns:rdf="http://www.w3.org/1999/02/22-rdf-syntax-ns#"
    xmlns="http://purl.org/rss/1.0/"
    xmlns:dc="http://purl.org/dc/elements/1.1/"
    xmlns:prism="http://prismstandard.org/namespaces/1.2/basic/">
<channel rdf:about=" http://newsline.net/rss_ln/rss.xml">
    <title>NewsLine London</title>
    <description>Your daily summary of the latest news and features from
NewLine London, with cumulative updates every eight hours, from our
European central desk.</description>
    <link>http://www.newsline/rss/rss.xml</link>
    <dc:publisher>NewsLine Inc</dc:publisher>
    <dc:language>en</dc:language>
    <prism:copyright>Copyright (C) 2003 NewsLine Inc</prism:copyright>
    <prism:publicationName>NewsLine Today</prism:publicationName>
    <prism:issn>0991-0645</prism:issn>
    <items>
        <rdf:Seq>
            <rdf:li rdf:resource="http://newsline.net/20031010_ln1235_xml"/>
            <rdf:li rdf:resource="http://newsline.net/20031010_ln1236_xml"/>
            <rdf:li rdf:resource="http://newsline.net/20031010_ln1237_xml"/>
            .
            .
        </rdf:Seq>
    </items>
</channel>
 <item rdf:about="http://newsline.net/20031010_ln1235_xml">
    .
    .
</item>
    .
    .
</rdf:RDF>
```

When it comes to the `item` element structure, there's a good deal of overlap with what's needed for the story archive. Here's an item instance:

```
<item rdf:about="http://newsline.net/20031010_ln1235_xml">
    <prism:publicationTime>2003-10-10T17:18:22</prism:publicationTime>
    <dc:identifier>20031010_ln1235_xml</dc:identifier>
    <dc:title>Blair defies Iraq critics in defiant conference speech</dc:title>
    <dc:creator>Martin Foley</dc:creator>
    <dc:description>At today's Labour Party conference UK prime minister
Tony Blair was resolute in his defence of government policy over the war in
Iraq.</dc:description>
    <dc:format>text/xml</dc:format>
    <dc:type>Article</dc:type>
    <prism:category>Feature</prism:category>
    <prism:person>Tony Blair</prism:person>
    <prism:event>Labour Party Conference 2003</prism:event>
    <prism:location>United Kingdom</prism:location>
</item>
```

RSS Transform

The data source for the feed is a copy of the aggregated meta data maintained by a desk editor. So the XSLT processing is basically similar to the Excel export process. The difference is in the selection and naming of elements and attributes.

First, you'll want to think through ways of making the transform easy to maintain. We did this in two ways in our example. One is to separate the variable information from script that applies to all transforms regardless of news desk origin. If anything changes for a particular desk, it will be easy to quickly modify the script. The second is to include some core meta data processing so that we can reuse it to create archive output.

This is the main transform:

```
<xsl:stylesheet version="1.0"
xmlns:xsl="http://www.w3.org/1999/XSL/Transform"
xmlns:dc="http://purl.org/dc/elements/1.1/"
xmlns:prism="http://prismstandard.org/namespaces/1.2/basic/"

xmlns:pcv="http://prismstandard.org/namespaces/pcv/1.2/"
xmlns:rdf="http://www.w3.org/1999/02/22-rdf-syntax-ns#">
    <xsl:include href="rss_variables.xsl"/>

    <xsl:include href="core_meta.xsl"/>
    <xsl:output method="xml"/>
    <xsl:variable name="date"
select="substring(resourceList/formHeader/@period,1,4)"/>
    <xsl:template match="/">
        <rdf:RDF xmlns:rdf="http://www.w3.org/1999/02/22-rdf-syntax-ns#"
xmlns="http://purl.org/rss/1.0/" xmlns:dc="http://purl.org/dc/elements/1.1/"
xmlns:prism="http://prismstandard.org/namespaces/1.2/basic/"

xmlns:sy="http://purl.org/rss/1.0/modules/syndication/">
        <channel>
            <xsl:attribute name="rdf:about"/>
            <xsl:value-of select="$deskURL"/>
            <title>
                <xsl:value-of select="$publication"/>
            </title>
            <description>Your daily summary of the latest news and
features
from <xsl:value-of select="$publication"/>, with cumulative updates every
eight hours, from our European central desk.</description>

            <sy:updatePeriod>hourly</sy:updatePeriod>
            <sy:updateFrequency>8</sy:updateFrequency>
            <sy:updateBase>2000-01-01T00:00Z</sy:updateBase>
            <link>
                <xsl:value-of select="$deskURL"/>
            </link>
            <dc:publisher>
                <xsl:value-of select="$publisher"/>
```

```
                    </dc:publisher>
                    <dc:language>eng</dc:language>
                    <prism:copyright>
                        <xsl:value-of select="concat('Copyright &#x00A9; ',$date,'
 ',$publisher)"/>
                    </prism:copyright>
                    <prism:publicationName>
                        <xsl:value-of select="$publication"/>
                    </prism:publicationName>
                    <prism:issn>
                        <xsl:value-of select="$issn"/>
                    </prism:issn>
                    <items>
                        <rdf:Seq>
                            <xsl:for-each select="//meta">
                                <xsl:sort select="identifier"/>
                                <rdf:li>
                                    <xsl:attribute name="rdf:resource">
                                        <xsl:value-of select=
                                        "concat($publisherURL,'/',identifier)"/>
                                    </xsl:attribute>

                                </rdf:li>
                            </xsl:for-each>
                        </rdf:Seq>
                    </items>
                </channel>
                <xsl:for-each select="//meta">
                    <xsl:sort select="identifier"/>
                    <xsl:apply-templates select="."/>
                </xsl:for-each>
            </rdf:RDF>
        </xsl:template>
    </xsl:stylesheet>
```

The file rss_variables.xsl uses xsl:variable to set values, but you could just as easily use an xsl:parameter element instead.

```
    <?xml version="1.0" encoding="UTF-8"?>
    <xsl:stylesheet version="1.0" xmlns:xsl="http://www.w3.org/1999/XSL/Transform">
        <!-- publisher URL -->
        <xsl:variable name="publisherURL">http://newsline.net</xsl:variable>
        <!-- publisher -->
        <xsl:variable name="publisher">NewsLine Inc</xsl:variable>
        <!-- desk URL-->
        <xsl:variable name="deskURL">http://newsline.net/rss_ln/rss.xml</xsl:variable>
        <!-- publication name -->
        <xsl:variable name="publication">NewsLine London</xsl:variable>
        <!-- ISSN -->
        <xsl:variable name="issn">0991-0645</xsl:variable>
    </xsl:stylesheet>
```

Our second include contains all the code to transform the meta element and its children. The processing is straightforward. Worth a note are the tests for status and rights, and the switch in element names for country and company. Also of interest is the use of some terms in the pcv namespace inside dc:creator, to preserve the details of a contributor's byline and the url of his or her Web page.

```xml
<?xml version="1.0" encoding="UTF-8"?>
<xsl:stylesheet version="1.0"
    xmlns:xsl="http://www.w3.org/1999/XSL/Transform"
    xmlns:dc="http://purl.org/dc/elements/1.1/"
    xmlns:prism="http://prismstandard.org/namespaces/1.2/basic/"
    xmlns:pcv="http://prismstandard.org/namespaces/pcv/1.2/"
    xmlns:rdf="http://www.w3.org/1999/02/22-rdf-syntax-ns#">
    <xsl:template match="meta">
        <item>
            <xsl:attribute name="rdf:about"><xsl:value-of
select="concat($publisherURL,'/',identifier)"/></xsl:attribute>

            <prism:publicationName>
                <xsl:value-of select="$publication"/>
            </prism:publicationName>
            <prism:publicationTime>
                <xsl:value-of select="publicationTime"/>
            </prism:publicationTime>
            <xsl:if test="status='Embargoed'">
                <prism:releaseTime>
                    <xsl:value-of select="releaseTime"/>
                </prism:releaseTime>
            </xsl:if>
            <xsl:choose>
                <xsl:when test="rights/copyright">
                    <prism:copyright>
<xsl:value-of select="concat('Copyright &#x00A9; ',$date,
                    ' ' ,rights/copyright)"/>

                    </prism:copyright>
                </xsl:when>
                <xsl:otherwise>
                    <prism:rightsAgent>
                        <xsl:value-of select="rights/rightsAgent"/>
                    </prism:rightsAgent>
                </xsl:otherwise>
            </xsl:choose>
            <link>
                <xsl:value-of select="identifier"/>
            </link>
            <dc:title>
                <xsl:value-of select="title"/>
            </dc:title>
            <dc:creator>
                <pcv:Descriptor>
                    <xsl:attribute name="rdf:about">
                        <xsl:value-of select="creator/@url"/>
                    </xsl:attribute>
                    <pcv:label>
```

```
                    <xsl:value-of select="creator/@byline"/>
                </pcv:label>
            </pcv:Descriptor>
        </dc:creator>
        <dc:description>
            <xsl:value-of select="description"/>
        </dc:description>
        <dc:format>
            <xsl:value-of select="format/@type"/>
        </dc:format>
        <dc:type>
            <xsl:value-of select="type/@type"/>
        </dc:type>
        <prism:category>
            <xsl:value-of select="category"/>
        </prism:category>
        <xsl:for-each select="subject/person">
            <prism:person>
                <xsl:value-of select="."/>
            </prism:person>
        </xsl:for-each>
        <xsl:for-each select="subject/event">
            <prism:event>
                <xsl:value-of select="."/>
            </prism:event>
        </xsl:for-each>
        <xsl:for-each select="subject/country">
            <prism:location>
                <xsl:value-of select="."/>
            </prism:location>
        </xsl:for-each>
        <xsl:for-each select="subject/organization | company">
            <prism:organization>
<xsl:value-of select="."/>
            </prism:organization>
        </xsl:for-each>
        <xsl:for-each select="subject/industry">
            <prism:industry>
                <xsl:value-of select="."/>
            </prism:industry>
        </xsl:for-each>
    </item>
  </xsl:template>
</xsl:stylesheet>
```

Archive Outputs

Our meta data archive design, as you'll recall from Chapter 16, involves storing quite a bit of XML data as a binary object and providing a number of keys for customer queries. A well-designed query on these keys should allow you to effectively reconstruct selections of the form data. This means that you can use RSS transforms similar to rss_feed.xsl as the basis for processes designed to handle archive data. Alternatively, with one or more transforms to HTML, you could output the results to standard sections of the NewsLine Web site, like finance or politics.

This case study isn't planned to get into the issues of how to handle other aspects of post-processing the meta data. However, we'll suggest one approach, without attempting to provide working code, that should get you thinking about possibilities.

If you're familiar with ASP.NET, you've probably had occasion to use the XSLTransform object to perform transforms on XML files on disk or on data stored in the XMLDocument object.

XMLTransform has two relevant methods, shown in the following table, which we'll illustrate.

Method	Description
Load	Loads the specifies XSL style sheet with any xsl:include or xsl:import declarations
Transform	Transforms the XML data using the loaded style sheet

Here, we'll assume you've constructed some core code for the Active Server Pages for the user interface, and to access the archive on SQL Server 2000 using the SQLXML feature. This feature allows you to pull a query result into an XMLTextReader object, using the ExecuteXmlReader method. Then you read the result to initialize the reader and append the remainder to a string that holds the XML output.

```
'define connection, select, and result string objects
.
.
.
Dim oCommand as New SqlCommand (strSelect, oConnect)
oXTReader = oCommand.ExecuteXmlReader()
oTXReader.Read()
oResultStr.append(oTXReader.GetRemainder().ReadToEnd())
.
.
'close the connection and other objects
```

The following example contains the code fragments for implementing a transform to RSS 1.0. Doing the transform requires just a few steps. First, define a transform object and an XSL path variable; then load the XSL. Now transform the XML with the output specified by strRSSPath.

```
.
.
Dim oTransform As New XslTransform()
Dim strXSLPath As string
strXSLPath = "\newsline\xslt\rss_archive.xsl"

oTransform.Load(strXSLPath)
oTransform.Transform(oResultStr,strRSSPath)
.
.
```

Summary

By now you should have some ideas about the potential for exporting data from InfoPath to external processes using XSLT and especially about the opportunities offered by integration with Excel. You've also seen how, with careful planning, you can use the semantics built into your schema to drive a variety of transforms, with plenty of flexibility.

This chapter winds up your work with the case study, and indeed everything else, apart from the reference sections in the appendixes. We've found that working with InfoPath and writing this book has been an interesting and stimulating journey. We hope that we've helped give you a head start with the newest tool in the Microsoft Office bag of tricks and that you'll enjoy plenty of success developing with InfoPath.

InfoPath XSF Schema

This is the XML schema for the Microsoft InfoPath 2003 form definition file. The schema is reproduced from the version of sd.xsd created December 4, 2003, at 22:44:26. Please read the legal notice that follows.

Legal Notice

Permission to copy, display and distribute the contents of this document (the "Specification"), in any medium for any purpose without fee or royalty is hereby granted, provided that you include the following notice on ALL copies of the Specification, or portions thereof, that you make:

Copyright © Microsoft Corporation. All rights reserved. Permission to copy, display and distribute this document is available at:

```
http://msdn.microsoft.com/library/en-us/odcXMLRef/html/odcXMLRefLegalNotice
.asp?frame=true.
```

No right to create modifications or derivatives of this Specification is granted herein.

There is a separate patent license available to parties interested in implementing software programs that can read and write files that conform to the Specification. This patent license is available at this location:

```
http://www.microsoft.com/mscorp/ip/format/xmlpatentlicense.asp.
```

THE SPECIFICATION IS PROVIDED "AS IS" AND MICROSOFT MAKES NO REPRESENTATIONS OR WARRANTIES, EXPRESS OR IMPLIED, INCLUDING, BUT NOT LIMITED TO, WARRANTIES OF MERCHANTABILITY, FITNESS FOR A PARTICULAR PURPOSE, NONINFRINGEMENT, OR TITLE; THAT THE CONTENTS OF THE SPECIFICATION ARE SUITABLE FOR ANY PURPOSE; NOR THAT THE IMPLEMENTATION OF SUCH CONTENTS WILL NOT INFRINGE ANY THIRD PARTY PATENTS, COPYRIGHTS, TRADEMARKS OR OTHER RIGHTS.

```xml
<?xml version="1.0" encoding="UTF-8" ?>
<xsd:schema xmlns:xsd="http://www.w3.org/2001/XMLSchema"
xmlns:xsf="http://schemas.microsoft.com/office/infopath/2003/solutionDefinition"
targetNamespace="http://schemas.microsoft.com/office/infopath/2003/solutionDefiniti
on" elementFormDefault="qualified" attributeFormDefault="unqualified">
    <!-- xdTitle type -->
    <xsd:simpleType name="xdTitle">
        <xsd:restriction base="xsd:string">
            <xsd:minLength value="1" />
            <xsd:maxLength value="255" />
            <xsd:pattern
value="([^\p{Z}\p{Cc}\p{Cf}\p{Cn}])(([^\p{Zl}\p{Zp}\p{Cc}])*([^\p{Z}\p{Cc}\p{Cf}\
p{Cn}]))?" />
        </xsd:restriction>
    </xsd:simpleType>
    <!-- xdViewName type -->
    <xsd:simpleType name="xdViewName">
        <xsd:restriction base="xsd:string">
            <xsd:minLength value="1" />
            <xsd:maxLength value="255" />
            <xsd:pattern
value="([^\p{Z}\p{C}/\\#&amp;&quot;&gt;&lt;])(([^\p{Zl}\p{Zp}\p{C}/\\#&amp;&quot;
&gt;&lt;])*([^\p{Z}\p{C}/\\#&amp;&quot;&gt;&lt;]))?" />
        </xsd:restriction>
    </xsd:simpleType>
    <!-- xdYesNo type -->
    <xsd:simpleType name="xdYesNo">
        <xsd:restriction base="xsd:NMTOKEN">
            <xsd:enumeration value="yes" />
            <xsd:enumeration value="no" />
        </xsd:restriction>
    </xsd:simpleType>
    <!-- xdFileName type -->
    <xsd:simpleType name="xdFileName">
        <xsd:restriction base="xsd:string">
            <xsd:minLength value="1" />
            <xsd:maxLength value="64" />
        </xsd:restriction>
    </xsd:simpleType>
    <!-- xdScriptLanguage type -->
    <xsd:simpleType name="xdScriptLanguage">
        <xsd:restriction base="xsd:NMTOKEN">
            <xsd:pattern
value="((([Jj][Aa][Vv][Aa])|([Jj])|([Vv][Bb]))([Ss][Cc][Rr][Ii][Pp][Tt]))" />
```

```xml
            </xsd:restriction>
        </xsd:simpleType>
        <!-- xdSolutionVersion type -->
        <xsd:simpleType name="xdSolutionVersion">
            <xsd:restriction base="xsd:string">
                <xsd:pattern value="(([0-9]{1,4}.){3}[0-9]{1,4})" />
            </xsd:restriction>
        </xsd:simpleType>
        <!-- xdEmptyString type -->
        <xsd:simpleType name="xdEmptyString">
            <xsd:restriction base="xsd:string">
                <xsd:maxLength value="0" />
            </xsd:restriction>
        </xsd:simpleType>

        <!-- xdErrorMessage type -->
        <xsd:simpleType name="xdErrorMessage">
            <xsd:restriction base="xsd:string">
                <xsd:maxLength value="1023" />
            </xsd:restriction>
        </xsd:simpleType>

        <!-- xDocumentClass -->
        <xsd:element name="xDocumentClass">
            <xsd:complexType>
                <xsd:all>
                    <xsd:element ref="xsf:package" minOccurs="1" />
                    <xsd:element ref="xsf:views" minOccurs="1" />
                    <xsd:element ref="xsf:scripts" minOccurs="0" />
                    <xsd:element ref="xsf:schemaErrorMessages" minOccurs="0" />
                    <xsd:element ref="xsf:documentSchemas" minOccurs="0" />
                    <xsd:element ref="xsf:applicationParameters" minOccurs="0" />
                    <xsd:element ref="xsf:fileNew" minOccurs="0" />
                    <xsd:element ref="xsf:customValidation" minOccurs="0" />
                    <xsd:element ref="xsf:domEventHandlers" minOccurs="0" />
                    <xsd:element ref="xsf:importParameters" minOccurs="0" />
                    <xsd:element ref="xsf:listProperties" minOccurs="0" />
                    <xsd:element ref="xsf:taskpane" minOccurs="0" />
                    <xsd:element ref="xsf:documentSignatures" minOccurs="0" />
                    <xsd:element ref="xsf:dataObjects" minOccurs="0" />
                    <xsd:element ref="xsf:query" minOccurs="0" />
                    <xsd:element ref="xsf:submit" minOccurs="0" />
                    <xsd:element ref="xsf:documentVersionUpgrade" minOccurs="0" />
                    <xsd:element ref="xsf:extensions" minOccurs="0" />
                </xsd:all>
                <xsd:attribute name="name" type="xsd:string" use="optional" />
                <xsd:attribute name="author" type="xsd:string" use="optional" />
                <xsd:attribute name="description" use="optional">
                    <xsd:simpleType>
                        <xsd:restriction base="xsd:string">
                            <xsd:maxLength value="255" />
                        </xsd:restriction>
                    </xsd:simpleType>
                </xsd:attribute>
```

```
            <xsd:attribute name="solutionVersion" type="xsf:xdSolutionVersion"
use="optional" />
            <xsd:attribute name="productVersion" type="xsd:string" use="optional" />
            <xsd:attribute name="solutionFormatVersion" type="xsf:xdSolutionVersion"
use="required" />
            <xsd:attribute name="dataFormSolution" type="xsf:xdYesNo" use="optional" />
            <xsd:attribute name="requireFullTrust" type="xsf:xdYesNo" use="optional" />
            <xsd:attribute name="publishUrl" type="xsd:string" use="optional" />
        </xsd:complexType>
    </xsd:element>
    <!-- UIContainer -->
    <xsd:group name="UIContainer">
        <xsd:choice>
            <xsd:element ref="xsf:toolbar" />
            <xsd:element ref="xsf:menu" />
            <xsd:element ref="xsf:menuArea" />
        </xsd:choice>
    </xsd:group>
    <!-- schemaErrorMessages -->
    <xsd:element name="schemaErrorMessages">
        <xsd:complexType>
            <xsd:sequence>
                <xsd:element ref="xsf:override" minOccurs="0" maxOccurs="unbounded" />
            </xsd:sequence>
        </xsd:complexType>
    </xsd:element>
    <!-- override -->
    <xsd:element name="override">
        <xsd:complexType>
            <xsd:sequence>
                <xsd:element ref="xsf:errorMessage" />
            </xsd:sequence>
            <xsd:attribute name="match" type="xsd:string" use="required" />
        </xsd:complexType>
    </xsd:element>
    <!-- applicationParameters-->
    <xsd:element name="applicationParameters">
        <xsd:complexType>
            <xsd:all>
                <xsd:element ref="xsf:solutionProperties" minOccurs="0" />
            </xsd:all>
            <xsd:attribute name="application" use="required">
                <xsd:simpleType>
                    <xsd:restriction base="xsd:string">
                        <xsd:enumeration value="InfoPath Design Mode" />
                    </xsd:restriction>
                </xsd:simpleType>
            </xsd:attribute>
        </xsd:complexType>
    </xsd:element>
    <!-- solutionProperties -->
    <xsd:element name="solutionProperties">
        <xsd:complexType>
            <xsd:attribute name="allowCustomization" type="xsf:xdYesNo" use="optional" />
            <xsd:attribute name="lastOpenView" use="optional" />
```

```
              <xsd:attribute name="scriptLanguage" type="xsf:xdScriptLanguage"
use="optional" />
              <xsd:attribute name="automaticallyCreateNodes" type="xsf:xdYesNo"
use="optional" />
              <xsd:attribute name="lastVersionNeedingTransform"
type="xsf:xdSolutionVersion" use="optional" />
              <xsd:attribute name="fullyEditableNamespace" type="xsd:anyURI"
use="optional" />
        </xsd:complexType>
    </xsd:element>
    <!-- dbInfo -->
    <xsd:element name="query">
        <xsd:complexType>
            <xsd:choice>
                <xsd:element ref="xsf:adoAdapter" />
                <xsd:element ref="xsf:webServiceAdapter" />
                <xsd:element ref="xsf:xmlFileAdapter" />
            </xsd:choice>
        </xsd:complexType>
    </xsd:element>
    <!-- scripts -->
    <xsd:element name="scripts">
        <xsd:complexType>
            <xsd:sequence>
                <xsd:element ref="xsf:script" minOccurs="0" maxOccurs="unbounded" />
            </xsd:sequence>
            <xsd:attribute name="language" type="xsf:xdScriptLanguage" use="required" />
        </xsd:complexType>
    </xsd:element>
    <xsd:element name="script">
        <xsd:complexType>
            <xsd:attribute name="src" type="xsf:xdFileName" use="required" />
        </xsd:complexType>
    </xsd:element>
    <!-- docObjects -->
    <xsd:element name="dataObjects">
        <xsd:complexType>
            <xsd:choice minOccurs="0" maxOccurs="unbounded">
                <xsd:element ref="xsf:dataObject" />
            </xsd:choice>
        </xsd:complexType>
    </xsd:element>
    <xsd:element name="dataObject">
        <xsd:complexType>
            <xsd:choice>
                <xsd:element ref="xsf:query" />
            </xsd:choice>
            <xsd:attribute name="name" type="xsf:xdTitle" use="required" />
            <xsd:attribute name="schema" type="xsd:string" use="optional" />
            <xsd:attribute name="initOnLoad" type="xsf:xdYesNo" use="optional" />
        </xsd:complexType>
    </xsd:element>
    <xsd:element name="adoAdapter">
        <xsd:complexType>
```

```xml
                <xsd:attribute name="name" type="xsd:string" use="optional" />
                <xsd:attribute name="connectionString" type="xsd:string" use="required" />
                <xsd:attribute name="commandText" type="xsd:string" use="required" />
                <xsd:attribute name="queryAllowed" type="xsf:xdYesNo" use="optional" />
                <xsd:attribute name="submitAllowed" type="xsf:xdYesNo" use="optional" />
            </xsd:complexType>
        </xsd:element>
        <xsd:element name="webServiceAdapter">
            <xsd:complexType>
                <xsd:choice>
                    <xsd:element ref="xsf:operation" />
                </xsd:choice>
                <xsd:attribute name="name" type="xsd:string" use="optional" />
                <xsd:attribute name="wsdlUrl" type="xsd:string" use="required" />
                <xsd:attribute name="queryAllowed" type="xsf:xdYesNo" use="optional" />
                <xsd:attribute name="submitAllowed" type="xsf:xdYesNo" use="optional" />
            </xsd:complexType>
        </xsd:element>
        <xsd:element name="operation">
            <xsd:complexType>
                <xsd:choice>
                    <xsd:element ref="xsf:input" minOccurs="0" />
                </xsd:choice>
                <xsd:attribute name="name" type="xsd:string" use="required" />
                <xsd:attribute name="soapAction" type="xsd:string" use="required" />
                <xsd:attribute name="serviceUrl" type="xsd:string" use="required" />
            </xsd:complexType>
        </xsd:element>
        <xsd:element name="input">
            <xsd:complexType>
                <xsd:choice minOccurs="0" maxOccurs="unbounded">
                    <xsd:element ref="xsf:partFragment" />
                </xsd:choice>
                <xsd:attribute name="source" type="xsd:string" use="required" />
            </xsd:complexType>
        </xsd:element>
        <xsd:element name="partFragment">
            <xsd:complexType>
                <xsd:attribute name="match" type="xsd:string" use="required" />
                <xsd:attribute name="replaceWith" type="xsd:string" use="required" />
            </xsd:complexType>
        </xsd:element>
        <xsd:element name="xmlFileAdapter">
            <xsd:complexType>
                <xsd:attribute name="name" type="xsd:string" use="optional" />
                <xsd:attribute name="fileUrl" type="xsd:anyURI" use="required" />
            </xsd:complexType>
        </xsd:element>
        <!-- documentSchemas -->
        <xsd:element name="documentSchemas">
            <xsd:complexType>
                <xsd:sequence>
                    <xsd:element ref="xsf:documentSchema" maxOccurs="unbounded" />
                </xsd:sequence>
```

```
                </xsd:complexType>
            </xsd:element>
            <xsd:element name="documentSchema">
                <xsd:complexType>
                    <xsd:attribute name="location" type="xsd:string" use="required" />
                    <xsd:attribute name="rootSchema" type="xsf:xdYesNo" />
                </xsd:complexType>
            </xsd:element>
            <!-- customValidation -->
            <xsd:element name="customValidation">
                <xsd:complexType>
                    <xsd:sequence>
                        <xsd:element ref="xsf:errorCondition" minOccurs="0"
maxOccurs="unbounded" />
                    </xsd:sequence>
                </xsd:complexType>
            </xsd:element>
            <xsd:element name="errorCondition">
                <xsd:complexType>
                    <xsd:sequence>
                        <xsd:element ref="xsf:errorMessage" />
                    </xsd:sequence>
                    <xsd:attribute name="match" type="xsd:string" use="required" />
                    <xsd:attribute name="expression" type="xsd:string" use="required" />
                    <xsd:attribute name="expressionContext" type="xsd:string" use="optional" />
                    <xsd:attribute name="showErrorOn" type="xsd:string" use="optional" />
                </xsd:complexType>
            </xsd:element>
            <xsd:element name="errorMessage">
                <xsd:complexType>
                    <xsd:simpleContent>
                        <xsd:extension base="xsf:xdErrorMessage">
                            <xsd:attribute name="type" use="optional">
                                <xsd:simpleType>
                                    <xsd:restriction base="xsd:NMTOKEN">
                                        <xsd:enumeration value="modal" />
                                        <xsd:enumeration value="modeless" />
                                    </xsd:restriction>
                                </xsd:simpleType>
                            </xsd:attribute>
                            <xsd:attribute name="shortMessage" use="required" >
                                <xsd:simpleType>
                                    <xsd:restriction base="xsd:string">
                                        <xsd:maxLength value="127" />
                                    </xsd:restriction>
                                </xsd:simpleType>
                            </xsd:attribute>
                        </xsd:extension>
                    </xsd:simpleContent>
                </xsd:complexType>
            </xsd:element>
            <!-- domEventHandlers -->
            <xsd:element name="domEventHandlers">
                <xsd:complexType>
```

```xsd
            <xsd:sequence>
                <xsd:element ref="xsf:domEventHandler" minOccurs="0"
maxOccurs="unbounded" />
            </xsd:sequence>
        </xsd:complexType>
    </xsd:element>
    <xsd:element name="domEventHandler">
        <xsd:complexType>
            <xsd:attribute name="match" type="xsd:string" use="required" />
            <xsd:attribute name="handlerObject" type="xsd:string" use="required" />
        </xsd:complexType>
    </xsd:element>
    <!-- importParameters -->
    <xsd:element name="importParameters">
        <xsd:complexType>
            <xsd:sequence>
                <xsd:element ref="xsf:importSource" minOccurs="0" maxOccurs="unbounded" />
            </xsd:sequence>
            <xsd:attribute name="enabled" type="xsf:xdYesNo" use="required" />
        </xsd:complexType>
    </xsd:element>
    <xsd:element name="importSource">
        <xsd:complexType>
            <xsd:attribute name="name" type="xsd:string" use="required" />
            <xsd:attribute name="schema" type="xsf:xdFileName" use="required" />
            <xsd:attribute name="transform" type="xsf:xdFileName" use="required" />
        </xsd:complexType>
    </xsd:element>
    <!-- listProperties -->
    <xsd:element name="listProperties">
        <xsd:complexType>
            <xsd:all>
                <xsd:element ref="xsf:fields" />
            </xsd:all>
        </xsd:complexType>
    </xsd:element>
    <xsd:element name="fields">
        <xsd:complexType>
            <xsd:sequence>
                <xsd:element ref="xsf:field" minOccurs="0" maxOccurs="unbounded" />
            </xsd:sequence>
        </xsd:complexType>
    </xsd:element>
    <xsd:element name="field">
        <xsd:complexType>
            <xsd:attribute name="type" type="xsd:NMTOKEN" use="required" />
            <xsd:attribute name="name" type="xsf:xdTitle" use="required" />
            <xsd:attribute name="columnName" type="xsf:xdTitle" use="required" />
            <xsd:attribute name="required" type="xsf:xdYesNo" use="optional" />
            <xsd:attribute name="viewable" type="xsf:xdYesNo" use="optional" />
            <xsd:attribute name="node" type="xsd:string" use="required" />
            <xsd:attribute name="maxLength" type="xsd:byte" />
            <xsd:attribute name="aggregation" use="optional">
                <xsd:simpleType>
```

```
                <xsd:restriction base="xsd:NMTOKEN">
                    <xsd:enumeration value="sum" />
                    <xsd:enumeration value="count" />
                    <xsd:enumeration value="average" />
                    <xsd:enumeration value="min" />
                    <xsd:enumeration value="max" />
                    <xsd:enumeration value="first" />
                    <xsd:enumeration value="last" />
                    <xsd:enumeration value="merge" />
                    <xsd:enumeration value="plaintext" />
                </xsd:restriction>
            </xsd:simpleType>
        </xsd:attribute>
    </xsd:complexType>
</xsd:element>
<xsd:element name="submit">
    <xsd:complexType>
        <xsd:all>
            <xsd:element ref="xsf:useHttpHandler" minOccurs="0" />
            <xsd:element ref="xsf:useScriptHandler" minOccurs="0" />
            <xsd:element ref="xsf:useQueryAdapter" minOccurs="0" />
            <xsd:element ref="xsf:webServiceAdapter" minOccurs="0" />
            <xsd:element name="successMessage" type="xsd:string" minOccurs="0" />
            <xsd:element name="errorMessage" type="xsd:string" minOccurs="0" />
        </xsd:all>
        <xsd:attribute name="caption" type="xsd:string" use="optional" />
        <xsd:attribute name="onAfterSubmit" use="optional">
            <xsd:simpleType>
                <xsd:restriction base="xsd:NMTOKEN">
                    <xsd:enumeration value="close" />
                    <xsd:enumeration value="keepOpen" />
                    <xsd:enumeration value="openNew" />
                </xsd:restriction>
            </xsd:simpleType>
        </xsd:attribute>
        <xsd:attribute name="showStatusDialog" type="xsf:xdYesNo" use="optional" />
        <xsd:attribute name="showSignatureReminder" type="xsf:xdYesNo"
use="optional" />
        <xsd:attribute name="disableMenuItem" type="xsf:xdYesNo" use="optional" />
    </xsd:complexType>
</xsd:element>
<xsd:element name="useHttpHandler">
    <xsd:complexType>
        <xsd:attribute name="method" use="required">
            <xsd:simpleType>
                <xsd:restriction base="xsd:NMTOKEN">
                    <xsd:enumeration value="POST" />
                </xsd:restriction>
            </xsd:simpleType>
        </xsd:attribute>
        <xsd:attribute name="href" type="xsd:anyURI" use="required" />
    </xsd:complexType>
</xsd:element>
<xsd:element name="useScriptHandler"></xsd:element>
```

```
<xsd:element name="useQueryAdapter">
    <xsd:complexType></xsd:complexType>
</xsd:element>
<!-- fileNew -->
<xsd:element name="fileNew">
    <xsd:complexType>
        <xsd:sequence>
            <xsd:element ref="xsf:initialXmlDocument" />
        </xsd:sequence>
    </xsd:complexType>
</xsd:element>
<xsd:element name="initialXmlDocument">
    <xsd:complexType>
        <xsd:attribute name="caption" type="xsf:xdTitle"
use="required"></xsd:attribute>
        <xsd:attribute name="href" type="xsf:xdFileName" use="required" />
    </xsd:complexType>
</xsd:element>
<!-- package -->
<xsd:element name="package">
    <xsd:complexType>
        <xsd:sequence>
            <xsd:element ref="xsf:files" />
        </xsd:sequence>
    </xsd:complexType>
</xsd:element>
<xsd:element name="files">
    <xsd:complexType>
        <xsd:sequence>
            <xsd:element ref="xsf:file" minOccurs="0" maxOccurs="unbounded" />
        </xsd:sequence>
    </xsd:complexType>
</xsd:element>
<xsd:element name="file">
    <xsd:complexType>
        <xsd:sequence>
            <xsd:element ref="xsf:fileProperties" minOccurs="0" maxOccurs="1" />
        </xsd:sequence>
        <xsd:attribute name="name" type="xsf:xdFileName" use="required" />
    </xsd:complexType>
</xsd:element>
<xsd:element name="fileProperties">
    <xsd:complexType>
        <xsd:sequence>
            <xsd:element ref="xsf:property" minOccurs="0" maxOccurs="unbounded" />
        </xsd:sequence>
    </xsd:complexType>
</xsd:element>
<xsd:element name="property">
    <xsd:complexType>
        <xsd:attribute name="name" type="xsd:string" use="required" />
        <xsd:attribute name="value" type="xsd:string" use="required" />
        <xsd:attribute name="type" type="xsd:QName" use="required" />
    </xsd:complexType>
```

```xml
    </xsd:element>
    <!-- View and Context-Driven Editing definitions -->
    <!-- attributeData -->
    <xsd:element name="attributeData">
        <xsd:complexType>
            <xsd:attribute name="attribute" type="xsd:string" use="required" />
            <xsd:attribute name="value" type="xsd:string" use="required" />
        </xsd:complexType>
    </xsd:element>
    <!-- button -->
    <xsd:element name="button">
        <xsd:complexType>
            <xsd:attribute name="caption" type="xsf:xdTitle" />
            <xsd:attribute name="icon" type="xsd:string" />
            <xsd:attribute name="tooltip" type="xsf:xdTitle" />
            <xsd:attribute name="name" type="xsd:NMTOKEN" />
            <xsd:attribute name="xmlToEdit" type="xsd:NMTOKEN" />
            <xsd:attribute name="action">
                <xsd:simpleType>
                    <xsd:restriction base="xsd:NMTOKEN">
                        <xsd:enumeration value="xCollection::insert" />
                        <xsd:enumeration value="xCollection::insertBefore" />
                        <xsd:enumeration value="xCollection::insertAfter" />
                        <xsd:enumeration value="xCollection::remove" />
                        <xsd:enumeration value="xCollection::removeAll" />
                        <xsd:enumeration value="xOptional::insert" />
                        <xsd:enumeration value="xOptional::remove" />
                        <xsd:enumeration value="xReplace::replace" />
                    </xsd:restriction>
                </xsd:simpleType>
            </xsd:attribute>
            <xsd:attribute name="showIf">
                <xsd:simpleType>
                    <xsd:restriction base="xsd:NMTOKEN">
                        <xsd:enumeration value="always" />
                        <xsd:enumeration value="enabled" />
                        <xsd:enumeration value="immediate" />
                    </xsd:restriction>
                </xsd:simpleType>
            </xsd:attribute>
        </xsd:complexType>
    </xsd:element>
    <!-- chooseFragment -->
    <xsd:element name="chooseFragment">
        <xsd:complexType mixed="true">
            <xsd:sequence>
                <xsd:any minOccurs="0" maxOccurs="unbounded" processContents="skip" />
            </xsd:sequence>
            <xsd:attribute name="parent" type="xsd:string" />
            <xsd:attribute name="followingSiblings" type="xsd:string" use="optional" />
        </xsd:complexType>
    </xsd:element>
    <!-- editWith -->
    <xsd:element name="editWith">
```

```xml
        <xsd:complexType>
            <xsd:sequence>
                <xsd:element ref="xsf:fragmentToInsert" minOccurs="0" maxOccurs="1" />
            </xsd:sequence>
            <xsd:attribute name="component" use="required">
                <xsd:simpleType>
                    <xsd:restriction base="xsd:NMTOKEN">
                        <xsd:enumeration value="xCollection" />
                        <xsd:enumeration value="xOptional" />
                        <xsd:enumeration value="xReplace" />
                        <xsd:enumeration value="xTextList" />
                        <xsd:enumeration value="xField" />
                        <xsd:enumeration value="xImage" />
                    </xsd:restriction>
                </xsd:simpleType>
            </xsd:attribute>
            <xsd:attribute name="caption" type="xsf:xdTitle" use="optional" />
            <xsd:attribute name="autoComplete" type="xsf:xdYesNo" use="optional" />
            <xsd:attribute name="proofing" type="xsf:xdYesNo" use="optional" />
            <xsd:attribute name="type" use="optional">
                <xsd:simpleType>
                    <xsd:restriction base="xsd:NMTOKEN">
                        <xsd:enumeration value="plain" />
                        <xsd:enumeration value="formatted" />
                        <xsd:enumeration value="plainMultiline" />
                        <xsd:enumeration value="formattedMultiline" />
                        <xsd:enumeration value="rich" />
                    </xsd:restriction>
                </xsd:simpleType>
            </xsd:attribute>
            <xsd:attribute name="field" type="xsd:string" use="optional" />
            <xsd:attribute name="removeAncestors" type="xsd:nonNegativeInteger"
use="optional" />
            <xsd:anyAttribute
namespace="http://schemas.microsoft.com/office/infopath/2003"
processContents="skip" />
        </xsd:complexType>
    </xsd:element>
    <!-- unboundControls -->
    <xsd:element name="unboundControls">
        <xsd:complexType>
            <xsd:sequence>
                <!-- button -->
                <xsd:element name="button" minOccurs="0" maxOccurs="unbounded">
                    <xsd:complexType>
                        <xsd:attribute name="name" use="required">
                            <xsd:simpleType>
                                <xsd:restriction base="xsd:NCName">
                                    <xsd:pattern value="[^\.\^-]*" />
                                </xsd:restriction>
                            </xsd:simpleType>
                        </xsd:attribute>
                    </xsd:complexType>
                </xsd:element>
```

```
                </xsd:sequence>
            </xsd:complexType>
        </xsd:element>
        <!-- editing -->
        <xsd:element name="editing">
            <xsd:complexType>
                <xsd:sequence>
                    <xsd:element ref="xsf:xmlToEdit" minOccurs="0" maxOccurs="unbounded" />
                </xsd:sequence>
            </xsd:complexType>
        </xsd:element>
        <!-- fragmentToInsert -->
        <xsd:element name="fragmentToInsert">
            <xsd:complexType>
                <xsd:sequence>
                    <xsd:element ref="xsf:chooseFragment" minOccurs="1" maxOccurs=
"unbounded" />
                </xsd:sequence>
            </xsd:complexType>
        </xsd:element>
        <!-- mainpane -->
        <xsd:element name="mainpane">
            <xsd:complexType>
                <xsd:attribute name="transform" type="xsf:xdFileName" use="required" />
            </xsd:complexType>
        </xsd:element>
        <!-- printSettings -->
        <xsd:element name="printSettings">
            <xsd:complexType>
                <xsd:attribute name="orientation">
                    <xsd:simpleType>
                        <xsd:restriction base="xsd:NMTOKEN">
                            <xsd:enumeration value="portrait" />
                            <xsd:enumeration value="landscape" />
                        </xsd:restriction>
                    </xsd:simpleType>
                </xsd:attribute>
                <xsd:attribute name="header">
                    <xsd:simpleType>
                        <xsd:restriction base="xsd:string">
                            <xsd:maxLength value="255" />
                        </xsd:restriction>
                    </xsd:simpleType>
                </xsd:attribute>
                <xsd:attribute name="footer">
                    <xsd:simpleType>
                        <xsd:restriction base="xsd:string">
                            <xsd:maxLength value="255" />
                        </xsd:restriction>
                    </xsd:simpleType>
                </xsd:attribute>
                <xsd:attribute name="marginUnitsType">
                    <xsd:simpleType>
                        <xsd:restriction base="xsd:NMTOKEN">
```

```
                    <xsd:enumeration value="in" />
                    <xsd:enumeration value="cm" />
                </xsd:restriction>
            </xsd:simpleType>
        </xsd:attribute>
        <xsd:attribute name="rightMargin">
            <xsd:simpleType>
                <xsd:restriction base="xsd:float">
                    <xsd:minInclusive value="0"/>
                    <xsd:maxInclusive value="100"/>
                </xsd:restriction>
            </xsd:simpleType>
        </xsd:attribute>
        <xsd:attribute name="leftMargin">
            <xsd:simpleType>
                <xsd:restriction base="xsd:float">
                    <xsd:minInclusive value="0"/>
                    <xsd:maxInclusive value="100"/>
                </xsd:restriction>
            </xsd:simpleType>
        </xsd:attribute>
        <xsd:attribute name="topMargin">
            <xsd:simpleType>
                <xsd:restriction base="xsd:float">
                    <xsd:minInclusive value="0"/>
                    <xsd:maxInclusive value="100"/>
                </xsd:restriction>
            </xsd:simpleType>
        </xsd:attribute>
        <xsd:attribute name="bottomMargin">
            <xsd:simpleType>
                <xsd:restriction base="xsd:float">
                    <xsd:minInclusive value="0"/>
                    <xsd:maxInclusive value="100"/>
                </xsd:restriction>
            </xsd:simpleType>
        </xsd:attribute>
    </xsd:complexType>
</xsd:element>
<!-- toolbar -->
<xsd:element name="toolbar">
    <xsd:complexType>
        <xsd:sequence>
            <xsd:group ref="xsf:UIItem" minOccurs="0" maxOccurs="unbounded" />
        </xsd:sequence>
        <xsd:attribute name="name" type="xsf:xdTitle" use="required" />
        <xsd:attribute name="caption" type="xsf:xdTitle" use="required" />
    </xsd:complexType>
</xsd:element>
<!-- menu -->
<xsd:element name="menu">
    <xsd:complexType>
        <xsd:sequence>
            <xsd:group ref="xsf:UIItem" minOccurs="0" maxOccurs="unbounded" />
```

```xsd
            </xsd:sequence>
            <xsd:attribute name="caption" type="xsf:xdTitle" use="required" />
        </xsd:complexType>
    </xsd:element>
    <!-- menuArea -->
    <xsd:element name="menuArea">
        <xsd:complexType>
            <xsd:sequence>
                <xsd:group ref="xsf:UIItem" minOccurs="0" maxOccurs="unbounded" />
            </xsd:sequence>
            <xsd:attribute name="name" use="required">
                <xsd:simpleType>
                    <xsd:restriction base="xsd:NMTOKEN">
                        <xsd:enumeration value="msoFileMenu" />
                        <xsd:enumeration value="msoEditMenu" />
                        <xsd:enumeration value="msoInsertMenu" />
                        <xsd:enumeration value="msoViewMenu" />
                        <xsd:enumeration value="msoFormatMenu" />
                        <xsd:enumeration value="msoToolsMenu" />
                        <xsd:enumeration value="msoTableMenu" />
                        <xsd:enumeration value="msoHelpMenu" />
                        <xsd:enumeration value="msoStructuralEditingContextMenu" />
                    </xsd:restriction>
                </xsd:simpleType>
            </xsd:attribute>
        </xsd:complexType>
    </xsd:element>
    <!-- UIContainer -->
    <xsd:group name="UIItem">
        <xsd:choice>
            <xsd:element ref="xsf:button" />
            <xsd:element ref="xsf:menu" />
        </xsd:choice>
    </xsd:group>
    <!-- taskpane -->
    <xsd:element name="taskpane">
        <xsd:complexType>
            <xsd:attribute name="caption" type="xsd:string" use="required" />
            <xsd:attribute name="href" type="xsd:string" use="required" />
        </xsd:complexType>
    </xsd:element>
    <!-- views -->
    <xsd:element name="views">
        <xsd:complexType>
            <xsd:sequence>
                <xsd:element ref="xsf:view" minOccurs="1" maxOccurs="unbounded" />
            </xsd:sequence>
            <xsd:attribute name="default" type="xsd:string" />
        </xsd:complexType>
        <xsd:unique name="views_name_unique">
            <xsd:selector xpath="./xsf:view" />
            <xsd:field xpath="@name" />
        </xsd:unique>
        <xsd:key name="view_name_key">
```

```xml
            <xsd:selector xpath="./xsf:view" />
            <xsd:field xpath="@name" />
        </xsd:key>
        <xsd:keyref name="view_printView" refer="xsf:view_name_key">
            <xsd:selector xpath="./xsf:view" />
            <xsd:field xpath="@printView" />
        </xsd:keyref>
        <xsd:keyref name="views_default" refer="xsf:view_name_key">
            <xsd:selector xpath="." />
            <xsd:field xpath="@default" />
        </xsd:keyref>
    </xsd:element>
    <!-- ViewContent -->
    <xsd:group name="ViewContent">
        <xsd:choice>
            <xsd:element ref="xsf:editing" minOccurs="0" />
            <xsd:element ref="xsf:mainpane" minOccurs="0" />
            <xsd:element ref="xsf:printSettings" minOccurs="0" />
            <xsd:group ref="xsf:UIContainer" minOccurs="0" maxOccurs="unbounded" />
            <xsd:element ref="xsf:unboundControls" minOccurs="0" />
        </xsd:choice>
    </xsd:group>
    <!-- view -->
    <xsd:element name="view">
        <xsd:complexType>
            <xsd:group ref="xsf:ViewContent" minOccurs="0" maxOccurs="unbounded" />
            <xsd:attribute name="caption" type="xsf:xdViewName" />
            <xsd:attribute name="name" type="xsf:xdViewName" use="required" />
            <xsd:attribute name="printView" type="xsd:string" />
        </xsd:complexType>
        <xsd:unique name="toolbar_name_unique">
            <xsd:selector xpath="./xsf:toolbar" />
            <xsd:field xpath="@name" />
        </xsd:unique>
        <xsd:unique name="menuArea_name_unique">
            <xsd:selector xpath="./xsf:menuArea" />
            <xsd:field xpath="@name" />
        </xsd:unique>
        <xsd:unique name="xmlToEdit_name_unique">
            <xsd:selector xpath="./xsf:editing/xsf:xmlToEdit" />
            <xsd:field xpath="@name" />
        </xsd:unique>
        <xsd:key name="xmlToEdit_name_key">
            <xsd:selector xpath="./xsf:editing/xsf:xmlToEdit" />
            <xsd:field xpath="@name" />
        </xsd:key>
        <xsd:keyref name="button_xmlToEdit_reference" refer="xsf:xmlToEdit_name_key">
            <xsd:selector xpath="./xsf:menuArea/xsf:button | ./xsf:menu/xsf:button |
./xsf:toolbar/xsf:button" />
            <xsd:field xpath="@xmlToEdit" />
        </xsd:keyref>
    </xsd:element>
    <!-- xmlToEdit -->
    <xsd:element name="xmlToEdit">
```

```
            <xsd:complexType>
               <xsd:sequence>
                  <xsd:element ref="xsf:editWith" minOccurs="0" maxOccurs="1" />
               </xsd:sequence>
               <xsd:attribute name="name" type="xsd:NMTOKEN" use="required" />
               <xsd:attribute name="item" type="xsd:string" use="required" />
               <xsd:attribute name="container" type="xsd:string" />
               <xsd:attribute name="viewContext">
                  <xsd:simpleType>
                     <xsd:restriction base="xsd:string">
                        <xsd:pattern value="((\.|\#|[a-zA-Z0-9_])[a-zA-Z0-9_]*)
(\s((\.|\#|[a-zA-Z0-9_])[a-zA-Z0-9_]*))*" />
                     </xsd:restriction>
                  </xsd:simpleType>
               </xsd:attribute>
            </xsd:complexType>
         </xsd:element>
         <!-- docDigitalSignatures -->
         <xsd:element name="documentSignatures">
            <xsd:complexType>
               <xsd:attribute name="signatureLocation" type="xsd:string" use="required" />
            </xsd:complexType>
         </xsd:element>
         <!-- Upgrade -->
         <xsd:element name="documentVersionUpgrade">
            <xsd:complexType>
               <xsd:choice>
                  <xsd:element ref="xsf:useScriptHandler" />
                  <xsd:element ref="xsf:useTransform" />
               </xsd:choice>
            </xsd:complexType>
         </xsd:element>
         <xsd:element name="useTransform">
            <xsd:complexType>
               <xsd:attribute name="transform" use="required">
                  <xsd:simpleType>
                     <xsd:union memberTypes="xsf:xdFileName xsf:xdEmptyString" />
                  </xsd:simpleType>
               </xsd:attribute>
               <xsd:attribute name="minVersionToUpgrade" type="xsf:xdSolutionVersion"
use="required" />
               <xsd:attribute name="maxVersionToUpgrade" type="xsf:xdSolutionVersion" />
            </xsd:complexType>
         </xsd:element>
         <!-- XSF Extensions -->
         <xsd:element name="extensions">
            <xsd:complexType>
               <xsd:sequence>
                  <xsd:element ref="xsf:extension" minOccurs="0" maxOccurs="unbounded" />
               </xsd:sequence>
            </xsd:complexType>
         </xsd:element>
         <xsd:element name="extension">
            <xsd:complexType mixed="true">
```

```
        <xsd:sequence>
            <xsd:any minOccurs="0" maxOccurs="unbounded" processContents="skip" />
        </xsd:sequence>
        <xsd:attribute name="name" type="xsd:NMTOKEN" use="required" />
        <xsd:anyAttribute processContents="skip" />
    </xsd:complexType>
  </xsd:element>
</xsd:schema>
```

Figure A-1 illustrates the schema. Most nodes are expanded fully. Only elements that are otherwise shown remain collapsed.

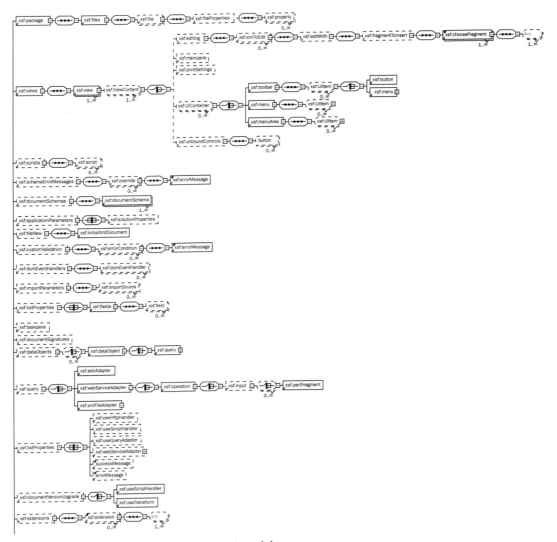

Figure A-1: The InfoPath XSF schema content model.

InfoPath Form Definition Reference

This reference lists the components in the form definition schema in four alphabetical sequences. Schema-defined data types are listed first, followed by groups. Then we list the elements and attributes.

A Web version of this reference is at www.Wrox.com.

The format of the entries follows.

Name [type]	The name of the element or attribute followed by its type. The xsf prefix is not used. Attributes of more than one element sharing the same name are listed separately with a note of the element they apply to.
Description	A short description of purpose or function.
Use	Notes on use.
Content	The content model for elements.
Used by	Parent element(s) of elements.
Attributes	Attributes of elements.
Attribute of	Parent element(s) of attributes.
Type	The XSD base type, element, or attribute type.
Example	Code snippet illustrating use.

All of the elements in the form definition file are namespace-qualified using the xsf namespace xmlns:xsf= http://schemas.Microsoft.com/office/infopath/2003/solutionsDefinition.

Types

The form definition schema provides several derived data types used to constrain attribute values.

xdEmptyString

Description

Used for attributes that specify an empty string.

Type

```
xsd:string
```

Example

```
<xsd:simpleType name="xdEmptyString">
    <xsd:restriction base="xsd:string">
        <xsd:maxLength value="0" />
    </xsd:restriction>
</xsd:simpleType>
```

xdErrorMessage Type

Description

Used for attributes that specify an error message no longer than 1,023 characters.

Type

```
xsd:string
```

Example

```
<xsd:simpleType name="xdErrorMessage">
    <xsd:restriction base="xsd:string">
        <xsd:maxLength value="1023" />
    </xsd:restriction>
</xsd:simpleType>
```

xdFileName

Description

Used for attributes that specify a filename of 1 to 64 characters in length.

Type

```
xsd:string
```

Example

```
<xsd:simpleType name="xdFileName">
  <xsd:restriction base="xsd:string">
    <xsd:minLength value="1" />
    <xsd:maxLength value="64" />
  </xsd:restriction>
</xsd:simpleType>
```

xdScriptLanguage

Description

Used for attributes that specify the name of a scripting language.

Type

xsd:NMTOKEN

Example

```
<xsd:simpleType name="xdScriptLanguage">
  <xsd:restriction base="xsd:NMTOKEN">
    <xsd:pattern value="((([Jj][Aa][Vv][Aa])|([Jj])|([Vv][Bb]))
        ([Ss][Cc][Rr][Ii][Pp][Tt]))" />
  </xsd:restriction>
</xsd:simpleType>
```

xdSolutionVersion

Description

Used for attributes that specify a version number.

Type

xsd:string

Example

```
<xsd:simpleType name="xdSolutionVersion">
  <xsd:restriction base="xsd:string">
    <xsd:pattern value="(([0-9]{1,4}.){3}[0-9]{1,4})" />
  </xsd:restriction>
</xsd:simpleType>
```

xdTitle

Description

Used for title attribute strings in the range 1 to 255 characters and that follow the prescribed pattern.

Type

xsd:string

Example

```
<xsd:simpleType name="xdTitle">
   <xsd:restriction base="xsd:string">
      <xsd:minLength value="1" />
      <xsd:maxLength value="255" />
      <xsd:pattern value="([^\p{Z}\p{Cc}\p{Cf}\p{Cn}])
         (([^\p{Zl}\p{Zp}\p{Cc}])*([^\p{Z}\p{Cc}\p{Cf}\p{Cn}]))?" />
   </xsd:restriction>
</xsd:simpleType>
```

xdViewName

Description

Used for viewattributes in the range 1 to 255 characters and that follow the prescribed pattern.

Type

```
xsd:string
```

Example

```
<xsd:simpleType name="xdViewName">
   <xsd:restriction base="xsd:string">
      <xsd:minLength value="1" />
      <xsd:maxLength value="255" />
      <xsd:pattern value="([^\p{Z}\p{C}/\\#&amp;&quot;&gt;&lt;])
         (([^\p{Zl}\p{Zp}\p{C}/\\#&amp;&quot;&gt;&lt;])*([^\p{Z}
         \p{C}/\\#&amp;&quot;&gt;&lt;]))?" />
   </xsd:restriction>
```

xdViewName

Description

Used for attributes that require "yes" or "no" values.

Type

```
xsd:NMTOKEN
```

Example

```
<xsd:simpleType name="xdYesNo">
   <xsd:restriction base="xsd:NMTOKEN">
      <xsd:enumeration value="yes" />
      <xsd:enumeration value="no" />
   </xsd:restriction>
</xsd:simpleType>
```

Groups

The form definition schema uses a few group declarations as shorthand in content models.

UIContainer

Description

Represents a collection of UI elements.

Example

```
<xsd:group name="UIContainer">
    <xsd:choice>
        <xsd:element ref="xsf:toolbar" />
        <xsd:element ref="xsf:menu" />
        <xsd:element ref="xsf:menuArea" />
    </xsd:choice>
</xsd:group>
```

UIItem

Description

Represents a collection of UI elements.

Example

```
<xsd:group name="UIItem">
    <xsd:choice>
        <xsd:element ref="xsf:button" />
        <xsd:element ref="xsf:menu" />
    </xsd:choice>
</xsd:group>
```

UIItem

Description

Represents a collection of elements used in a view.

Example

```
<xsd:group name="ViewContent">
    <xsd:choice>
        <xsd:element ref="xsf:editing" minOccurs="0" />
        <xsd:element ref="xsf:mainpane" minOccurs="0" />
        <xsd:element ref="xsf:printSettings" minOccurs="0" />
        <xsd:group ref="xsf:UIContainer" minOccurs="0" maxOccurs="unbounded" />
        <xsd:element ref="xsf:unboundControls" minOccurs="0" />
    </xsd:choice>
</xsd:group>
```

Elements

adoAdapter

Description

Defines an ActiveX Data Objects (ADO) data adapter used to retrieve the data from an ADO data source.

Use

The required `connectionString` attribute contains all the parameter values needed to connect to the data source, and the `commandText` attribute contains the SQL command for querying the data source.

`queryAllowed` is an optional attribute that states whether data can be retrieved using the query method of the data adapter object. Allowed values are `"yes"` and `"no"` (default). `submitAllowed` specifies the same options for the submit method.

Attributes

`commandText`, `connectionString`, `name`, `queryAllowed`, `submitAllowed`

Type

`xsd:complexType`

Example

```
<xsf:query>
    <xsf:adoAdapter
        connectionString="Provider=Microsoft.Jet.OLEDB.4.0;
            Password=&quot;&quot;;;User ID=Admin;
            Data Source=infnwind.mdb;Mode=Share Deny None;
            Extended Properties=&quot;&quot;;;..."
        commandText="select [EmployeeID],[LastName],[FirstName]
            from [Employees] as [Employees]"
        queryAllowed="yes"
        submitAllowed="yes">
    </xsf:adoAdapter>
</xsf:query>
```

applicationParameters

Description

Optional top-level child of the `xDocumentClass` element. The contained `solutionProperties` element specifies how a form should be used in design mode.

Use

The required `application` attribute identifies the name of the application used to design the InfoPath form. The value must be `"InfoPath Design Mode"`.

Content

solutionProperties

Attributes

application

Type

xsd:complexType

attributeData

Description

Specifies the name, and associated value, of an attribute that will be inserted, or modified if it already exists, by the insert action of the xCollection or xOptional editing components.

Use

The required attribute and value attributes contain the name and value.

Attributes

attribute, value

Type

xsd:complexType

Example

```
<xsf:chooseFragment parent="report">
   <xsf:attributeData attribute="author" value="author name"/>
</xsf:chooseFragment>
```

button

Description

Defines a button that has an associated action. Each button element corresponds to a button in a toolbar or a menu item in a menu. These buttons or menu items can be dynamically enabled, disabled, or hidden, based on the user's selection in the view. The element also specifies either an associated editing component action or an associated script.

Use

If the caption attribute is not specified, the value defaults to the caption provided by the corresponding editWith element, which itself defaults to the empty string. If no icon is specified, the caption alone will be used. If both caption and icon are specified, both will be displayed. If neither is specified, a blank button is displayed.

If the `OnClick` event for the button is intended to fire an editing component action, the `action` and `showIf` attributes are used.

The `name` attribute associates the `OnClick` event handler of the button with a scripting function. Although `name` is optional, it is required for buttons that use scripting code.

The `tooltip` attribute provides the pop-up text for toolbar buttons. If the button is a menu item, this attribute has no effect.

The `xmlToEdit` attribute is optional, but it is required for buttons used with editing components to associate the `OnClick` event with the component.

Attributes

`action, caption, icon, name, name, showIf, tooltip, xmlToEdit`

Type

`xsd:complexType`

Example

```
<xsf:menuArea name="msoInsertMenu">
    <xsf:menu caption="&amp;Section">
        <xsf:button action="xCollection::insert" xmlToEdit="CD_10"
            caption="CD" icon="cd.bmp" showIf="always" tooltip="Insert a CD."/>
        <xsf:button action="xCollection::insert" xmlToEdit="Track_14"
            caption="Track" icon="track.bmp" showIf="always"/>
        <xsf:button action="xOptional::insert" xmlToEdit="Label_16"
            caption="Label" icon="label.bmp"/>
    </xsf:menu>
</xsf:menuArea>
```

chooseFragment

Description

Container for an XML fragment.

Use

The `chooseFragment` element has an open-content model. In addition to, or instead of, XML data being inserted directly as a fragment, it can contain one or more `attributeData` elements. In this case the `attributeData` elements are not included as inserted content but are each used to specify setting an attribute value.

The `parent` attribute is an XPath expression to the node under which the fragment should be inserted. The default value is `"."`.

The insertion will be as a child of the parent node, but before the position defined in the `followingSiblings` attribute. If no nodes are found, the insertion acts as an append.

followingSiblings is only used during an insert when the current context is not in an item. The behavior is to append to the content of the parent node, unless the followingSiblings attribute is specified, in which case the insertion is still within the content of the parent, but prior to any followingSiblings nodes.

chooseFragment elements are typically ordered in increasing size. The first will be the data fragment to be inserted by the insertBefore and insertAfter actions, when there is already at least one item in the collection. The insert action, on the other hand, can be invoked when there is currently a node in the XML tree corresponding to container, but no node corresponding to item (i.e., it can be used to insert the first "item").

Any element content within the xmlFragment (other than attributeData) corresponds to new content to be inserted into the source XML and should be in the appropriate namespace. In particular, if the default namespace of the XSF file is http://schemas.microsoft.com/office/infopath/2003/solutionDefinition, then the inserted elements should be namespace-qualified, or else the default namespace should be set appropriately within xmlFragment.

Attributes

followingSiblings, parent

Type

xsd:complexType

Example

```
<xsf:xmlToEdit name="workItem" unit="workItem" container="issue">
    <xsf:editWith component="xCollection">
        <xsf:fragmentToInsert>
            <xsf:chooseFragment parent="workitems" followingSiblings="X|Y">
                <workItem/>
            </xsf:chooseFragment>
            <xsf:chooseFragment followingSiblings="B|C">
                <workItems><workItem/></workItems>
            </xsf:chooseFragment>
        </xsf:fragmentToInsert>
    </xsf:editWith>
</xsf:xmlToEdit>
```

customValidation

Description

Defines rule-based validation in addition to the validation enforced by the XML schema.

Use

To create multiple error conditions on a field, you need to edit the XSF file directly. These will not appear in the Data Validation dialog box in design mode.

Content

```
errorCondition
```

Example

```
<xsf:customValidation>
    <xsf:errorCondition
        match="/exp:expenseReport"
        expressionContext="exp:reportDate"
        expression="msxsl:string-compare(., ../exp:startDate) < 0 and
            ../exp:startDate != """
        showErrorOn=".">
        <xsf:errorMessage
            type="modeless"
            shortMessage="The report date occurs before the end of the expense
                period.">
            The report date occurs before the end of the expense period. Verify that
                this is correct.
        </xsf:errorMessage>
    </xsf:errorCondition>
</xsf:customValidation>
```

dataObject

Description

Defines a secondary data object used in a form template.

Use

Multiple dataObject elements are allowed within a form. Each data object is an XML node set popu-lated from an external data source. Each dataObject can be accessed using the name from the XSLT view code and any scripts in the form.

The required name attribute is the unique name for this object (maximum length = 255 characters).

In design mode, InfoPath automatically packages the schema for each secondary data object as part of the form template. An entry is made for the schema files under the files element, and this filename is referred to from the schema attribute in the dataObject element.

The optional initOnLoad attribute specifies whether the data object should be initialized on document load, using the query method for the object. Allowed values are "yes" and "no" (default).

Content

```
query
```

Attributes

```
initOnLoad, name, schema
```

Type

```
xsd:complexType
```

Example

```
<xsf:dataObjects>
    <xsf:dataObject
        name="EmployeeNames"
        schema="EmployeeNames.xsd"
        initOnLoad="yes">
      <xsf:query>
          .
          .
          .
      </xsf:query>
    </xsf:dataObject>
</xsf:dataObjects>
```

dataObjects

Description

Defines all secondary data objects used in a form template.

Use

The dataObjects element contains a collection of data objects that are used to populate XML nodes from external data sources.

Content

```
dataObject
```

documentSchema

Description

Defines an XML Schema for a form. One element is present for each declared schema for the form.

Use

If an XML schema refers to other schema modules using xsd:import or xsd:include elements, the modules do not have to be listed in the documentSchemas element. However, they must be included in the form template with their references changed to relative filenames.

The required location attribute contains the namespace URI and location URL, relative to the form definition file, as well as the filename of the schema, delimited by a space. Schemas without a namespace are listed with just the schema filename.

If a form's underlying XML document contains references to multiple XML schemas, they are listed with separate documentSchema elements and the top-level XML Schema has its rootSchema attribute set to "yes".

Attributes

```
location, rootSchema
```

Type

```
xsd:complexType
```

Example

```
<xsf:documentSchemas>
    <xsf:documentSchema
        location="urn:schema:custom:Namespace customFilename.xsd"
        rootSchema="yes"/>
</xsf:documentSchemas>
```

documentSchemas

Description

Container for one or more `documentSchema` elements.

Use

`documentSchemas` should only contain the top-level root schema reference and any other independently referred to schemas from the XML document. Included and imported schemas should not be listed here.

Content

```
xsf:documentSchema
```

documentSignatures

Description

Defines the location of a digital signature node in the form.

Use

The required `signatureLocation` attribute contains an XPath expression pointing to the form node that stores the digital signature.

Attributes

```
signatureLocation
```

Type

```
xsd:complexType
```

Example

```
<xsf:documentSignatures signatureLocation="/contributors/contrib1"/>
```

documentVersionUpgrade

Description

Defines how forms created with an older version of the form template can be upgraded to the latest version of the form template.

Content

useScriptHandler, useTransform

Example

```
<xsf:documentVersionUpgrade>
   <xsf:useTransform
      transform="upgrade.xsl"
      minVersionToUpgrade="0.0.0.0"
      maxVersionToUpgrade="1.0.0.5"/>
</xsf:documentVersionUpgrade>
```

domEventHandler

Description

Defines an event handler for one or more XML nodes.

Use

The required `match` attribute identifies the XML node for which this handler is declared. The XPath expression in the attribute cannot contain predicates.

The required `handlerObject` identifies the handler object in the script. The script must use this name to define event handler functions for the specified node.

Attributes

handlerObject, match

Type

xsd:complexType

Example

```
<xsf:domEventHandlers>
   <xsf:domEventHandler
      match="TravelReport/Expenses"
      handlerObject="TravelExpenses"/>
</xsf:domEventHandlers>
```

domEventHandlers

Description

Contains a collection of pointers to event handlers.

Content

```
domEventHandler
```

editing

Description

Contains information about the editing components used in a view.

Use

The editing section of the form definition file specifies how and when users are able to edit nodes of the underlying XML document. Only one editing element is allowed per view.

Content

```
xmlToEdit
```

editWith

Description

Specifies an instance of an editing component and provides the parameters to determine its behavior.

Use

If the `viewContext` attribute of the parent `xmlToEdit` element is defined, the parameters of `editWith` are associated with the specified view context.

Allowed values for the `autoComplete` are `"yes"` and `"no"` (default).

Allowed values for the `proofing` are `"yes"` (default) and `"no"`.

The value for the `removeAncestors` must be a nonnegative integer. The default is `"0"`.

The `component` attribute is the name of the editing component that will be referenced by the `action` attribute of a button element. Valid component names are `xCollection`, `xOptional`, `xReplace`, `xTextList`, `xField`, and `xImage`.

The `caption` specifies an identifier for alternate forms of XML data to be used in the editing component.

The `field` attribute refers to an XML node displayed as an editable field for an `xText` list editing component. The default value is `"."`.

The following values are allowed for the type attribute: `"plain"` (default), `"plainMultiline"`, `"formatted"`, `"formattedMultiline"`, and `"rich"`.

Content

```
fragmentToInsert
```

Attributes

autoComplete, caption, component, field, proofing, removeAncestors, type

Type

```
xsd:complexType
```

Example

```
<xsf:xmlToEdit name="workItem" item="workItems/workItem" container="workItems">
<xsf:editWith component="xCollection">
     <xsf:fragmentToInsert>
       <xsf:chooseFragment>
          <workItem description="create visuals" effort="2"/>
       </xsf:chooseFragment>
     </xsf:fragmentToInsert>
   </xsf:editWith>
</xsf:xmlToEdit>
```

errorCondition

Description

Defines a custom validation or error condition for a XML node in a form.

Use

The required expression attribute contains an XPath expression (relative to the expressionContext attribute, if specified) that must be evaluated to validate the XML node specified in the match attribute. If the specified expression evaluates to TRUE, then it is considered to be an error condition and the specified error message is displayed.

expressionContext is a relative XPath expression that identifies the node on which the expression is rooted and therefore should be evaluated. The default value is ".". This is the same as the matched node.

The required match attribute identifies the XML node on which this custom validation is declared.

showErrorOn contains an XPath expression relative to the expressionContext node. The default is ".".

Content

```
errorMessage
```

Attributes

expression, expressionContext, match, showErrorOn

Type

```
xsd:complexType
```

Example

```
<xsf:errorCondition
        match="/exp:expenseReport"
        expressionContext="exp:reportDate"
        expression="msxsl:string-compare(., ../exp:startDate) < 0 and
           ../exp:startDate != """
        showErrorOn=".">
        <xsf:errorMessage
           type="modeless"
           shortMessage="The report date occurs before the end of the expense
              period.">
           The report date occurs before the end of the expense period. Verify that
              this is correct.
        </xsf:errorMessage>
</xsf:errorCondition>
```

errorMessage

Description

Defines a custom validation or error condition for a XML node in a form.

Use

You can supply both long and short error messages as values. The long error message is the content for the element. Its maximum length is 1,023 characters. The short message is contained in the shortMessage attribute and is limited to 127 characters.

If the error message type attribute is set to "modal", the long error message is displayed when the user right-clicks Full error description on the shortcut menu. The short message value is ignored. If the attribute is set to "modeless" (default), the short message is displayed as a ToolTip.

Attributes

```
shortMessage, type
```

Type

```
xsf:xdErrorMessage
```

Example

```
<xsf:errorMessage
   type="modeless"
   shortMessage="The report date occurs before the end of the expense period.">
      The report date occurs before the end of the expense period. Verify that
         this is correct.
</xsf:errorMessage>
```

extension

Description

Specifies a reserved, open-content model element for InfoPath upgrades.

Use

It is intended to include minor upgrades to the InfoPath 2003 XSF format that can be used by future releases of InfoPath or by specific forms. It can contain elements of an open-content model, and the restriction of such extensions within the extensions element means that InfoPath 2003 can ignore these and continue to open the forms in the InfoPath 2003 application.

The name is a unique name identifying the extension being specified.

Attributes

name

Type

xsd:complexType

Example

```
<xsf:extensions>
    <xsf:extension
        name="someValue"
        anyAttributesHere="someValue">
        ...open content model here...
    </xsf:extension>
<xsf:extensions>
```

extensions

Description

Container for extension elements.

Content

extension

field

Description

Defines a single field for form library columns.

Specifies a relative XPath expression from the item attribute of the xmlToEdit element.

Use

The required `node` attribute contains an XPath expression that identifies the XML node or nodes in the form from which the data is read for list display. Maximum length = 255 characters.

The required `name` attribute is the label to be used on the list header.

The `type` attribute is the XML Schema data type.

`columnName` identifies the column name in the SQL table containing the list view. Maximum length = 255 characters.

`maxlength` gives the maximum size of the field in bytes.

`required` indicates if NULL values are allowed. Allowed values are `"yes"` and `"no"` (default).

`viewable` indicates whether the field should be added to the default list view. Allowed values are `"yes"` and `"no"` (default).

`aggregation` specifies how form property data should be processed to obtain a single value for a form library report. It can either be an aggregation action or an indication of the particular element in the collection.

Attributes

`aggregation, columnName, maxLength, name, node, required, type, viewable`

Type

`xsd:complexType`

Attribute of

`editWith`

Type

`xsd:string`

Example

```
<xsf:listProperties>
    <xsf:fields>
        <xsf:field
            type="xsd:date"
            name="TravelDate"
            columnName="TravelDate"
            required="yes"
            viewable="yes"
            node="TravelReport/Header/travelDate"
            aggregation="first"/>
    </xsf:fields>
</xsf:listProperties>
```

fields

Description

Contains one or more fields for form library columns.

Content

```
field
```

file

Description

Identifies a file as one of the files making up a form template. It may include specific property names and values for each file.

Use

The required name attribute specifies the filename.

Content

```
xsf:fileProperties
```

Attributes

```
name
```

Type

```
xsd:complexType
```

Example

```
<xsf:package>
    <xsf:files>
        <xsf:file name="view_1.xsl">
            <xsf:fileProperties>
                <xsf:property
                    name="lang"
                    type="string"
                    value="1033"/>
            </xsf:fileProperties>
        </xsf:file>
    </xsf:files>
</xsf:package>
```

fileNew

Description

Contains the information used when the user creates a form based on a template.

Content

```
initialXmlDocument
```

fileProperties

Description

Wrapper element for all file properties defined for the current file.

Content

```
property
```

files

Description

Lists all files that are used by the form.

Content

```
file
```

fragmentToInsert

Description

Sources of XML data that can be used within an associated editing component.

Content

```
chooseFragment
```

importParameters

Description

Contains all the parameters that define how the import/merge files feature works for a form. If the element is not present, then import/merge files is disabled.

Use

If the `importSource` element is not defined, the XSLT transform defined in the `mainpane` is used.

The required `enabled` attribute specifies if form merging is enabled. Allowed values are `"yes"` (default) or `"no"`.

Content

```
importSource
```

Attributes

```
enabled
```

Type

```
xsd:complexType
```

importSource

Description

Specifies all the parameters to be used when merging a form of a specific schema into the form described by this template.

Use

The `name` attribute identifies the URL of the source form as defined in its processing instruction.

The `schema` attribute identifies a schema URN. If the source form belongs to the schema, the XSLT specified in the `transform` attribute is used for merging into the current form.

Attributes

```
name, schema, transform
```

Type

```
complexType
```

Example

```
<xsf:importParameters
    enabled="yes"
    defaultTransform="defaultschematransform.xslt">
    <xsf:importSource
        name="addedform"
        schema="urn:some-schema:namespace"
        transform="schematransform.xslt" />
</xsf:importParameters>
```

initialXMLDocument

Description

Contains a reference to an XML file containing sample data to populate a new form created by a user.

Use

The required `href` attribute specifies the URL of the XML sample data to be used by the `File⇨New` command.

`caption` defines the text string to be used as the name of the form in the Template Gallery and in the most recently used list.

Example

```
<xsf:fileNew>
    <xsf:initialXMLDocument caption="Travel Report
    href=http://server/folder/TravelReportTemplate.xml" />
</xsf:fileNew>
```

input

Description

Contains the substitution information for parts of the input SOAP message to the Web service.

Use

Specified parts in the SOAP message are replaced when the form template is being filled out with data from within the form. It is used when a secondary data source is being populated from a Web service call and InfoPath needs some input arguments in order to make the Web service calls.

The required `source` attribute contains the name of the resource file in the form template that contains the XML schema for the input SOAP message of the selected operation of the Web service.

Content

`partFragment`

Attributes

`source`

Type

`xsd:complexType`

listProperties

Description

Contains properties that appear in a list view in a form library.

Use

XML documents belonging to a form can be placed in a single folder or library. Depending on the underlying support in the file system/server, this information can be used to create meaningful list views on a set of forms. For example, when InfoPath forms are saved into a Windows SharePoint Services form library that is based on an InfoPath form as a template, then form properties specified in this section are automatically made available to the default view of the form library.

Content

```
fields
```

mainpane

Description

Determines what is displayed in the main form area, as opposed to secondary UI, task panes, and so on.

Use

The required `transform` attribute contains the relative URL to the XSL Transformation (XSLT) used for the view.

Attributes

```
transform
```

Type

```
xsd:complexType
```

Example

```
<xsf:view name="View" caption="View">
   <xsf:mainpane transform="input.xsl">
</xsf:mainpane>
   .
   .
</xsf:view>
```

menu

Description

Menus can contain both buttons and nested menus.

Use

Custom menus are placed in the order they are declared in the form definition, between the Table and Help menus. If a menu contains no visible menu items and has no visible submenus, then its caption will be hidden.

The required `caption` attribute is used as the caption for a menu.

Attributes

```
caption
```

Type

```
xsd:complexType
```

menuArea

Description

Contains information about the InfoPath built-in menus used in a view.

- ❑ msoFileMenu
- ❑ msoEditMenu
- ❑ msoInsertMenu
- ❑ msoViewMenu
- ❑ msoFormatMenu
- ❑ msoToolsMenu
- ❑ msoTableMenu
- ❑ msoHelpMenu
- ❑ msoStructuralEditingContextMenu

Use

Multiple buttons or menus can be declared within a menuArea element. Each button element adds a menu item to the built-in menu and has an action (or command) associated with it. A menu element contained in a menuArea creates a cascading menu.

The name attribute must be one of the built-in InfoPath named menu areas.

Attributes

name

Type

xsd:complexType

Example

```
<xsf:menuArea name="msoInsertMenu">
   <xsf:menu caption="&amp;Section">
      <xsf:button action="xCollection::insert"
 xmlToEdit="CD_10" caption="CD" showIf="always">
      </xsf:button>
      <xsf:button action="xCollection::insert" xmlToEdit="Track_14"
caption="Track" showIf="always"></xsf:button>
      <xsf:button action="xOptional::insert" xmlToEdit="Label_16"
caption="Label"></xsf:button>
   </xsf:menu>
</xsf:menuArea>
```

operation

Description

Defines the method on a Web service to be used for retrieving/submitting form data.

Use

The name attribute is the unique name of the method.

The required serviceUrl attribute contains the Web service URL to which the request should be sent.

The required soapAction attribute contains the value of the SOAPAction attribute in the SOAP request message.

Content

input

Attributes

name, serviceUrl, soapAction

Type

xsd:complexType

Example

```
<xsf:webServiceAdapter
    wsdlUrl="http://localhost/webservicesample/infopathwebservicesample.asmx?WSDL"
    queryAllowed="yes"
    submitAllowed="no">
    <xsf:operation
        name="getOrders"
        soapAction="http://tempuri.org/getOrders"
        serviceUrl="http://localhost/webservicesample/sample.asmx">
        <xsf:input source="Submit.xml"/>
    </xsf:operation>
</xsf:webServiceAdapter>
```

override

Description

Each override element defines one overriding error message for schema data type errors for an individual XML node.

Use

The required match attribute identifies the XML node for which the override is defined.

Content

```
errorMessage
```

Attributes

```
match
```

Type

```
xsd:complexType
```

package

Description

Contains information about all of the files used in an InfoPath form.

Content

```
xsf:files
```

Example

```
<xsf:package>
    <xsf:files>
        <xsf:file name="input.xslt" />
        <xsf:file name="report.xslt" />
    </xsf:files>
</xsf:package>
```

partFragment

Description

Describes one substitution group for a specific part of the input SOAP message.

Use

The `match` attribute contains an XPath expression that identifies nodes in the input SOAP message schema to be substituted/replaced.

The required `replaceWith` attribute contains an XPath expression that identifies the values in the source document that should be used to replace parts of the input SOAP message.

Attributes

```
match, replaceWith
```

Type

```
xsd:complexType
```

Example

```
<xsf:input source="Submit.xml">
   <xsf:partFragment
      match="/dfs:myFields/dfs:dataFields/s0:IsPrime/s0:inValue"
      replaceWith="/dfs:myFields/dfs:dataFields/s0:IsPrime"/>
</xsf:input>
```

printSettings

Description

Specifies the printer settings used when printing a view.

Use

All the attributes are optional, and some correspond to values set in the Print Settings dialog box. `header`header and `footer`footer are text strings.

Allowed values for `orientation` are `"portrait"` and `"landscape"`.

`marginUnitsType` gives the unit of measurement for the four margin values; allowable values are `"in"` (inch) and `"cm"` (centimeter). Along with the four margin values, it must be set by editing the XSF file manually.

Attributes

`bottomMargin, footer, header, leftMargin, marginUnitsType, orientation, rightMargin, topMargin`

Type

`xsd:complexType`

Example

```
<xsf:view name="View" caption="View">
   <xsf:printSettings
      header="Header text goes here."
      footer="Footer text goes here."
      orientation="portrait"
      marginUnitsType="in"
      topMargin="1"
      leftMargin="2"
      rightMargin="2"
      bottomMargin="1"
   </xsf:printSettings>
   .
   .
</xsf:view>
```

property

Description

Defines one specific property for the specified file.

Use

name defines the name of the property. For simple properties, the value is included in the value attribute. For complex (and multivalued) properties, value is defined in a container XML tree using an open-content model. type defines the XML Schema data type of the element.

Attributes

name, type, value

Type

xsd:complexType

Example

```
<xsf:package>
    <xsf:files>
        <xsf:file name="view.xslt" >
            <xsf:fileProperties>
                <xsf:property name="size" type="xs:integer value="4286" />
            </xsf:fileProperties>
        </xsf:file>
    </xsf:files>
</xsf:package>
```

query

Description

Associates a data adapter with a data object or a form's underlying XML document.

Use

Only one data adapter definition is allowed in a query.

Content

adoAdapter, webServiceAdapter, xmlFileAdapter

schemaErrorMessages

Description

Used to specify custom error messages to be returned for XML Schema data type errors. Otherwise, some default error messages (specific to data types) are returned by InfoPath.

Content

```
override
```

script

Description

Defines the source scripting file containing all the data-level script content referenced in the form.

Use

The required `src` attribute is the relative URL of the script file.

Attributes

```
src
```

Type

```
xsd:complexType
```

scripts

Description

Defines the source of all business logic scripts used at the document level in the form.

Use

All scripts should be written in the language declared here and must be included in the form template. You should ensure you use unique names across script source files.

InfoPath supports the following values for the `language` attribute: `"JavaScript"`, `"JScript"`, or `"VBScript"`.

Content

```
script
```

Attributes

```
language
```

Type

```
xsd:complexType
```

Example

```
<xsf:scripts language="jscript">
    <xsf:script src="myscripts.js" />
</xsf:scripts>
```

solutionProperties

Description

Optional child of the `applicationParameters` element used to store design-time information about the form.

Use

All attributes are optional. `allowCustomization` indicates whether the form can be modified or customized. `automaticallyCreateNodes` indicates whether XML nodes will be automatically generated when controls are inserted in the view in design mode. `fullyEditableNamespace` identifies the namespace of an XML schema in the form template that can be entirely modified in design mode. `lastOpenView` identifies the name of the view that was last open in InfoPath when a form was being designed. `lastVersionNeedingTransform` identifies, temporarily, the value of the `maxVersionToUpgrade` attribute in the `documentVersionUpgrade` element for upgrade with an XSLT file. `scriptLanguages` identifies the name of the scripting language used to implement the business logic of the form.

Attributes

`allowCustomization`, `automaticallyCreateNodes`, `fullyEditableNamespace`, `lastOpenView`, `lastVersionNeedingTransform`, `scriptLanguage`

Type

`xsd:complexType`

Example

```
<xsf:applicationParameters application="InfoPath Design Mode">
   <xsf:solutionProperties
      allowCustomization="no"
      lastOpenView="view1"
      scriptLanguage="JScript"
      automaticallyCreateNodes="no"
      lastVersionNeedingTransform="1.1.0.10"
      fullyEditableNamespace="urn:names?pace1:mynames"/>
</xsf:applicationParameters>
```

submit

Description

Contains information about submit functionality for a form's data.

Use

`caption` defines the name of the submit button and corresponding menu item that will appear on the File menu.

`disableMenuItem` specifies whether the menu item for the submit operation should be disabled.

`onAfterSubmit` specifies the action after a submission was successful. Allowed values are `"Close"`, `"KeepOpen"` (default), or `"OpenNew"`. If the submit operation is not successful, then the attribute is ignored and the form is kept open.

`showSignatureReminder` specifies whether a dialog box should be displayed to prompt the user to digitally sign the form before submitting it.

`showStatusDialog` specifies whether the status dialog box should be shown after the submit operation. Values include `"yes"` (default) and `"no"`. If the attribute is set to `"yes"` and no custom messages are defined, default submit messages are displayed.

Content

errorMessage, submitMessage, useHttpHandler, useQueryAdapter, useScriptHandler, webServiceAdapter

Attributes

caption, disableMenuItem, onAfterSubmit, showSignatureReminder, showStatusDialog

Type

xsd:complexType

Example

```
<xsf:submit
    caption="Su&amp;bmit"
    disableMenuItem="no"
    onAfterSubmit="KeepOpen"
    showStatusDialog="yes"
    showSignatureReminder="yes">
    <xsf:successMessage>Submit was successful.</xsf:successMessage>
    <xsf:errorMessage>Submit was not successful.</xsf:errorMessage>
</xsf:submit>
```

successMessage

Description

Specifies the text used to notify the user that the submission was successful.

Use

The message is displayed in the case when `onAfterSubmit="KeepOpen"`. If `onAfterSubmit="Close"` or `onAfterSubmit="OpenNew"`, it is ignored.

Type

xsd:string

Example

```
<xsf:successMessage>success string</xsf:successMessage>
```

taskpane

Description

Defines an optional form-specific task pane.

Use

The task pane is a modeless panel that appears by default to the right of the main form area. Task panes contain commands specific to completing tasks that are related to a single form. InfoPath supports the use of a single custom task pane.

To get multiple task pane behavior, you can include multiple HTML files in the form template and use the Navigate method of the HTMLTaskPane object in the InfoPath object model to navigate to different HTML files.

The required caption attribute defines the caption used in the task pane drop-down list box.

The required href attribute specifies the relative or absolute URL to an HTML file.

Attributes

caption, href

Type

xsd:complexType

Example

```
<xsf:xDocumentClass>
    .
    .
    <xsf:taskpane
        caption="Metadata"
        href="taskpanes/tp_meta.html"/>
    .
    .
</xsf:xDocumentClass>
```

toolbar

Description

Custom toolbars or top-level menus are declared using the toolbar and menu elements, which themselves each contain zero or more button elements. In addition, nesting is allowed to provide for submenus, and for drop-down menus off toolbars. The menu in a toolbar is implemented as a button in the toolbar, displaying the caption together with a downward triangle to the right. Clicking on the button displays a drop-down menu. If the drop-down contains no visible menu items and has no visible submenus, then the button will be hidden.

Use

The required `caption` attribute is used as the title of the toolbar, when the toolbar is not docked to the user interface.

The `name` attribute is used to identify toolbars so that placement information can be remembered. This also enables docking and undocking, placement, and so forth. to be maintained when switching between views, when a toolbar of the same name is defined in both views. The name must be unique within a given view.

Attributes

`caption, name`

Type

`xsd:complexType`

Example

```
<xsf:toolbar caption="Design Issues Form">
   <xsf:menu caption="Insert">
      <xsf:button action="xCollection::insert" xmlToEdit="issue" caption="Issue"/>
      <xsf:button action="xCollection::insert" xmlToEdit="workItem caption="Work
         Item"/>
   </xsf:menu>
      <xsf:button action="xOptional::insert" xmlToEdit="header" caption="Header"/>
      <xsf:button action="xOptional::insert" xmlToEdit="approvalInfo"
         caption="Approval Info"/>
</xsf:toolbar>
```

unboundControls

Description

Defines the unbound button controls that are used in the view.

Use

Unbound controls are the buttons that are dragged from the Controls task pane onto the view in design mode. The name assigned to the button control is used in the `name` attribute of the button element, and when a user clicks on the button, the scripting code associated with the button will be called.

Content

`button`

Attributes

`name`

Type

`xsd:complexType`

Example

```
<xsf:view>
    <xsf:unboundControls>
        <xsf:button name="MyButton">
        </xsf:button>
    </xsf:unboundControls>
        .
        .
        .
</xsf:view>
```

useHTTPHandler

Description

Declares that the form data will be submitted to the specified URL using the specified HTTP method.

Use

The required href attribute specifies the URL to which the form should be submitted.

The required method attribute specifies the HTTP method to use for the submit operation.

Example

```
<xsf:useHttpHandler>
        href="http://MyServer/InfoPathScripts/MyScript.asp"
        method="POST"/>
```

useQueryAdapter

Description

Declares that the form data will be submitted using the same data adapter as the one specified to initially load the document.

Use

The query element used is the child element of the xDocumentClass element, not the element that is a child of the dataObject element.

useScriptHandler

Description

Use

When used with the submit element, it declares that the form data will be processed by script code in the OnSubmitRequest event handler.

When used with the documentVersionUpgrade element, it means that the upgrade of older forms will be processed by scripting code in the OnVersionUpgrade event handler in the form's primary scripting file.

useTransform

Description

Specifies that the upgrade will be handled by an XSLT file supplied by the newer version of the form template.

Use

When a user fills out a form, InfoPath automatically runs the specified XSLT on the form's underlying XML document and uses the output as the XML data to be edited, if the version of the form is greater than or equal to the `minVersionToUpgrade` attribute and the version is less than or equal to the `maxVersionToUpgrade` attribute.

Attributes

`maxVersionToUpgrade, minVersionToUpgrade, transform`

Type

`xsd:complexType`

Example

```
<xsf:documentVersionUpgrade>
   <xsf:useTransform
      transform="upgrade.xsl"
      minVersionToUpgrade="0.0.0.0"
      maxVersionToUpgrade="1.0.0.5"/>
</xsf:documentVersionUpgrade>
```

view

Description

This specifies the name identifier of the view chosen to be the default view.

Use

The `name` attribute identifies the view, including OM calls for switching views and for specifying the default view.

Attributes

`caption, name, printView`

Type

`xsd:complexType`

views

Description

Container for a sequence of one or more `view` elements.

Use

If not specified, the default view is the first view element found within the views element. This view is loaded when an InfoPath is initially opened.

In forms that use ADO or a Web service as their primary data source, the default view is set by the initialView attribute in the processing instruction of the form's XML template file. This attribute cannot be changed while in design mode.

Content

view

Attributes

default

Type

xsd:complexType

Example

```
<views default="meta_input">
    <view name="meta_input" caption="Story summary" printView="story_summary">
        <mainpane transform="metadata.xslt"/>
    </view>
</views>
```

webServiceAdapter

Description

Defines a Web service data adapter to be used to retrieve the data from a Web service for the specified data object. It can also be used to define a Web service adapter used to submit the main form data.

Content

operation

Attributes

name, queryAllowed, submitAllowed, wsdlUrl

Type

xsd:complexType

Example

```
<xsf:webServiceAdapter
    wsdlUrl="http://server1/bvtService/Service1.asmx?wsdl"
    queryAllowed="no"
```

```
        submitAllowed="yes">
          .
          .
          .
    </xsf:webServiceAdapter>
```

xDocumentClass

Description

The root element in the InfoPath Form Definition schema.

Use

The `name` provides a unique (URN-based) name to the form defined in this file. If this attribute is missing, then the form is named from the URL or the filename of the XSF file contained in the `href` attribute of the processing instruction of the XML document or template being loaded.

The `author` attribute names the author of the form definition. The optional `description` attribute contains a brief description of the form. `dataformSolution` specifies that the form is based on an ADO or Web service data sources. Allowed attribute values are `"yes"` and `"no"` (default). You should set the value to `"yes"` for forms with a `"yes"` view in order for them to work correctly.

`publishUrl` is set automatically when a form is published or deployed using InfoPath design mode. When you open a form, InfoPath checks this value against its original location and prevents new forms being created if the template was moved. To enable the template again, you need to set the attribute to the current location.

`requireFullTrust` specifies that the form is a fully trusted URN form. Possible values are `"yes"` and `"no"` (default). If this attribute is set to `"yes"`, the form will get full trust security privileges and a URN in the name attribute must identify the form.

`solutionVersion` gives the version number of the form definition file. It allows InfoPath to find if the current form is compatible with the product version. `productVersion` contains the version number of the form. The format of these two version numbers is nnnn.nnnn.nnnn.nnnn (major.minor.revision.build).

The required `xmlns` attribute declares all the global namespaces. Elements in the XSF schema are from the namespace `http://schemas.microsoft.com/office/InfoPath/2003/solutionDefinition`.

Content

`applicationParameters`, `customValidation`, `dataObjects`, `documentSchemas`, `documentSignatures`, `documentVersionUpgrade`, `domEventHandlers`, `extensions`, `fileNew`, `importParameters`, `listProperties`, `package`, `query`, `schemaErrorMessages`, `scripts`, `submit`, `taskpane`, `views`

Attributes

`author`, `dataFormSolution`, `description`, `name`, `productVersion`, `publishUrl`, `requireFullTrust`, `solutionFormatVersion`, `solutionVersion`

Type

```
xsd:complexType
```

Example

```
<xsf:xDocumentClass
    xmlns:xsf="http://schemas.microsoft.com/office/infopath/2003/solutionDefinition"
    name="urn::myTravelReport.microsoft.com"
    author="MichaelAllen"
    description="Travel Report form for entering travel reports, issues, expenses,
etc."
    dataFormSolution="yes"
    solutionVersion = "1.0.1.1"
    productVersion="11.0.1.1"
    solutionFormatVersion="0.9.0.0">
</xsf:xDocumentClass>
```

xmlFileAdapter

Description

Defines a data adapter for retrieving data from a static XML file for a data object.

Use

The required `fileUrl` attribute contains the URL of the XML file.

Attributes

```
fileUrl, name
```

Type

```
xsd:complexType
```

Example

```
<xsf:query>
        <xsf:xmlFileAdapter fileUrl="currencies.xml" />
</xsf:query>
```

xmlToEdit

Description

Specifies an instance of an editing component. The `xmlToEdit` element corresponds to an XML editing control in the design mode view.

Also a `button` attribute that specifies the name of an `xmlToEdit` element.

Use

The attributes specify where the control is in the view.

If the current selection or insertion point maps to an XML node that satisfies the `container` attribute XPath expression, the control is enabled. Otherwise, all actions are disabled. It is not sufficient for the container node to exist.

The `item` attribute is the XPath to the node to be edited.

The required `name` attribute identifies the contained editing component as the target for button actions. There should be no more than one `xmlToEdit` block with the same name in a given view.

The HTML element named in the `viewContext` must have the attribute `xd:CtrlId` set to that string. So `viewContext="myID"` in the form corresponds to `xd:CtrlId="myID"` in the HTML.

Content

editWith

Attributes

container, item, name, viewContext

Type

xsd:complexType

Attribute of

button

Type

xsd:NMTOKEN

Example

```
<xsf:xmlToEdit name="CD_10"
    item="/CustomUISample/CDCollection/CD"
    container="/CustomUISample">
    viewContext="cdID"
    <xsf:editWith caption="CD"
        xd:autogeneration="template"
        component="xCollection">
        .
        .
        .
    </xsf:editWith>
</xsf:xmlToEdit>
```

Attributes

action

Description

Specifies an action on an editing component, initiated by an `onClick` event, using the syntax `Component::Action`.

Attribute of

`button`

Type

`xsd:NMTOKEN`

aggregation

Description

Specifies how form property data should be processed to obtain a single value for a form library report.

Use

The `aggregation` attribute can either be an aggregation action or an indication of the particular element in the collection. It uses the following aggregation actions: `sum`, `count`, `average`, `min`, `max`, `first`, `last`, `merge`, and `plaintext`.

Attribute of

`field`

Type

`xsd:NMTOKEN`

allowCustomization

Description

Determines if the form can be modified or customized by users.

Attribute of

`solutionProperties`

Type

`xsf:xdYesNo`

application

Description

Identifies the name of the application used to design the Microsoft Office InfoPath 2003 form.

Use

In InfoPath 2003 the only allowed value is `"InfoPath Design Mode"`.

Attribute of

applicationParameters

Type

xsd:string

attribute

Description

Required attribute of `attributeData`. Specifies the name of the attribute to be inserted or modified.

Attribute of

attributeData

Type

xsd:string

author

Description

Identifies the author of the form definition.

Attribute of

xDocumentClass

Type

xsd:string

autoComplete

Description

Switches the auto-completion of controls on or off.

Attribute of

editWith

Type

xsf:xdYesNo

automaticallyCreateNodes

Description

Defines whether XML nodes will be automically generated when controls are inserted in the view in design mode. This attribute corresponds to the Automatically create data source check box at the bottom of the controls task pane.

Attribute of

solutionProperties

Type

xsf:xdYesNo

bottomMargin

Description

Specifies the bottom margin when printing a view.

Use

This attribute must be set by editing the XSF file, since there is no design mode interface.

Attribute of

printSettings

Type

xsd:float

caption (button element)

Description

Provides the display caption for a button.

Use

If caption attribute is not specified, the caption for the corresponding editWith element is used. If no icon is specified, the caption alone is used. If both caption and icon are specified, both are displayed. If neither is specified, a blank button is displayed.

caption (editWith element)

Description

Specifies an identifier for alternate forms of XML data to be used in the editing component.

caption (initialXmlDocument element)

Description

Defines the text string to be used as the name of the form in the Template Gallery and in the most recently used list.

caption (menu element)

Description

The caption for a menu.

caption (submit element)

Description

The name of the submit button and corresponding menu item that will appear on the File menu.

caption (taskpane element)

Description

The caption used in the task pane drop-down list box.

caption (toolbar element)

Description

The title of the toolbar, when the toolbar is floating.

caption (view element)

Description

The caption for the view in the view list.

columnName

Description

Identifies the column name in the SQL table underlying the form list view.

Attribute of

field

Type

xsf:xdTitle

commandText

Description

The SQL command for querying an ADO data source.

Attribute of

adoAdapter

Type

xsd:string

component

Description

The name of the editing component referenced with the action attribute of a button element.

Attribute of

editWith

Type

xsd:NMTOKEN

connectionString

Description

The connection string containing all the parameters needed to connect to the ADO data source.

Attribute of

adoAdapter

Type

xsd:string

container

Description

An XPath expression that sets the context in which a form control can be selected and its actions enabled.

Use

In design mode, InfoPath generates XPath patterns giving the full path from the root of the document. If you edit the form definition manually, you can use relative paths and predicates in your expressions.

Attribute of

xmlToEdit

Type

xsd:string

dataFormSolution

Description

Identifies the form as a database form.

Use

Allowed attribute values are "yes" and "no" (default). Forms with a primary data source based on ADO or Web services connection that have a query view should have this attribute set to "yes" in order for them to work properly.

Attribute of

xDocumentClass

Type

xsf:xdYesNo

default

Description

The identifier of the view chosen to be the default view. If not specified, the view will default to the first view element in document order. When a document instance is loaded, the default view is loaded initially.

Attribute of

views

Type

```
xsd:string
```

description

Description

A description of the form displayed in the File⇨New and File⇨Open dialog boxes.

Attribute of

```
xDocumentClass
```

Type

```
xsd:string
```

disableMenuItem

Description

Enables or disables the File⇨Submit menu item.

Attribute of

```
submit
```

Type

```
xsf:xdYesNo
```

enabled

Description

Specifies whether form merging is enabled for a form.

Attribute of

```
importParameters
```

Type

```
xsf:xdYesNo
```

expression

Description

An XPath expression used to validate the XML node specified in the match attribute of an errorCondition element.

Attribute of

errorCondition

Type

xsd:string

expressionContext

Description

Specifies the node on which the expression specified in the expression attribute of an errorCondition element is rooted.

Attribute of

errorCondition

Type

xsd:string

field

Description

Defines a single field for form library columns.

Specifies a relative XPath expression from the item attribute of the xmlToEdit element.

Attribute of

editWith

Type

xsd:string

fileUrl

Description

Contains the URL of a static XML file used as a data source.

Attribute of

xmlFileAdapter

Type

xsd:anyURI

followingSiblings

Description

Specifies a relative XPath expression for the XML nodes prior to which the insertion of an XML fragment should occur.

Attribute of

chooseFragment

Type

xsd:string

footer

Description

The content of the page footer for a print view.

Attribute of

printSettings

Type

xsd:string

fullyEditableNamespace

Description

Defines the namespace for a form's XML schema that can be edited in design mode.

Attribute of

solutionProperties

Type

xsd:anyURI

handlerObject

Description

Identifies the unique name of the domEventHandler object in the script code.

Use

The referenced script must use this name to define event handler functions for the specified XML node. For example, a script may contain functions such as onValidate and onAfterChange that are called whenever the specified events occur at the matching XML node.

Attribute of

domEventHandler

Type

xsd:string

header

Description

The content of the page header in a print view.

Attribute of

printSettings

Type

xsd:string

href (initialXmlDocument element)

Description

Specifies the name of the XML template file to be used when a user chooses File⇨Fill Out a Form.

href (taskpane element)

Description

The URL of the HTML file containing the task pane data.

href (useHttpHandler element)

Description

The URL to which the form should be submitted.

icon

Description

Contains a URL or identifier for an image used for a button.

Use

If a URL is used, the image must be in BMP or GIF format. If the value is an integer, it will be interpreted as a system ID, allowing access to internal system icons (.ico).

Attribute of

```
button
```

Type

```
xsd:string
```

initOnLoad

Description

Specifies if a data object should be initialized automatically on form load.

Attribute of

```
dataObject
```

Type

```
xsf:xdYesNo
```

item

Description

An XPath expression that specifies the nodes to be edited with components in the contained `editWith` elements.

Attribute of

```
xmlToEdit
```

Type

```
xsd:string
```

language

Description

Identifies the name of the scripting language used to implement the business logic of a form.

Attribute of

```
scripts
```

Type

```
xsf:xdScriptLanguage
```

lastOpenView

Description

The name of the view that was last open in the application while editing/viewing the form. The next time the form is opened in the application, this view is automatically opened.

Attribute of

solutionProperties

Type

lastVersionNeedingTransform

Description

Identifies, temporarily, the value of the maxVersionToUpgrade in the documentVersionUpgrade for upgrade with an XSLT file if the script is currently being used for the upgrade.

Attribute of

solutionProperties

Type

xsf:xdSolutionVersion

leftMargin

Description

Specifies the left margin when printing a view.

Use

This attribute must be set by editing the XSF file, since there is no design mode interface.

Attribute of

printSettings

Type

xsd:float

location

Description

Contains the namespace URI and URL of the XML schema for a form, followed by a space and the filename. Schemas without namespaces are listed with just the XSD filename.

Attribute of

```
documentSchema
```

Type

```
xsd:string
```

marginUnits

Description

Specifies the margin unit size when printing a view.

Use

This attribute must be set by editing the XSF file, since there is no design mode interface.

match (domEventHandler element)

Description

Identifies the XML node for which the event handler is declared.

match (errorCondition element)

Description

Identifies the XML node on which the custom validation is declared.

match (override element)

Description

Identifies the XML node for which the error message override is defined.

match (partFragment element)

Description

An XPath expression that identifies the elements and attributes inside the input SOAP message that are to be replaced at run time.

maxLength

Description

Defines the length of a field (number of bytes).

Attribute of

field

Type

xsd:byte

maxVersionToUpgrade

Description

Inclusive value for the latest form that needs to be upgraded.

method

Description

Specifies the HTTP method to use for a form submit operation.

Attribute of

useHttpHandler

Type

xsd:NMTOKEN

minVersionToUpgrade

Description

Inclusive value for the oldest XML that can be upgraded. This is defined to prevent running an upgrade XSLT on XML documents so different from the current one that the XSLT may cause data loss.

Attribute of

useTransform

Type

xsf:xdSolutionVersion

name (button element)

Description

Associates the OnClick event handler of a button with a script function.

Use

Although name is optional, it is required for buttons that use scripting code.

name (dataObject element)

Description

The unique name for the data object.

name (extension element)

Description

The unique name for the specified InfoPath extension.

name (field element)

Description

The name of the field to be used on the form list view.

name (file element)

Description

The name of the file.

name (importSource element)

Description

The name of the source form defined in the processing instruction of the XML document.

name (menuArea element)

Description

A name that corresponds to one of the built-in InfoPath top-level menus.

name (operation element)

Description

The unique name of the Web service method.

name (property element)

Description

The name of the property.

name (toolbar element)

Description

The name of a toolbar, which must be unique within a form.

name (view element)

Description

Identifies the view.

name (xDocumentClass element)

Description

Unique URN for the form.

name (xmlToEdit element)

Description

Associates actions on an editing component with buttons defined in menus and toolbars.

node

Description

Defines the XPath expression needed to extract the value of the specified property from the XML document.

Attribute of

field

Type

xsd:string

onAfterSubmit

Description

Specifies whether the form should be closed or kept open, or if a new form should be created after a successful submission.

Attribute of

submit

Type

```
xsd:NMTOKEN
```

orientation

Description

The orientation of the page in a print view.

Attribute of

```
printSettings
```

Type

```
xsd:NMTOKEN
```

parent

Description

This attribute gives a relative XPath from the `xmlToEdit` container node. It refers to the node in the XML under which this fragment should be inserted. The default value is ".".

Attribute of

```
chooseFragment
```

Type

```
xsd:string
```

printView

Description

Specifies the name of an alternate view to use for printing a view.

Attribute of

```
view
```

Type

```
xsd:string
```

productVersion

Description

Identifies the version (build) number of the InfoPath application with which a form has been created. It is represented in the format nnnn.nnnn.nnnn.nnnn (major.minor.revision.build).

Attribute of

xDocumentClass

Type

xsd:string

proofing

Description

Switches the proofing features, such as the spelling checker, on or off.

Attribute of

editWith

Type

xsf:xdYesNo

publishUrl

Description

Identifies the publish location of a URL-based, sandboxed solution. This is set automatically when a form is published or deployed using InfoPath design mode. When a form is opened, the value is used to check if it has been moved from its original published location.

Attribute of

xDocumentClass

Type

xsd:string

queryAllowed

Description

Optional attribute of adoAdapter that specifies whether data can be retrieved from the data source through the query method of the data adapter object.

Use

Allowed values are "yes" (default) and "no".

Attribute of

adoAdapter, webServiceAdapter

Type

```
xsf:xdYesNo
```

removeAncestors

Description

Specifies the number of ancestor (parent) elements to be removed when the last item is removed.

Attribute of

```
editWith
```

Type

```
xsd:nonNegativeInteger
```

replaceWith

Description

Contains an XPath expression that identifies a unique node inside the InfoPath 2003 main document DOM that should be used at specified locations inside the input SOAP message when making the Web service call.

Attribute of

```
partFragment
```

Type

```
xsd:string
```

required

Description

Identifies whether a `field` element accepts NULL values. Allowed values are `"yes"` and `"no"` (default).

Attribute of

```
field
```

Type

```
xsf:xdYesNo
```

requireFullTrust

Description

Identifies the form to be a fully trusted URN solution.

Use

Allowed values are `"yes"` and `"no"`. If set to `"yes"`, the form must be identified by a URN specified in the `name` attribute.

Attribute of

xDocumentClass

Type

xsf:xdYesNo

rightMargin

Description

Specifies the right margin when printing a view.

Use

This attribute must be set by editing the XSF file, since there is no design mode interface.

Attribute of

printSettings

Type

xsd:float

rootSchema

Description

Identifies an XML schema as the top-level schema of the form.

Attribute of

documentSchema

Type

xsf:xdYesNo

schema (dataObject element)

Description

Refers to a schema file associated with a data object.

schema (importSource element)

Description

Identifies a schema URN for a form that is the source of an import or merge operation.

scriptLanguage

Description

Identifies the name of the scripting language used to implement the business logic of the form.

Attribute of

```
solutionProperties
```

Type

```
xsf:xdScriptLanguage
```

serviceUrl

Description

The Web service URL where the request should be sent.

Attribute of

```
operation
```

Type

```
xsd:string
```

shortMessage

Description

Short error message to return in case of invalid data.

Attribute of

```
errorMessage
```

Type

```
xsd:string
```

showErrorOn

Description

Identifies XML nodes on which an error should be displayed when the form is filled out.

Attribute of

errorCondition

Type

xsd:string

showIf

Description

Optional attribute that specifies the display property of a button.

Use

The showIf attribute only applies to buttons used with editing components.

Allowed values are as follows:

- ❑ always (default).
- ❑ enabled. Shows the button only if the action is contextually enabled.
- ❑ immediate. Shows the button only if the action is contextually immediate

Attribute of

button

Type

xsd:NMTOKEN

showSignatureReminder

Description

Specifies if a dialog box should be shown reminding the user that the form should be signed before submitting.

Attribute of

submit

Type

xsf:xdYesNo

showStatusDialog

Description

Specifies if the status dialog box should be shown after the submit operation.

Attribute of

submit

Type

xsf:xdYesNo

signatureLocation

Description

An XPath expression that points to the node that is used for storing the digital signature.

Attribute of

documentSignatures

Type

xsd:string

soapAction

Description

The value of the SOAPAction attribute in the SOAP request message.

Attribute of

operation

Type

xsd:string

solutionFormatVersion

Description

The version number that represents the format of the form definition file in the form nnnn.nnnn.nnnn.nnnn (major.minor.revision.build). Version number of InfoPath form definition format will be updated for major format upgrades, and it helps InfoPath in determining if the current form is compatible with the current product version in which it is being opened.

Attribute of

`xDocumentClass`

Type

`xsf:xdSolutionVersion`

solutionVersion

Description

Identifies the version number of the form. It is represented in the format nnnn.nnnn.nnnn.nnnn (major.minor.revision.build).

Attribute of

`xDocumentClass`

Type

`xsf:xdSolutionVersion`

source

Description

Points to a resource file in the form template that contains the schema for the input SOAP message of the selected operation of the Web service.

Attribute of

`input`

Type

`xsd:string`

src

Description

Provides a relative URL to the specified script source file.

Attribute of

`script`

Type

`xsf:xdFileName`

submitAllowed (adoAdapter element)

Description

Optional attribute of adoAdapter that specifies whether data can be submitted to the data source through the submit method of the data adapter object.

Use

Allowed values are "yes" and "no" (default).

submitAllowed (webServiceAdapter element)

Description

Optional attribute of adoAdapter that specifies whether data can be submitted to the data source through the submit method of the data adapter object.

Use

Allowed values are "yes" and "no" (default).

tooltip

Description

Optional attribute of the button element that provides the pop-up text for a toolbar button.

Attribute of

button

Type

xsf:xdTitle

topMargin

Description

Specifies the top margin when a view is printed.

Use

This attribute must be set by editing the XSF file, since there is no design mode interface.

Attribute of

printSettings

Type

xsd:float

transform (importSource element)

Description

Identifies the XSLT transform to be used during a merge operation.

transform (mainpane element)

Description

Specifies the XSLT transform for the main part of the form.

transform (useTransform element)

Description

Specifies the upgrade XSLT filename relative to the form template.

type (editWith element)

Description

Specifies the formatting of a text field. The following values are allowed: `"plain"` (default), `"plainMultiline"`, `"formatted"`, `"formattedMultiline"`, and `"rich"`.

type (errorMessage element)

Description

Specifies whether a short or a long error message is displayed.

type (field element)

Description

The XML Schema data type of a `field` element.

type (property element)

Description

Associates actions on an editing component with buttons defined in menus and toolbars.

value (attributeData element)

Description

Specifies the value of the attribute to be inserted.

value (property element)

Description

Specifies the value of a file property.

viewable

Description

Identifies whether this field should be added to the default view or not. Allowed values are `"yes"` and `"no"` (default).

Attribute of

field

Type

xsf:xdYesNo

viewContext

Description

Use

This corresponds to a condition on the current selection in the view. The condition is satisfied if there is some common ancestor of the current selection (in the HTML tree) that has the corresponding xd:CtrlId.

This can be used to disambiguate controls when two instances of the same control have the same XML context, so that the XML context is identical.

Attribute of

xmlToEdit

Type

xsd:string

wsdlUrl

Description

Contains the URL of the WSDL file describing the Web service.

Attribute of

webServiceAdapter

Type

xsd:string

InfoPath Object Model Reference

This appendix lists the methods, properties, and events of InfoPath's object model.

Object Model Diagram

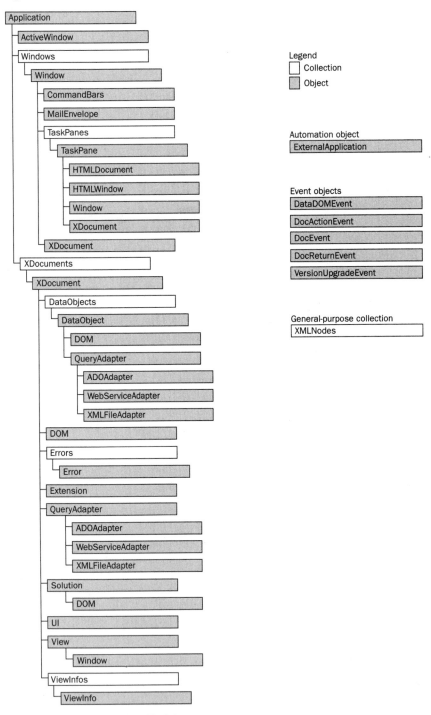

Figure C-1: InfoPath Object Model.

Objects

Name	Description
ADOAdapter	Represents a connection to a Microsoft ADO/OLEDB data source.
Application	Represents the Microsoft Office InfoPath 2003 application.
DataDOMEvent	Parameter to the OnBeforeChange, OnValidate, and OnAfterChange events
DataObject	This is the link object between the data adapter and InfoPath form
DocActionEvent	Parameter of OnClick button event.
DocEvent	Parameter to the OnSwitchView and OnAfterChange events of an InfoPath form.
DocReturnEvent	Parameter to the OnLoad and OnSubmitRequest events of an InfoPath form.
Error	Is an error in InfoPath form associated with an XML DOM node.
ExternalApplication	Represents the Microsoft Office InfoPath 2003 application from external scripts.
HTMLTaskPane	Custom task pane associated with a window
HTMLTaskPaneExternal	Is used to expose the InfoPath Object Model to the Dynamic HTML (DHTML) scripting code in a custom task pane.
MailEnvelope	Custom e-mail message.
Solution	Is a InfoPath form template.
TaskPane	Is a task pane associated to a window.
UI	Represents various user interface components that can be used in an InfoPath form.
VersionUpgradeEvent	Parameter to the OnVersionUpgrade event of an InfoPath form.
View	Is the current view of the form.
ViewInfo	Contains descriptive information about a view.
WebServiceAdapter	Represents a connection to an XML Web service.
Window	Represents a window that is used in the InfoPath application.
XDocument	Is underlying XML document of an InfoPath form.
XMLFileAdapter	Represents a connection to an XML file.

Collections

Name	Description
DataObjects	Contains a DataObject instance for each secondary data source used in the form.
Errors	Contains an Error object for each errors within a form.
TaskPanes	Contains a list of TaskPane object for each task pane used in the form.
ViewInfos	List of ViewInfo within the form.
Windows	List of Window object within the form.
XDocuments	Contains an XDocument for each underlying XML document currently open.
XMLNodes	Collection of XML DOM nodes.

Events

Name	Description
OnAfterChange	Occurs after changes to a form's underlying XML document have been accepted and after the OnValidate event has occurred.
OnAfterImport	Occurs after the import (or merge) operation has successfully completed.
OnBeforeChange	Occurs after changes to a form's underlying XML document have been made but before the changes are accepted.
OnLoad	Occurs after a form has been loaded, but before any views have been initialized.
OnSubmitRequest	Occurs when the submit operation is invoked either from the InfoPath user interface or by using the Submit method of the XDocument object in the InfoPath Object Model.
OnSwitchView	Occurs after a view in a form has been successfully switched.
OnValidate	Occurs after changes to a form's underlying XML document have been accepted but before the OnAfterChange event occurs.
OnVersionUpgrade	Occurs when the version number of a form being opened is older than the version number of the form template on which it is based.

Objects

ADOAdapter

Properties

Name	Type	Description
Connection	String	Connection string for ADO
Command	String	Command string for ADO
Timeout	Long	Timeout slice for both connection and command timeouts

Methods

Name	Return Type	Parameters	Description
BuildSQLFromXMLNodes	String	IXMLDOMNode	Returns a string containing an SQL command text fragment using the specified XML node.

Application

Properties

Name	Type	Description
ActiveWindow	Window	Returns active Window object.
Name	String	Returns the name of application.
LanguageSettings	LanguageSettings	Returns LanguageSettings MSO object.
Version	String	Returns InfoPath version string.
Windows	Windows	Returns windows collection object.
XDocuments	XDocuments	Returns XDocuments collection object.

Methods

Name	Return Type	Parameters	Description
FormatString	String	VARIANT varUnput String bstrCategory String bstrOptions	Converts the specified string according to specified Category and Options.
NewADODBConnection	ADODBConnection		Creates and returns a reference to an empty ADO Connection object.
NewADODBRecordset	ADODBRecordset		Creates and returns a reference to an empty ADO Recordset object.
Quit		Boolean vfForce (optional: 0)	Closes the application; If vfForce is set to true, all documents will be closed without saving even if they are currently dirty. If vfForce is set to false, regular procedure of document closing will run.

DataDOMEvent

Properties

Name	Type	Description
Site	XMLDOMNode	XML node where the event is currently processed.
MatchExpression	String	Returns context string for the XML node where the event is currently processed.
Parent	XMLDOMNode	Returns parent for the XML node where the event was fired.
Source	XMLDOMNode	Returns the XML node where the event was fired.
Operation	String	Returns name of the event action. Name can be one of the keywords: Delete, Insert, and Update.
IsUndoRedo	Boolean	Returns true if event is fired within Undo or Redo activity.
OldValue	VARIANT	In the case of updating or deleting leaf node returns its old value.

Name	Type	Description
NewValue	VARIANT	In the case of updating or inserting leaf node returns its new value.
XDocument	XDocument	Returns the XDocument object.
ReturnStatus	Boolean	Indicates if the event return status: TRUE—There was no error detected. FALSE—Changes were not accepted due to an error being detected.
ReturnMessage	String	Get or set the error message text.

Methods

Name	Return Type	Parameters	Description
Report Error()	Validation Error	VARIANT varNode String bstrShortErrorMessage Boolean fSiteDependent String bstrDetailedError (optional: " ") Long ErrorCode (optional: 0) String bstrType (optional: "modeless")	Creates Error object and adds it to the Errors collection.

DataObject

Properties

Name	Type	Description
DOM	XMLDOMDocument	Returns a reference to the Document Object Model (DOM).
NAME	String	Name of the associated.
QueryAdapter	IDispatch	Returns a reference to one of the following data adapter: ADOAdapter, WebServiceAdapter, or XMLFileAdapter object.

Methods

Name	Return Type	Parameters	Description
Query			Read data from specified Adapter into DOM associated with DataObject.

DocActionEvent

Properties

Name	Type	Description
ReturnStatus	Boolean	Indicates if the event return status: TRUE—There was no error detected. FALSE—Changes were not accepted due to an error being detected.
Source	XMLDOMNode	Returns the XML node where the event was fired.
XDocument	XDocument	Returns the XDocument object.

DocEvent

Properties

Name	Type	Description
XDocument	XDocument	Returns the XDocument object.

DocReturnEvent

Properties

Name	Type	Description
ReturnStatus	Boolean	Indicates if the event return status: TRUE—There was no error detected. FALSE—Changes were not accepted due to an error being detected.
XDocument	XDocument	Returns the XDocument object.

Error

Properties

Name	Type	Description
ConditionName	String	For USER_SPECIFIED type, returns the name of the error condition For SCHEMA_VALIDATION and SYSTEM_GENERATED type, it returns NULL.
DetailedErrorMessage	String	Get/set the error message's detailed message.

Name	Type	Description
ErrorCode	Long	Get/set error code value.
Node	XMLDOMNode	Returns the XML node associated with an error.
ShortErrorMessage	String	Get/set the error message's `ScreenTip`.
Type	String	Returns the type of error object: `SCHEMA_VALIDATION`—Schema validation error (generated by the platform). `SYSTEM_GENERATED`—Template error based on declarative programming (generated by platform following constraints declared in the template manifest) or created from script using the `Event.ReportError()` method call `USER_SPECIFIED`—Generated from template script using `Errors.Add()` method call.

ExternalApplication

Methods

Name	Return Type	Parameters	Description
CacheSolution		String bstrSolutionURI	Examines the form template in the cache and, if necessary, updates it from the published location of the form template.
Close		String bstrDocument	Closes (unconditionally) the specified document.
New		String bstrDocumentURI Long XdDocumentVersionMode (optional: "xdFailOnVersionOlder")	Creates a new form from the XML file.
NewFromSolution		BSTR* bstrSolutionURI	Creates a new form from the template. `bstrSolutionURI` parameter can specify either XSF or XSN template files.
Open		String bstrDocumentURI Long XdDocumentVersionMode (optional: "xdFailOnVersionOlder")	Opens the specified XML form.

Table continued on following page

Name	Return Type	Parameters	Description
Quit			Closes an application. Runs the regular document closing procedure
Register Solution		String bstrSolutionURL String bstrBehavior (optional: "overwrite")	Installs a form template. If bstrBehavior = overwrite (default) the platform will update existing registration record. If bstrBehavior = new-only the method will fail if the form template is already registered.
Unregister Solution		String bstrSolutionURN	Uninstalls the registered template.

HTMLTaskPane

Properties

Name	Type	Description
HTMLDocument	Document	Returns a reference to an HTML document object.
HTMLWindow	Window	Returns a reference to an HTML window object.
Type	TaskPane	Returns the type of task pane object.
Visible	Boolean	Specifies or returns if the task pane is visible or not.

Methods

Name	Return Type	Parameters	Description
Navigate		String bstrURL	Loads the specified HTML document into InfoPath task pane.

HTMLTaskPaneExternal

Properties

Name	Type	Description
Window	Window	Returns taskpane Window object.
XDocument	XDocument	Returns XDocument object associated to the current form.

MailEnvelope

Properties

Name	Type	Description
BCC	String	Get/put value of BCC mail envelope field.
CC	String	Get/put value of CC mail envelope field.
Subject	String	Get/put value of Subject mail envelope field.
To	String	Get/put value of To mail envelope field.
Visible	Boolean	Show/Hide mail header of the window.

Solution

Properties

Name	Type	Description
PackageURL	String	Returns URL of the local folder with un-cabbed template form files.
URI	String	Returns template form's original URL or URN (from where it was loaded).
Version	String	Returns template version.
DOM	XMLDOMDocument	Returns DOM object of the template form's manifest XML file.

TaskPane

Properties

Name	Type	Description
Type	TaskPane	Returns the type of task pane object.
Visible	Boolean	Specifies or returns if the task pane is visible or not.

UI

Methods

Name	Return Type	Parameters	Description
Alert()		String bsrtAlertString	Displays message box with specified Alert string.
ShowModal Dialog()		String bstrName, VARIANT vArguments (optional) VARIANT* vHeight (optional) VARIANT* vWidth (optional) VARIANT* vXPos (optional) VARIANT* vYPos (optional)	Displays a modal message box with specified HTML.
Show Signature Dialog()			Opens a dialog box for processing form digital signatures.
ShowMail Item()		String bstrTo String bstrCC String bstrBCC String bstrSubject String bstrBody	Creates a mail item with the specified parameters. Attaches an XML document. Makes the mail header visible.

VersionUpgradeEvent

Properties

Name	Type	Description
DocumentVersion	String	A read-only property that returns a string containing the version number of a Microsoft Office InfoPath 2003 form.
ReturnStatus	Boolean	Indicates if the event return status: TRUE—There was no error detected. FALSE—Changes were not accepted due to an error being detected.

Name	Type	Description
SolutionVersion	String	A read-only property that returns a string containing the version number of a form template.
XDocument	XDocument	Returns the XDocument object.

View

Properties

Name	Type	Description
Name	String	Returns the name of the current view.
Window	Window	Returns the Window object associated with the view.

Methods

Name	Return Type	Parameters	Description
DisableAutoUpdate			Notifies platform that document DOM changes should stop being synced with the view.
EnableAutoUpdate			Notifies platform that document DOM changes should start being synced with the view.
ExecuteAction		String bstrAction VARIANT varXMLToEdit (optional)	Executes an editing command, exactly equivalent to clicking on a button with corresponding xmlToEdit and action attributes. As with the button, the action will be based on the current selection. It will act on the selected context, and in the case where the selection would lead the button to be disabled, ExecuteAction will have no effect.
Export		String bstrURL String bstrFormat	Exports View as a file with specified format. Saves the file to specified URL.

Table continued on following page

Name	Return Type	Parameters	Description
ForceUpdate			Notifies platform that changes made to DOM need to be synced with the view.
GetContextNodes	XMLNodes	VARIANT varNode (optional) VARIANT varViewContext (optional)	Returns the context (within the View) of the selection that would be created by calling SelectNodes (varNode, null, varViewContext), in the form of the collection of XML nodes mapped from the view, starting at the selection and walking up.
GetSelectedNodes	XMLNodes		Returns collection of XML nodes to which the selected view elements are mapped. Otherwise returns an empty collection
SelectNodes		XMLDOMNode pxnStartNode VARIANT varEndNode (optional) VARIANT varViewContext (optional)	Attempts to set selection in the View, corresponding to a range of selectable view elements, the first of which maps to xnStartNode and the last of which maps to varEndNode.
SelectText		XMLDOMNode pxnField VARIANT varViewContext (optional)	Attempts to set selection on the text content of an editable field bound to the specified xnField.
SwitchView		String bstrName	Switches to the specified view. If the specified string is empty, InfoPath switches to the default view.

ViewInfo

Properties

Name	Type	Description
Name	String	Returns the view name.
IsDefault	Boolean	Returns true if the view is defined as default in template xsf; otherwise returns false.

WebServiceAdapter

Properties

Name	Type	Description
Input	String	Get/Set XML node corresponding to defined in xsf: WSAdapter/Operation/Input.
Operation	String	Get/Set Web service command string.
WSDLURL	String	Returns URL of the WSDL file.

Window

Properties

Name	Type	Description
Active	Boolean	Returns true if window is currently active, otherwise returns .
CommandBars	CommandBars	Returns MSO CommandBars object.
MailEnvelope	MailEnvelope	Returns the MailEnvelope object.
TaskPanes	TaskPanes	Returns TaskPanes collection object.
Type	Long	Returns 0 for Editor window; returns 1 for Designer window.
XDocument	XDocument	Returns the XDocument object tied to window.

Methods

Name	Return Type	Parameters	Description
Activate		Activates the window	Notifies platform that document DOM changes should stop being synced with the view.
Close		Boolean varForce (optional: false)	Closes the window and documents. If varForce is set to true, all document will be closed without saving even if it is currently dirty. If varForce is set to false, regular procedure of document closing will run.

XDocument

Properties

Name	Type	Description
DataObjects	Boolean	Returns `DataObjects` collection object tied to the document.
DOM	XMLDOMDocument	Returns document XML content DOM.
Errors	ValidationErrors	Returns `Errors` collection object tied to the document.
Extension	IDispatch	Returns document business logic functions and global variables.
IsDirty	Boolean	Returns `true` if the document is dirty (it has been modified after the last save); otherwise returns `false`.
IsDOMReadOnly	Boolean	Returns `true` if the document DOM is in read-only mode.
IsNew	Boolean	Returns `true` if the document was not saved after it was created; otherwise returns `false`.
IsReadOnly	Boolean	Returns `true` if the form file is in read-only mode.
IsSigned	Boolean	Return `true` if form is signed; otherwise returns `false`.
Language	String	Get/Set document language value.
QueryAdapter	DataAdapter	Returns the `DataAdapter` object used for `Query()` call.
Solution	Solution	Returns `Template` object tied to the document.
UI	UI	Returns `UI` object tied to the document.
Uri	String	Returns the URI location.
View	View	Returns `View` object tied to the document.
ViewInfos	ViewInfos	Returns `ViewInfos` collection object tied to the document.

Methods

Name	Return type	Parameters	Description
GetDataVariable	String	Long VariableNumber	Returns string value of the specified variable; in the case the variable value is not defined or is empty method will return `NULL`.

Name	Return type	Parameters	Description
GetDOM	XMLDOM Document	String bstrName	Returns the DOM object tied to DataObject specified by name.
ImportFile		String bstrFileURI	Imports specified XML file into document.
PrintOut			Prints the document as it is rendered in the view
Query			Queries the data using DataAdapter associated with document and stores retrieved data to the document DOM.
Save			Saves the document to the URL address with which it is associated.
SaveAs		String bstrFileUrl	Saves the form to specified URL.
SetDataVariable		Long VariableNumber String bstrVariableValue	Sets the value of the enumerated variable to the document API.
Submit			Performs submit operation defined in template xsf. This can be: —HttpHandler —QueryAdapter —ScriptHandler

Events

Name	Parameters	Description
OnAfterImport	DocEvent pEvent	Occurs after the import (or merge) operation has successfully completed.
OnLoad	DocReturnEvent pEvent	Occurs after a form has been loaded, but before any views have been initialized.
OnSubmitRequest	DocReturnEvent pEvent	Occurs when the submit operation is invoked.
OnSwitchView	DocEvent pEvent	Occurs after a view in a form has been successfully switched.
OnVersionUpgrade	VersionUpgradeEvent pEvent	Occurs when the version number of a form being opened is older than the version number of the form template on which it is based.

XMLFileAdapter

Properties

Name	Type	Description
FileURL	String	Get/Set XML File location address.

Collections

DataObjects

Properties

Name	Type	Description
Count	Long	Returns number of DataObjects in the DataObjects collection.
Item	DataObject	Returns the DataObject; method has VARIANT parameter that is Long for enumeration and String for accessing DataObject by name.

Errors

Properties

Name	Type	Description
Count	Long	Returns the number of error objects in the errors collection.
Item	ValidationError	Returns the error object corresponding to the specified index.

Methods

Name	Return Type	Parameters	Description
Add	Validation Error	VARIANT varNode String bstrConditionName String bstrShortErrorMessage String bstrDetailedErrorMessage Long ErrorCode (optional) String bstrType (optional: "modeless")	Creates an error object and adds it to the errors collection.

Name	Return Type	Parameters	Description
Delete		VARIANT varNode String bstrConditionName	Deletes all error objects associated with the specified XML Node and Condition Name.
DeleteAll			Deletes all error objects in the collection.

TaskPanes

Properties

Name	Type	Description
Count	Long	Returns the number of TaskPane objects in the task pane collection
Item	TaskPane	Returns the TaskPane object by its type value (not by its index in the collection).

ViewInfos

Properties

Name	Type	Description
Count	Long	Returns number of ViewInfo objects in collection

Methods

Name	Return Type	Parameters	Description
Item	ViewInfo	VARIANT Index	Returns ViewObject by specified index: LONG for enumeration and BSTR for accessing ViewObjects by name.

Windows

Properties

Name	Type	Description
Count	Long	Returns number of Window objects in collection.

Methods

Name	Return Type	Parameters	Description
Item	Window	VARIANT Index	Returns Window specified by LONG index.

XDocuments

Properties

Name	Type	Description
Count	Long	Returns the number of XDocument objects in collection.
Item	XDocument	Returns XDocument object by specified index: String for enumeration access; String for accessing XDocuments by URL.

Methods

Name	Return Type	Parameters	Description
Close		VARIANT varIndex	Closes the document specified by: Long collection index XDocument object Document file URL
New	XDocument	VARIANT varTemplateURI Long XdDocument VersionMode (optional: xdFail OnVersionOlder)	Creates new document by specified template XML file.
NewFrom Solution	XDocument	VARIANT varSolutionURI	Creates a new form using the specified template package.
Open	XDocument	VARIANT varDocumentURI Long XdDocument VersionMode (optional: xdFailOnVersionOlder)	Opens the form specified by URI.

XMLNodes

Properties

Name	Type	Description
Count	Long	Returns the number of XML Nodes in the collection.
Item	XMLDOMNode	Returns XMLDOMNode object by specified collection index.

References

In this section we included references to the primary standards and specifications likely to be of interest to InfoPath developers.

Also included are relevant Microsoft developer center URLs, and Web sites on meta data standards.

Date and Time Formats
A note posted by Reuters and made available by the W3 Consortium for discussion. ISO 8601 describes a large number of date/time formats. This profile defines a few formats, likely to satisfy most requirements.
`www.w3.org/TR/NOTE-datetime`

DCMI Metadata Terms
The authoritative specification of all meta data terms maintained by the Dublin Core Metadata Initiative—elements, element refinements, encoding schemes, and vocabulary terms.
Dublin Core Metadata Initiative. Recommendation. 2003-03-04.
`www.dublincore.org/documents/dcmi-terms/`

Expressing Simple Dublin Core in RDF/XML
Gives an encoding for the DC element set in XML using simple RDF, provides a DTD and W3C XML schemas to validate the documents and describes a method to link them from Web pages.
Dublin Core Metadata Initiative. Recommendation. 2002-07-31.
`www.dublincore.org/documents/2002/07/31/dcmes-xml/`

Extensible Markup Language (XML) 1.0 (Second Edition)
The second edition of XML (first published February 10, 1998) is not a new version of the specification. It incorporates the first-edition errata.
World Wide Web Consortium. Recommendation. 2000-10-06.
`www.w3.org/TR/2000/REC-xml-20001006`

InfoPath
MSDN center for InfoPath.
Microsoft.
`www.msdn.microsoft.com/library/default.asp?url=/library/`
`en-us/dnanchor/html/odc_ancInfo.asp`

ISO 3166 code lists
Lists extracted from ISO 3166-1 containing all short country names and alpha-2 code elements officially published by ISO.
International Standards Organization.
`www.iso.org/iso/en/prods-services/iso3166ma/index.html`

PRISM 1.2
Defines a meta data standard based on XML for use in traditional and electronic publishing.
Publishing Requirements for Industry Standard Metadata. Working Draft. 2003-07-29.
`www.prismstandard.org/`

RDF Primer
Introduces the basic concepts of RDF and describes its XML syntax. It describes how to define RDF vocabularies using the RDF Vocabulary Description Language.
World Wide Web Consortium. Working Draft. 2003-09-05.
`http://www.w3.org/TR/2004/REC-rdf-primer-20040210`

RDF Site Summary (RSS) 1.0
An XML application providing lightweight meta data description and syndication format.
RSS Developer's Working Group. Recommendation. 2001-05-30.
`web.resource.org/rss/1.0/spec`

RDF Site Summary 1.0 Modules
Guidelines for namespace-based modularization that allows RSS to be extended.
RSS Developer's Working Group. Recommendation. 2001-03-20.
`http://web.resource.org/rss/1.0/modules/`

RDF/XML Syntax Specification (Revised)
Defines the XML syntax for RDF graphs, which was originally defined in the 1999 RDF Model and Syntax Specification.
World Wide Web Consortium. Working Draft. 2003-09-05.
`http://www.w3.org/TR/2004/REC-rdf-syntax-grammar-20040210/`

Resource Description Framework (RDF): Concepts and Abstract Syntax
Defines an abstract syntax on which RDF is based, and that serves to link its concrete syntax to its formal semantics.
World Wide Web Consortium. Working Draft. 2003-09-05.
`http://www.w3.org/TR/2004/REC-rdf-concepts-20040210/`

SOAP Version 1.2 Part 1: Messaging Framework
Defines an extensible messaging framework containing a message construct that can be exchanged over a variety of underlying protocols.
World Wide Web Consortium. Proposed recommendation. 2003-05-07.
`www.w3.org/TR/2003/PR-soap12-part1-20030507/`

SOAP Version 1.2 Part 2: Adjuncts
Defines a set of adjuncts that may be used with SOAP Version 1.2 Part 1: Messaging Framework.
World Wide Web Consortium. Proposed recommendation. 2003-06-24.
`ww.w3.org/TR/2003/REC-soap12-part2-20030624/`

UDDI Version 3.0
Describes the Web services, data structures, and behaviors of all instances of a UDDI registry. 2002-06-19.
`http://uddi.org/pubs/uddi_v3.htm`

Uniform Resource Identifiers (URI): Generic Syntax
Defines the generic syntax of URI, including both absolute and relative forms, and guidelines for their use.
World Wide Web Consortium. 1998-08.
`www.ietf.org/rfc/rfc2396.txt`

Uniform Resource Locators (URL)
Specifies a Uniform Resource Locator (URL), the syntax and semantics of formalized information for location and access of resources via the Internet.
World Wide Web Consortium. 1994-12.
`www.w3.org/Addressing/rfc1738.txt`

URN Syntax
Sets out the canonical syntax for Uniform Resource Names.
World Wide Web Consortium. 1997-05.
`www.ietf.org/rfc/rfc2141.txt`

Web Services Description Language (WSDL) Version 1.2 Part 1: Core Language
WSDL is an XML language for describing Web services. The specification defines the core language that can be used to describe Web services.
World Wide Web Consortium. Working Draft. 2003-06-11.
`www.w3.org/TR/2003/WD-wsdl12-20030611`

Web Services Description Language (WSDL) Version 1.2 Part 2: Message Patterns
Describes Web Services Description Language (WSDL) Version 1.2 message patterns.
World Wide Web Consortium. 2003-06-11.
`www.w3.org/TR/wsdl12-patterns/`

Web Services Description Language (WSDL) Version 1.2 Part 3: Bindings
Describes how to use Web Services Description Language (WSDL) in conjunction with SOAP 1.2.
World Wide Web Consortium. Working Draft. 2003-06-11.
`www.w3.org/TR/2003/WD-wsdl12-bindings-20030611`

Windows Script
MSDN center for Windows Scripting.
Microsoft.
`www.msdn.microsoft.com/library/default.asp?url=/nhp/default`
`.asp?contentid=28001169`

XML

MSDN center for XML.

Microsoft.

`www.msdn.microsoft.com/library/default.asp?url=/nhp/default`
`.asp?contentid=28000438`

XML Path Language (XPath) Version 1.0

XPath is a language for addressing parts of an XML document, designed to be used by both XSLT and XPointer.

World Wide Web Consortium. Recommendation. 1999-11-16.

`www.w3.org/TR/1999/REC-xpath-19991116`

XML Schema Part 0: Primer

Provides a readable description of the XML Schema features and shows how to create schemas using the XML Schema language.

World Wide Web Consortium. Recommendation. 2001-05-02.

`www.w3.org/TR/2001/REC-xmlschema-0-20010502/`

XML Schema Part 1: Structures

Specifies the XML Schema definition language for describing the structure and constraining the contents of XML 1.0 documents.

World Wide Web Consortium. Recommendation. 2001-05-02.

`www.w3.org/TR/2001/REC-xmlschema-1-20010502/`

XML Schema Part 2: Datatypes

Specifies the XML Schema definition language for describing the structure and constraining the contents of XML 1.0 documents.

World Wide Web Consortium. Recommendation. 2001-05-02.

`www.w3.org/TR/2001/REC-xmlschema-2-20010502/`

XML-Signature Syntax and Processing

Specifies XML digital signature processing rules and syntax.

World Wide Web Consortium. 2002-02-12.

`www.w3.org/TR/xmldsig-core/`

XSL Transformations (XSLT) Version 1.0

XSLT is a language for transforming XML documents into other XML documents.

World Wide Web Consortium. Recommendation. 1999-11-16.

`www.w3.org/TR/1999/REC-xslt-19991116`

Glossary

In the glossary we include terms and definitions that are specific to InfoPath, as well as those relating to the world of XML and its multitude of standards and specifications. Also included are a small number of definitions relating to XML in Microsoft Excel. For InfoPath element and attribute names, you should see Appendix A.

Each entry includes an acronym if there is one, and acronyms are entered in alphabetical order with "see" references to the full term.

active field   The field on an InfoPath form in which the cursor is located.

ActiveX Data Objects (ADO)   A data access interface that communicates with OLE DB-compliant data sources to connect to, retrieve, manipulate, and update data.

ADO   *See* ActiveX Data Objects.

aggregation   The process of merging a set of InfoPath forms. Usually the forms will have an identical structure, but it is possible to merge forms with different schemas using XSLT.

attribute   XML name-value pair included in an element that sets its properties.

attribute field   A field in an InfoPath data source that is an attribute.

bind   To associate a control in an InfoPath form with an element or attribute in a data source. Data contained in bound controls is saved to the underlying XML document.

cascading style sheets (CSS)   A W3C specification for applying style to HTML or XML elements. CSS can be embedded in an XSL or HTML file or stored in a separate linked file.

CDATA section   A section in an XML document where the characters represent text content as distinct from markup.

Glossary

child element   An element contained by another element in an XML tree structure.

class   The definition of an object, including the name, properties and methods, and any events that it has. An instance of a class has all of the defined characteristics of the class.

COM   *See* Component Object Model.

Component Object Model (COM)   A specification developed by Microsoft for software components that can be assembled into programs or can add functionality to existing programs.

conditional formatting   Rules that change the appearance of an InfoPath form control, including its visibility.

content model   The description of the set of elements and attributes contained inside another XML element. If an XML element can have child elements and attributes that are not declared in a schema, it is said to have an open-content model.

CSS   *See* cascading style sheets.

data adapter   An InfoPath object used to submit data to and retrieve data from databases, Web services, and XML files.

data source   Fields and groups bound to controls on an InfoPath form that define and store the data.

data validation   The process of testing the accuracy of form data. In InfoPath, validation can be applied from an XML Schema, a form control, or scripting code.

DC   *See* Dublin Core.

declarative programming   Programming based on independent rules. The order in which rules are declared or executed is not significant. XSLT is an example.

design mode   InfoPath design mode allows you to design the form interface and extract the files that make up a form.

dialog box alert   An InfoPath validation alert that opens a dialog box with a custom error message.

Document Object Model (DOM)   Formal definition of what XML syntax represents. Once a document is parsed, the DOM can be processed using script.

DOM   *See* Document Object Model.

Dublin Core (DC)   A recommendation for the content of resource meta data by the Dublin Core Metadata Initiative.

editing component   In an InfoPath form definition file, an editing component, associated with a form control, provides actions that allow users to edit XML nodes. It also exposes actions like "insert" and "remove" in menu and toolbar buttons.

element   XML text structure marked up with start and end tags. Elements can have attributes and can contain other elements.

event   An action recognized by a system or form object, for which you can define a response. Examples include opening a form, a button click, and merging forms.

event handler   A script function in an InfoPath form that responds to a form or data validation event.

expression box   A read-only InfoPath form control that displays calculated data based on an XPath expression.

Extensible Hypertext Markup Language (XHTML)   A reformulation of HTML to conform with XML 1.0.

Extensible Markup Language [XML]   A subset of Standard Generalized Markup Language (SGML) designed by the W3C for delivering information on the Web. The W3C XML recommendation defines a set of rules for the creation of customized elements and attributes for specific applications.

Extensible Stylesheet Language Transformation (XSLT)   An XSLT style sheet describes how an XML instance document is transformed into an XML document using a different vocabulary.

external data source   *See* secondary data source.

field   An element or attribute in an InfoPath form data source that can contain data. If the field is an element, it may contain attribute fields.

form   An InfoPath document with a set of controls into which users can enter information. Controls include rich text boxes, date pickers, and optional and repeating sections.

form definition file (XSF)   The file automatically generated by InfoPath when a new template is created and saved in design mode. It contains information about the form as a whole, together with all of the other files and components used in a form. The file extension is .xsf.

form template (XSN)   The compressed file format that packages all the InfoPath form files into one file. The file extension is .xsn.

group   An element in an InfoPath data source that can contain fields and other groups. Controls that contain other controls, such as repeating tables and sections, are bound to groups.

hyperlink   An InfoPath control that can link users to another location—often a Web page. The link data may be partly or entirely based on an XPath expression.

IMT   *See* Internet media type.

InfoPath data type   An InfoPath field property that defines the kinds of data the field can store. Data types include hyperlink, date, time, date and time, and picture.

inline alert   An InfoPath validation alert that marks a control with a dashed red border. Users can right-click to display a custom error message.

Internet media type (IMT)   Internet media type encodings.

ISO 639-1   Specifies the two-letter codes for languages. The scheme is a subset of ISO 639-2.

ISO 639-2   Specifies the three-letter codes for languages. It represents all the ISO 639-1 languages. The three-letter structure allows more codes and finer granularity.

ISO 3166   Contains a two-letter code that is recommended as the general-purpose code, a three-letter code that has better mnemonic properties, and a numeric three-digit code that can be useful if script independence of the codes is important.

JavaScript   A cross-platform, World Wide Web scripting language. Code may be inserted directly into an HTML page or linked to it.

Joint Photographic Expert Group (JPEG)   A compressed graphics file format supported by many Web browsers. It was developed for storing photographic images and is best used for high-resolution color Images. The file extension is .jpg.

JPEG   *See* Joint Photographic Expert Group.

Jscript   An interpreted, object-based scripting language that borrows from C, C++, and Java. It is the Microsoft implementation of the ECMA 262 language specification.

layout table   A tabular structure used to lay out InfoPath form content.

mapped cell   A cell in an Excel 2003 spreadsheet that is related to a single-occurring element in an XML schema.

meta data   Data that describes other data. For example, the author, title, and extent of a Web page are meta data.

method   A programming procedure that operates on a specific object and is encapsulated in it.

Microsoft Script Editor   A programming environment used to create, edit, and debug Microsoft JScript or Microsoft VBScript code in an InfoPath form.

namespace declaration   An attribute on an element in an XML document that a given namespace prefix will refer to a namespace URI in the form `xmlns:prefix="uri"`.

node   A node in a tree that represents an element or attribute in an XML document.

object model [OM]   A class hierarchy of objects and collections that represents the content and functionality of an application.

object model diagram   A graphical representation of an object model.

OM   *See* object model

Optional section   An InfoPath form control bound to a group. The content is usually hidden by default. Users can insert and remove optional sections when filling out the form. The editing component is xOptional.

parent element   An element containing one or more elements in an XML tree structure.

PRISM   *See* Publishing Requirements for Industry Standard Metadata.

processing instruction   A statement in an XML document containing instructions for the software that will process it. A common use is to identify an XSL style sheet, for example `<?xml-stylesheet href="view_1.xsl" type="text/xsl"?>`.

publish   To make an InfoPath form available for others to complete, by saving it to a shared public location.

Publishing Requirements for Industry Standard Metadata (PRISM)   Defines a standard for content description in traditional and electronic publishing.

RDF   *See* Resource Definition Framework.

RDF Site Summary (RSS)   A format for syndication and descriptive meta data. An RSS summary describes a "channel" consisting of items and their URLs.

RDF/XML   RDF/XML is an XML syntax for expressing RDF statements about resources.

reference field   A field that is associated with another, such that if the properties in one are changed, those in the other field are updated to match.

reference group   A group that is associated with another, such that if the properties in one are changed, those in the other group are updated to match.

repeating field   An InfoPath form control bound to a data source field that can repeat.

repeating group   An InfoPath form control bound to a data source group that can occur more than once.

repeating section   An InfoPath form control that contains other controls and that repeats as needed.

repeating table   An InfoPath form control that contains other controls in a tabular layout where rows repeat as required.

Resource Definition Framework [RDF]   A general-purpose language for representing information in the Web, intended for describing and exchanging meta data about online resources.

Resource Manager   A design mode feature in InfoPath that allows you to add or remove files from a form template.

RFC 3066   Internet RFC 3066 *Tags for the Identification of Language* specifies the syntax for the two-letter (lowercase) code taken from ISO 639, or a three-letter code if there is no two-letter code, followed optionally by a two-letter (uppercase) country code taken from ISO 3166.

RSS   *See* RDF Site Summary.

scripting language   A simple programming language designed to perform special or limited tasks.

secondary data source (external data source)   An XML data file, database, or Web service that is bound to a control on an InfoPath form.

section   A control on an InfoPath form that contains other controls.

Simple Object Access Protocol [SOAP]   SOAP Version 1.2 is a lightweight protocol intended for exchanging structured information in a decentralized, distributed environment.

SOAP   *See* Simple Object Access Protocol.

SQL   *See* Structured Query Language.

Structured Query Language (SQL)   A syntax for creating queries on databases.

task pane   A secondary pane in a Microsoft Office application. In InfoPath, a custom task pane is an HTML file providing form-specific commands and content.

text field   An InfoPath form control containing text or rich text. The editing component is xField.

UDDI   *See* Universal Description Discovery and Integration.

Uniform Resource Identifier (URI)   A compact string of characters for identifying an abstract or physical resource. A URI is the superset of URLs and URNs.

Uniform Resource Locator (URL)   The text representation of a resource available over an Internet protocol such as HTTP. An absolute URL contains the full address, including the protocol, the domain, the path, and the filename. In a relative URL, the domain and some or all of the path is omitted.

Uniform Resource Name (URN)   Names intended to serve as persistent, location-independent resource identifiers.

Universal Description Discovery and Integration [UDDI]   A specification for registering and discovering Web services.

URI   *See* Uniform Resource Identifier.

URL   *See* Uniform Resource Locator.

URN   *See* Uniform Resource Name.

VBScript *See* Visual Basic Scripting Edition.

view InfoPath forms may contain multiple views of the form data. Each view is generated from the form data by an XSLT transform.

Visual Basic Scripting Edition (VBScript) An interpreted, object-based scripting language that is a subset of Microsoft Visual Basic.

Web Service Description Language [WSDL] An XML language for describing Web services.

WSDL *See* Web Service Description Language.

WSX *See* XML Schema.

W3C Schema Datatype Properties defined in an XML schema that specify the kinds of data that elements and attributes can contain.

W3C-DTF A proposal for dates and times encoded with a profile based on ISO 8601. Equivalent to `xsd:dateTime` in XML Schema Part 2: Datatypes.

XHTML *See* Extensible Hypertext Markup Language.

XML *See* Extensible Markup Language.

XML list A list in an Excel 2003 spreadsheet where a column is related to a repeating element in an XML schema.

XML map Abstract object created each time a schema is added to an Excel 2003 workbook. The map relates between schema objects and spreadsheet locations. A workbook can support multiple maps, which have distinct names.

XML Path Language (XPath) An expression language used by XSLT to access or refer to parts of an XML document. For example, /book/chapter[5]/section[2] selects the second section of the fifth chapter of a book.

XML schema Note the lower-case "s" in schema. A description of the order, cardinality, and relationship of elements and attributes in a class of XML documents.

XML Schema (WSX) The W3C XML Schema definition language for describing the structure and constraining the contents of XML 1.0 documents. InfoPath form files are usually based on a single schema, though multiple schemas are supported. Additional schemas for secondary data sources are also required. The file extension is .xsd.

XML Signature XML Signatures provide integrity, message authentication, and/or signer authentication services for data of any type, whether located within the XML that includes the signature or elsewhere.

XML template   The XML InfoPath file that contains any default data that is displayed in a view when a new form is created by a user.

XPath   *See* XML Path Language.

XSF   *See* form definition file.

XSLT   *See* Extensible Stylesheet Language Transformation.

XSN   *See* form template.

Index

D